Alcohol, Society, and the State

—2—

A report of the International Study of Alcohol Control Experiences, in collaboration with the World Health Organization Regional Office for Europe.

Alcohol, Society, and the State

-2-

THE SOCIAL HISTORY OF CONTROL POLICY IN SEVEN COUNTRIES

Edited by Eric Single, Patricia Morgan, and Jan de Lint

Contributors

Poland:	Jacek Moskalewicz
Finland:	Klaus Mäkelä, Esa Österberg, Pekka Sulkunen
Switzerland:	Monique Cahannes, Richard Müller
Holland:	Jan de Lint
Ireland:	Dermot Walsh, Brendan Walsh
Ontario:	Eric Single, Norman Giesbrecht, Barry Eakins
California:	Richard Bunce, Tracey Cameron, Gary Collins, Patricia Morgan, James Mosher, Robin Room

ADDICTION RESEARCH FOUNDATION

Toronto, Canada

iii

Canadian Cataloguing in Publication Data

Alcohol, society and the state

A report of the International Study of Alcohol Control
Experiences, in collaboration with the World Health
Organization Regional Office for Europe.
Includes bibliographical references and index.
Contents: v. 1. A comparative study of alcohol control /
Klaus Mäkelä . . . (et al.) — v. 2. The social history of
control policy in seven countries / edited by Eric Single,
Patricia Morgan, and Jan de Lint.
ISBN 0-88868-061-9 (v. 1). — ISBN 0-88868-060-0 (v. 2)

1. Liquor traffic — History — 20th century. 2. Liquor
laws — History — 20th century. 3. Liquor problem —
History — 20th century. I. Addiction Research Foun-
dation of Ontario. II. International Study of Alcohol
Control Experiences. III. World Health Organization.
Regional Office for Europe.

HV5082.A42   363.4'1   C82-094059-3

Printed and bound in Canada.

Contents

List of Tables

List of Figures

Foreword

Over the last decade, the growing concern felt by member states regarding alcohol-related problems has been reflected in a number of WHO documents. In 1975, the 28th World Health Assembly drew attention to the association between the level of alcohol consumption and certain forms of health damage (Resolution WHA 28.81). In 1979, the 32nd World Health Assembly recognized problems related to alcohol as ranking among the world's major public health problems and urged member states to take all appropriate measures to reduce its consumption among all sectors of the population (Resolution WHA 32.40).

The background to this renewed interest in alcohol-related policies is threefold. First, the rapid post-war increase in overall alcohol consumption was accompanied by an increased magnitude of problems related to drinking. Second, it was realized that many alcohol problems cannot be conceptualized as manifestations of an underlying entity, that of alcohol dependence. Alcohol dependence, while widespread and worrying, constitutes only a small part of the total of alcohol-related problems. And third, the limited efficacy and high cost of existing treatment systems gave impetus to the search for strategies of prevention.

The prevention of alcohol-related and drug-related problems has been one of the main objectives of the medium-term programme in mental health for the European Region. In 1975, an international group of researchers reviewed the scientific evidence on the relationships between alcohol control policies, levels of aggregate consumption, and chronic health ailments related to drinking. The report had a considerable impact on international scientific debate, and it was felt that more information on related topics, not directly dealt with in this first project, was needed. In view of the wide variety of alcohol problems, it was deemed important to study the significance of cultural patterns of drinking as well as consequences of single-drinking occasions. It also became evident that, in order to be realistic, alcohol control policies pursuing public health goals require a deeper understanding of the historical processes lying behind the relaxation of controls over the last decades.

In an effort to examine these issues, the International Study of Alcohol Control Experiences was conceived. It originated as a collaborative enterprise between the Addiction Research Foundation of Ontario, the Alcohol Research Group in Berkeley, and the Finnish Foundation for Alcohol Studies. Research groups from Ireland, the Netherlands, Poland, and Switzerland joined the project, and the international aspect of the project was carried out under an agreement between the WHO Regional Office for Europe and the Finnish Foundation for Alcohol Studies.

In order to understand the social dynamics of the post-war increase in alcohol consumption and to study the control measures in their historical context, the project was carried out as a series of comparative case studies.

The results of the project are drawn together in this report and its companion volume. The first report is an international discussion of the post-war experiences (1950-1975) of the seven societies. The second report summarizes each of the seven case studies.

The societies studied in these two volumes all belong to the industrialized part of the world but the analysis sheds light on genuinely international processes that are likely to have a global influence. The report is also unique in that it analyses the social dynamics and structural constraints of control policies, considerations essential to the design of realistic measures for strengthening the impact of public health concerns but which are often not taken into account. I hope that the conclusions of the study will be of value to public health authorities throughout the world.

Leo A. Kaprio, M.D.
Regional Director for Europe
World Health Organization
Copenhagen, October 1981

1. Introduction

This book presents the alcohol control experiences in seven different settings — Poland, Finland, Switzerland, the Netherlands, Ireland, Ontario, and California. Given the predominance of clinical and treatment-oriented alcohol research, a collection of case studies such as this is unusual both in its comparative approach and in its emphasis on primary rather than secondary prevention.

With the almost universal increase in alcohol consumption throughout the world since World War II, a corresponding increase in concern over alcohol-related problems, and the limited success of treatment approaches, there has been increasing interest in the use of control measures to limit the incidence of alcohol-related problems (WHO, 1975, 1979a, 1979b, 1979c, 1980). The interest in alcohol control measures for primary prevention has been particularly evident in countries with a strong temperance tradition such as Canada, Sweden, and the United Kingdom. In 1975, an international group of alcohol researchers reviewed selected aspects of consequences related to alcohol use and concluded that "changes in the overall consumption of alcoholic beverages have a bearing upon the health of the people in any society. Alcohol measures can be used to limit consumption. Thus, control of alcohol availability becomes a public health issue" (Bruun et al., 1975: 90).

It was against this background of growing interest in alcohol control policy that the International Study of Alcohol Control Experiences (ISACE) was conceived.* The basic purpose of the International Study of Alcohol Control Experiences has been (1.) to trace the historical development of alcohol control policy, its determinants, and its effects on the levels and patterns of alcohol consumption in different societies, and (2.) to as-

---

*The following research institutes and groups have participated in the study:

    Addiction Research Foundation of Ontario, Toronto
    Finnish Foundation for Alcohol Studies, Helsinki
    Foundation for Scientific Research of Alcohol and Drug Use, Amsterdam
    Medico-Social Research Board, Dublin
    Psychoneurological Institute, Warsaw
    Social Research Group, University of California, School of Public Health, Berkeley
    Swiss Institute for the Prevention of Alcoholism, Lausanne

The project group has functioned as a scientifically autonomous body, while benefiting from the collaboration and support of the WHO Regional Office for Europe, under an agreement between the Regional Office and the Finnish Foundation for Alcohol Studies. The national projects were carried out independently by the participating groups. The international collaboration was organized around a series of working meetings held in Toronto, Ontario, in 1976; Helsinki, Finland, 1978; Pacific Grove, California, in 1979; Serock, Poland, in 1980; and Niagara-on-the-Lake, Ontario, in 1981.

sess the potentials of control policy to influence the consumption of alcohol and its adverse consequences.

In order to achieve these goals, the participating research groups have carried out case studies of recent trends regarding alcohol consumption, alcohol-related problems, and alcohol control systems, specifically focusing on the period from 1950 to the late 1970s. In three of the areas studied — Canada, Switzerland, and the United States — the major alcohol control policy decisions are made at the provincial or cantonal or state level rather than at the federal level. Whereas the case studies of the alcohol control experiences in the United States and Canada focus specifically on the state of California and the province of Ontario, the Swiss report focuses on the entire country.

The project has resulted in two complementary volumes. The theoretical and policy implications of the case studies presented in this book are discussed in *Alcohol, Society, and the State: A Comparative Study of Alcohol Control*, by Klaus Mäkelä et al. (Addiction Research Foundation, 1981).

THE EVOLUTION OF THE PROJECT

The International Study of Alcohol Control Experiences thus developed, in part, to continue and expand on the work of the 1975 international group. However, a markedly different perspective on alcohol control was adopted.

The 1975 working group deliberately focused on the effects of control measures. The authors show a clear awareness of the necessity of taking into account concrete historical circumstances when assessing control measures, but these were not taken up in the report. As the discussion was limited to chronic health ailments, the focus was on the average consumption level and the number of heavy consumers as determinants of alcohol problems. In this context, control was looked upon from a policy perspective as something that could be manipulated. Control measures, alcohol consumption, and alcohol-related problems were kept conceptually distinct and were separately studied.

In the International Study of Alcohol Control Experiences the focus was instead on the origins and nature of control mechanisms as they develop within particular cultural and historical circumstances. It became clear that controls are not rigid systems of legal regulations which are easily manipulated. Rather, they are elaborate networks of cultural, economic, and political structures which are both a response to and a determinant of the magnitude of alcohol-related problems. Controls are more than formal rules. They involve economics. They involve culture and history. Most of all, they involve politics and the state apparatus.

The evolution of the project also led to a broadening of our perspective on alcohol-related problems, placing them in their historical and cultural context. It became increasingly evident that, along with changes in alcohol control mechanisms, there are corresponding shifts in the ways alcohol-related problems are identified and managed. Indeed, alcohol control policies and the management of alcohol appear to be linked to alcohol consumption and consequences through a network of cultural and economic determinants not easily recognized.

The historical descriptions of alcohol policy presented in these chapters are relevant to wider social issues. For example, the alcohol control experiences illustrate the emergence of state intervention into public health. Also, the integration of alcohol issues into working-class movements of the 19th century reflected the belief that these issues were an integral part of social reform. Thus, an examination of alcohol's role within a particular society may help us discern major shifts in a given historical period.

THE CULTURAL AND HISTORICAL BASIS OF ALCOHOL CONTROL

The importance of the cultural context to any system of control measures is almost self-evident. Both the patterns of drinking and the social reactions to drinking vary from one context to another. Further, the cultural perceptions of consequences of drinking differ markedly. In some countries, there seems to be considerable attention paid to alcohol-related chronic disease, while in others there appears to be greater concern with social conflicts arising from single incidents of intoxication.

Not only do perceptions of alcohol problems vary from culture to culture, but there is also a great deal of variation in the efficacy of control measures. What works in one setting may not necessarily work in another. For example, an intriguing feature of the Irish situation is the inordinately high proportion of personal income expended on alcoholic beverages. The demand for beer, the popular form of alcoholic beverage in Ireland, appears to be relatively insensitive to price increases. In this context the use of price increases to influence aggregate consumption is debatable.

The insensitivity of consumption to price in the Irish context is but one example of the importance of viewing alcohol control in its cultural and historical context. There is considerable variability in the seven case studies regarding the meaning of drinking, the predominate manner in which alcohol is consumed, definitions of appropriate activities and behaviours associated with drinking, and social conventions regarding who may drink, how much, and when.

Although the seven case studies clearly demonstrate many divergencies in alcohol culture, they also illustrate common trends: the general increase in alcohol consumption, the increase in alcohol availability, the liberalization of alcohol controls, and the convergence in drinking patterns. Perhaps the most important convergence in the different alcohol cultures is the common tendency for alcohol to be viewed less and less as a special commodity. This trend can only be understood in the context of broader historical changes. In particular, the liberalization of alcohol policy is linked to growing involvement of government in all aspects of the economy.

The special status of alcohol is gradually slipping as traditions based on temperance or other moral sentiments give way to efforts to rationalize and insure the efficient operation of the market. Indeed, in the Netherlands, alcohol is generally treated as any other commodity. Nonetheless, the Dutch have a complex and extensive control system due to the development of elaborate regulations governing *all* commodities and *all* aspects of the economy. Thus, despite the erosion of its special status, alcohol is nonetheless subjected to considerable control simply by virtue of the fact that it is a commodity and subject to the normal regulations intended to insure the orderly functioning of the economy. Hence, the determination of control mechanisms must detail not only those regulations which pertain solely to alcohol, but also the system of economic control in general.

ALCOHOL AND THE STATE

In view of the cultural divergencies noted above, it is not surprising that state involvement in alcohol control varies a great deal between the seven jurisdictions. In the Netherlands, there are few special controls on alcohol. In California, Switzerland, and Ireland, controls are relatively liberal and mainly concern retail trade in alcohol. Ontario has a provincial monopoly on retail sales of alcoholic beverages for off-premise consumption and strictly controls on-premise consumption. In Finland and Poland, both the production and distribution of alcohol are government controlled. Thus, the extent to which control measures may be applied differs considerably between societies.

On the other hand, the case studies demonstrate a uniform trend toward increased state involvement with alcohol-related problems. Whether living in the Netherlands, California, or Poland, a person suffering from a social or health problem associated with the immoderate use of alcohol can expect some form of intervention, either by officials of the state or by professionals funded by the state. In an increasing number of communities, state officials no longer ignore the problems of alcoholism or deem them to be issues which the individual and the individual's family must deal with alone.

The increased state involvement with alcohol-related problems is interrelated with two further common trends: the rise of the welfare state and the medicalization of alcohol problems. With the rise of the welfare state, the state has gradually become more involved not only in regulating the economy, but also in assuming responsibility for the management of all kinds of social problems, including those deemed to be alcohol-related. Whereas skid row inebriates once were either ignored or put into gaol, now they are treated (albeit not always successfully) by state-operated or funded medical agencies. Moral condemnation has been, in part, replaced by a medical diagnosis, and the state has assumed the major responsibility for the rehabilitation of the patient.

Further, increasing welfare state bureaucracies and professionalized alcohol treatment systems have developed as alternative means of social control. Increased state responsibility over the management of alcohol-related problems has, in this framework, allowed the state to broaden the definition of, and the intervention into, "alcohol-related" social problems. Thus, alcohol treatment modalities are being used to address problems of youth, family, disorders, and crime — problems which may have once called for coercive rather than treatment-oriented responses.

The assumption of this responsibility can be and is a very expensive proposition. Indeed, it has been predicted that the assumption of too many social welfare responsibilities will precipitate a crisis in the welfare state in which the state is forced to abandon or sharply reduce its involvement in areas such as alcoholism treatment.

Other factors related to the state's assumption of increased responsibility for alcohol-related problems are its considerable fiscal and economic interests in the production and distribution of alcoholic beverages. For example, there are direct taxes on the beverages and on establishments which sell alcohol. There is also the economic significance of the industry to consider. Large numbers of workers (who are taxpayers) are employed and depend on the alcohol industry. Further, there are often special considerations such as the impact of alcohol availability on tourism or the impact of alcohol exports on the balance of trade.

Several case studies illustrate the noteworthy lack of integration between those agencies of the state concerned with the revenue aspects of alcohol and those agencies responsible for the management of alcohol-related problems. When conflicts occur, they tend to be dealt with at the highest levels (inter-ministerial) where the short-term economic considerations usually carry the greater weight. Thus, we frequently find the state liberalizing its controls on the alcohol industry while expanding treatment facilities and incurring greater costs for the management of alcohol-related problems.

Our case studies also show how alcohol controls signify the cultural acceptance of drinking behaviours. Prevailing conceptions of appropriate and inappropriate drinking represent major restraints on the state's ability to influence consumption behaviour and manage alcohol-related problems. Thus, the official response to the availability of alcohol and the management of alcohol-related problems is limited not only by the state's fiscal and economic interests, but also by the cultural place of drinking in society.

THE CASE STUDIES

There is no particular rationale for ordering chapters. Chapter 2 presents the experience of Poland and highlights the tension between society and state which exists to varying degrees in all settings. In this study, Poland is unique both in terms of its socialist economy and in terms of the extreme social upheavals of World War II and the post-war period. Although there is greater potential for strict alcohol controls in a planned economy, alcohol has nonetheless assumed a significant role in the Polish society, and controls on availability have been relatively lax. Despite the many fascinating and unique aspects of the alcohol culture in Poland, there are remarkable similarities to other settings concerning trends in aggregate alcohol consumption as well as in the management of alcohol-related problems.

The Finnish alcohol experience is well-known among alcohol researchers. Indeed, the term ''Finnish pattern of drinking'' has often been used to describe Saturday night binge drinking. For every five adult Finnish males, one has been arrested for public drunkenness. Attempts by the state monopoly to manipulate the traditional hard-drinking pattern of Finns have met with very limited success. The 1969 legislation introducing medium beer in grocery stores and ending rural prohibition was followed by a dramatic increase in consumption but left intact the core patterns of drinking. The traditional alcohol culture has thus far prevailed over attempts to moderate drinking patterns.

Switzerland is typified by its multicultural society, decentralized economy, and the politics of compromise. There are marked differences in rates of consumption and patterns of drinking among the three major language groups, despite the fact that all are subject to essentially the same system of controls. Consumption has increased despite a decline in the number of outlets where alcoholic beverages are sold, counter to the generally positive relationship between availability and consumption.

In the Netherlands, the rapid increase in alcohol use during the post-war period cannot be attributed to the liberalization of its control system since this was already very lax. Rather, it is argued that the erosion of informal controls, specifically the decline of temperance sentiments, appears to be a more important cause.

Ireland also experienced a marked increase in alcohol consumption. Relevant factors undoubtedly include increased national prosperity with enhanced personal disposable income and the erosion of traditional restraints on drinking by women and young people. In spite of heavy taxation, the Irish consumer appears willing to devote a relatively high proportion of personal expenditures to purchasing alcohol. However, it must be recognized that despite recent prosperity, alcohol remains an expensive commodity relative to earnings.

The Ontario experience highlights the responsive nature of alcohol control policy. In the post-war period, alcohol consumption was relatively low and associated with working class, urban males. The alcoholic was typically treated with moral condemnation and the availability of alcohol was strictly controlled. By the end of the 1970s, the drinking culture had changed radically. Alcohol use was considered normal and acceptable behaviour. New groups of drinkers had emerged: women, youth, immigrants. Alcohol was made more available and alcoholics were given treatment rather than gaol sentences. Just as previously strict controls were congruent with prevailing social attitudes, so too it may be claimed that the liberalization of controls in Ontario has been consistent with changes in public attitudes towards alcohol.

In California, alcohol consumption grew steadily but not dramatically during the study period. Supermarkets, lunch counters, restaurants, and sports arenas became increasingly dependent on revenue from alcohol sales, as alcohol availability was expanded. The state's role in managing alcohol problems, meanwhile, grew tremendously and was carefully separated from the state's alcohol control functions. Industry interests largely determined the content of alcohol control policies, which focused on retail practices. The powerful wine industry in particular was able to fashion state control policies to protect its own interests.

If there is one overriding conclusion which can be derived from these case studies, it is that specific policy recommendations are rarely, if ever, applicable to the situation prevailing in a given jurisdiction. The applicability of control mechanisms must take cognizance of the cultural, economic, and political systems in which it is to be applied. These comprehensive case studies are presented in the hope that they might stimulate similar studies in other countries.

REFERENCES

Bruun, K., Edwards, G., Lumio, M., Mäkelä, K., Pan, L., Popham, R.E., Room, R., Schmidt, W., Skog, O-J., Sulkunen, P., & Österberg, E., 1975, *Alcohol Control Policies in Public Health Perspective.* The Finnish Foundation for Alcohol Studies, Volume 25. Forssa: Aurasen Kirjapaino.

Mäkelä, K., Room, R., Single, E., Sulkunen, P. & Walsh, B., with Bunce, R., Cahannes, M., Cameron, T., Giesbrecht, N., de Lint, J., Makinen, H., Morgan, P., Mosher, J., Moskalewicz, J., Müller, R., Österberg, E., Wald, I., & Walsh, D., 1981, *Alcohol, Society, and the State 1: A Comparative Study of Alcohol Control.* Toronto: Addiction Research Foundation.

World Health Organization (WHO), 1975, *WHO Official Records No. 226,* 48 (Resolution WHA 28.81).

World Health Organization (WHO), 1978, *Alcohol-related Problems: The Need to Develop Further the WHO Initiative.* Report to the Executive Board, WHO Document EB 63/23.

World Health Organization (WHO), 1979a, *Thirty-second World Health Assembly, 7-25 May 1979. Resolutions and Decisions.* Geneva, 37 (Resolution WHA 32.40).

World Health Organization (WHO) Regional Office for Europe, 1979b, *Public Health Aspects of Alcohol and Drug Dependence. Report of a WHO Conference.* Copenhagen, EURO Reports and Studies 8.

World Health Organization (WHO), 1979c, *Prevention of Alcohol-related Problems: An International Review of Preventive Measures, Policies, and Programmes.* Moser, J., compiler. WHO Document MNH/79.16.

World Health Organization (WHO), 1980, *Report of a WHO Expert Committee on Problems Related to Alcohol Consumption.*

2. Alcohol: Commodity and Symbol in Polish Society

Jacek Moskalewicz*

ECONOMIC AND SOCIAL CONTEXT

Poland is a Central European country comprised of 312,520 square kilometres. From 1950 to 1975, Poland's population increased by 36%, from 25 to 34 million. The rate of population growth showed a particularly rapid upswing from 1948 to 1956, when live births rose to 30 per 1,000 inhabitants. Since the early 1960s there has been a gradual aging of society and a considerable drop in the birth rate to 16.6 in 1970, and a doubling of the population above the age of 65.

During World War II, Poland suffered great human and material losses. After the war, the country's borders were shifted west and its political and economic system underwent deep changes: nationalization of the means of production and reorientation towards socialism, as well as intensive industrialization. The latter started in the early 1950s. In the years 1950 to 1975, the number of people employed in industry grew 2.5 times, while employment in agriculture remained unchanged. In 1950, the employment structure in Poland was still that of an agriculture country, with over 50% of the total working population employed in agriculture. By 1975, the largest proportion of workers were employed in industry: approximately 39%, with 32% in agriculture, and 28% in services. In the study period, the national income per capita in fixed prices grew more than four times, whereas consumption rose only 3.5 times. This is due primarily to the increasing role of capital goods in the structure of national income: in the 1970s capital goods accounted for close to 40% of the total expenditures of national income. Another characteristic of post-war Polish society was the increased mobility — both vertical and horizontal — of the

*Psychoneurological Institute, Warsaw, Poland. The author would like to acknowledge all those whose assistance, advice, and encouragement contributed to this study, particularly his colleagues at the Department of Studies in Alcoholism and Drug Dependency of the Psychoneurological Institute. Specifically, gratitude is extended to Antoni Bielewicz for his help in the description of Polish drinking culture, to Jacek Morawski for collecting and interpreting many data on alcohol-related problems, to Leszek Stafiej and Maria Guz for translation services, and to Ignacy Wald for his encouragement and advice throughout this project.

9

population. This was a result of the shift in the country's borders west leading to the migration of about one-third of the population; of industrialization; and of sociopolitical changes.

Intensive industrialization was accompanied by quick urbanization. In 1950, town dwellers still amounted to not much more than one-third of the total population. This was followed by a swift tide of migration from rural areas to towns and larger urban centres. In 1975, the urban population constituted 55.7% of the total. The quick momentum of urbanization helped to spread the urban lifestyle throughout the country, introducing, as well, rural cultures into the towns and cities. Involving more than the mere transformation of lifestyle, this process also brought about the cumulation of traditional rural and urban patterns of culture.

Increased social mobility, cumulation of traditional cultural lifestyles, and the demands of an industrial workforce all affected changes in the structure and functions of the family. The traditional multigenerational extended family model was almost completely replaced by the nuclear family with fewer children (Dodziuk-Lityńska and Markowska, 1971). The employment of women, adding to their hitherto "internal" functions in the family, become more and more widespread, equalizing the proportion of men and women in the workforce today. In 1975, female employment amounted to 42.3% of total employment in the state-owned and cooperative economy.

All in all, the economic and social changes contributed to homogenization of the society rather than to its cultural diversification. Thus, in the period following World War II, Poland has become a homogenous country ethnically, in language and religion. The non-Polish population amounts to 1 to 2% of the total (as compared to 30% in the inter-war period) and the vast majority now identify themselves as Roman Catholics.

ALCOHOL PRODUCTION AND TRADE

The basic agricultural crops are potato and rye, which also serve as cheap raw material for the production of spirits. Harsh winters and the absence of tradition account for the scarcity of viticulture. A few vineyards in the southwest region of the country provide small amounts of grapes for the production of domestic grape wine which comprised in the early 1970s only about 1% of grape wine consumption in Poland. The production of cheaper fruit wine, based chiefly on apples, witnessed an eightfold increase in crop production from 1950 to 1975. The brewing industry utilizes domestic raw materials, requiring only a small amount of imported hops and brewing barley.

The distilling of spirits in Poland is monopolized by the state enterprise POLMOS which is directly supervised by the Ministry of Food, Industry, and Purchase. POLMOS runs 17 plants all over the country, four of them providing about 50% of the overall spirits production. POLMOS also deals with production of yeast, soft drinks, vinegar, and mustard, which comprise a rather insignificant share of total output. Unrectified spirits are manufactured chiefly by distillers which are not run by POLMOS. In the 1970s, there were more than 900 distilleries operating in Poland, most of them situated at state-owned farms. Unlike that of spirits, the production of wine and beer is less centralized, considerable amounts of fruit wines being made in cooperative establishments.

The retailing of alcoholic beverages is handled separately from production. Sales of spirits are monopolized by the state and cooperative trade establishments, but sales of wines and beer are allowed in private shops. In 1970, there were about 10,000 licensed spirits outlets (mostly general food shops), only 1,832 of which dealt exclusively with alcoholic beverages. In the 1970s, there were 38,000 shops selling alcoholic beverages (vodkas and wines), with a fractional percentage of private victuallers among them licensed for wines only. No statistics are available in Poland for the number of shops selling beer, for which no license is required.

The on-premise retail network is far less developed; and the number of such outlets is four times less than that of off-premises. In the 1970s, close to 70% (9,000) of the country's on-premise establishments had licenses for either the sale of wine only, or vodka and wine.

State monopoly over the production of spirits and a general control over alcohol distribution would seem to provide a good opportunity to effectively control alcohol supply. In practice, however, the situation is much more complicated. The production and sale of alcohol are an integral part of the growth-oriented economic system, in which economic mechanisms to award quantitative growth have been firmly established. The use of other criteria in respect to alcohol would require the adoption of different cost-and-outcome calculation and awarding systems. Such systems would not be in line with the now existing economic practice and expectations of alcohol industry management and workers. The creation of such systems, although possible, would require great organizational efforts. Thus, arbitrary decisions of central planning agencies to limit alcohol supply without close consideration of the above questions would cause many side-effects. In the study period, several attempts have been made to do this — such as attempts to deter waiters from serving alcohol by discontinuing sales commissions on alcohol served by them. These attempts were perceived as unfair by restaurant staff and brought about illegal sales of alcohol in these establishments. Waiters instead served alcohol bought in shops for lower prices, and catering margins were pocketed (Podgórecki, 1968).

In the 25 years from 1950 to 1975, the production of spirits in Poland grew 3.2 times, wines 11 times, and beer 3.7 times. The rapid growth in the production of wine should not be overstressed, because of the extremely low production volumes in 1950. In spite of this rapid up-swing, the role of wine in alcohol production is still negligible, and its share of alcohol consumption is limited to 12% (up from 1.7% in 1950). The rapid growth in production of alcoholic beverages accompanied the growth of the industry as a whole. At the end of the 25-year study period, the production of spirits, wine, and beer was around 1.2-1.3% of the total value of industrial production. In the 1970s, about 10% of the state budget revenue came from private expenditure on alcohol, mostly in the form of turnover tax paid by the producer. The spirits industry is the most profitable, providing about 70% of budget revenues from alcoholic beverages.

Apart from their fiscal significance, alcoholic beverages have played an increasingly important role as home market stabilizers, particularly in the 1970s, when the demand for many consumer goods exceeded supply. The lack of balance of the market was due to the rapid jump in population incomes in those years and the implementation of a vast investment program. In 1975, alcoholic beverages accounted for 12.8% of retail trade and nearly 30% of the value of sales in on-premise outlets; one could hardly point to any other single commodity that attracted as much of the population's buying power. In 1975, only private expenditures on meat and cloth slightly surpassed those on alcohol. Alcohol expenditures grew more than twofold in the years 1970-75, and their share of private consumption exceeded 10%.

Employment in alcohol production and distribution is of negligible significance in the country's labour force, constituting a fractional percentage of total industrial employment and a few percentage points of trade employment. As Poland suffers a considerable shortage of labour power, any possible cuts in the production or distribution of alcohol would pose no threat of unemployment.

Alcoholic beverages are not a significant export commodity in Polish trade. Their share in various years fluctuated from 0.3 to 0.5% of exports value and from 0.3 to 0.8% of import values. Spirits yielded the highest export profit among alcoholic beverages. Grape wines constitute the highest volume of imports among alcoholic beverages, as there is virtually no domestic wine production. The production of spirits, fruit wines, and beer satisfies 98-100% of their consumption. In the 1970s, when the volume of alcohol exports was relatively higher, the share of spirits and beer sold abroad made up respectively about 5% and 2% of their overall production.

The state, which controls all foreign trade, also supervises imports of alcoholic beverages and is able to freely shape their supply depending on the domestic industry requirements. Centrally established prices for imported alcoholic beverages are 50-100% higher than their domestic counterparts. Transportation of alcohol into and out of the country by individual tourists has a negligible impact on the domestic alcohol consumption level. Worth stressing, however, is the impact that private "imports" of whisky, gin, or grape wines have on the diffusion in Poland of non-traditional consumption patterns. This has been intensified by the production of tonic water and cola, as well as the increased supply of grapefruit and orange juices in the 1970s.

ALCOHOL CONSUMPTION

Since World War II, consumption of alcoholic beverages in Poland has increased. As early as 1950, alcohol consumption in litres per capita, though relatively low by international standards, was twice as high as in 1938. In 1975, alcohol consumption reached the level of 6.9 litres of 100% alcohol per capita (Figure 1). However, this was not a steady rise. Between 1950 and 1953, four price increases for alcohol were introduced which, along with other factors, stabilized alcohol consumption during that period. The consumption rise which followed in the next four years was crowned by a rapid jump from 3.4 litres per capita in 1956 to 4.1 litres in 1957. From then on consumption stabilized for nine years in spite of the introduction in that period of only three price increases. Since the mid-1960s alcohol consumption has been on the steady rise with particular momentum in the 1970s (Wald et al., 1981).

Interesting, from an international perspective, are changes in the structure of consumption by beverage type. Between 1950 and 1960, consumption patterns in Poland diversified considerably with the proportion of spirits falling from 78.4 to 62.1%. The consumption of wine rose in that period by a factor of five. Since the mid-1960s a revival of the traditional consumption structure has been observed, with the share of spirits in alcohol consumption surpassing 70% again in 1977. These recent changes have been accompanied by the rapid growth in consumption of all alcoholic beverages.

The structure of spirits consumption in terms of distribution channels was more stable. In the years 1951 to 1968, the share of on-premise consumption slightly exceeded 20%. Since the late 1960s drinking in public has decreased, its share in consumption falling from 20.7% in 1968 to 12.2% in 1975 and to 9.6% in 1978. At the beginning of that process (first four years) changes in the structure of consumption were additive. Following the increase in alcohol prices in 1974, drinking in public has been more and more clearly replaced by private drinking.

The data discussed are based on sales statistics and reflect quite precisely the real level of alcohol consumption. It is estimated that illicit spirits production has no significant impact on the total consumption figures (Galarski, 1976). Consumption of non-beverage alcohol is marginal, too. Even among patients treated for alcoholism, the proportion of those who drink non-beverage alcohol does not exceed 2 or 3% (Bielewicz and Sikorska, 1979).

FIGURE 1   *Per Capita Alcohol Consumption: 1950-1975*

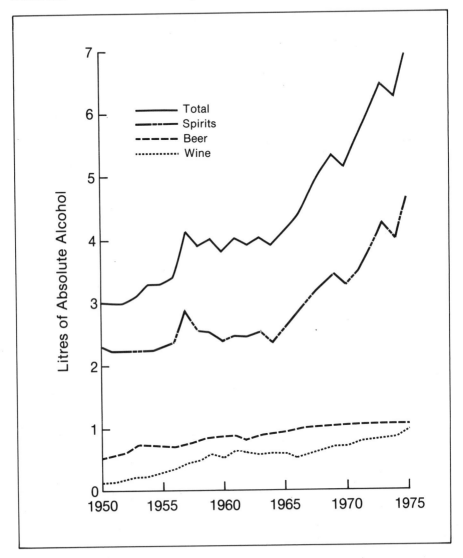

Drinking Populations

The only data on the distribution of alcohol consumption in the population were collected in the 1960s (e.g., Świecicki, 1963), and are out of date. A later survey on alcohol (Janik, 1976) was a quick public opinion poll and failed to provide a deeper analysis of the problem. It is known only that from 1961 to 1976 the percentage of abstainers did not change, remaining about 20%. The slightly higher proportion of abstainers in 1976 can be due to the fact that the recent survey covered the population aged 16 and over, whereas the 1961 data referred to persons 20 and over. In both samples, women are much more frequent abstainers than men. In the 1976 study there was a higher percentage of abstaining men as compared to the 1961 survey. However, the same percentages of women reported abstention in both samples, which may indicate the increasing popularity of alcohol among women. Higher alcohol consumption among women may be associated with the adoption by women of many functions traditionally performed by men.

One may speculate that demographic factors contributed to alcohol consumption growth and the increase of alcohol-related problems in the late sixties and seventies. The post-war baby boom generation which reached the drinking age in that time remarkably enlarged the drinking population. The proportion of that age group in the total changed from 15.2% in 1960 to 18.7% in 1975, but the impact of the post-war generation on mean alcohol consumption levels is better explained by its "wetness" than by its numbers. The growth in the numbers of elderly, who usually drink less than average, suggests that the rise in alcohol consumption per drinker may have been higher than indicated by per capita figures. The highest mean alcohol consumption was registered in the regions populated mainly by those who immigrated after the war due to the shift in the country's borders. This may indicate the significance of weaker social control and the breakdown of traditional community ties in the trends toward increased alcohol consumption.

Drinking Patterns

The gradual overlapping of rural and urban lifestyles after World War II had significant impact on societal drinking patterns. There is some evidence that traditionally, Polish peasants drank large amounts of alcohol on a limited number of well-defined drinking occasions. In contrast, urban populations consumed alcohol more frequently but in smaller doses. The combination of those two drinking patterns may have contributed to the growth in alcohol consumption. The development of a more homogenous culture in Poland has also contributed to greater similarity in drinking patterns between regions.

Despite some changes in the structure of alcohol consumption during the 1950s and early 1960s, vodka has remained the traditional drink of choice. Poles drink less frequently than others, yet once they do, it is "to the bottom," both literally — vodka is drunk in one gulp — and metaphorically; almost every drinking occasion ends in drunkenness.

Alcohol is not drunk at daily meals in Poland but at special dinners, underscoring the extraordinary meaning of the event and the meal. Usually a large amount of alcohol is on hand for such celebrations. This is reflected in responses given in Janik's survey to the question: "What amount of vodka would you prepare for a Saturday party (per one man and per one woman)?" Thirty-five percent of the informants think that 0.25 litres of vodka should be prepared per one man; 30% think that 0.5 litres are required. The amount of alcohol per one woman is smaller, yet 27% of the subjects prepare 0.25 litres of vodka per one woman invited. Serving spirits in this amount must make the majority of guests drunk. Passing the intoxication threshold is more probable in that refusal to drink at a party is not socially accepted. Close to 40% of persons questioned in Stocka's study (1975) think that to avoid a drink at a party is "exaggeration" and those studied by Janik (1976) quite often say they drink: "not to differ from others," "instigated by the community," "not to offend others." The social imperative to drink and do it to the last drop is often reflected in drinking songs: "Who won't drink will be beaten by sticks" or "If we are to drink at all it has to be to the last drop."

The stereotype of a drunken person functioning in society differs from the legal definition of insobriety. Among those studied by Janik (1976), 45% define a drunken person as one who "stammers" and is "not able to fully control his movements," and 27% give even more liberal criteria: a drunken person being one who has "a clearly upset balance, staggers, jabbers."

Drinking is important in Polish social, occupational, and family life. It is socially accepted to get drunk at family occasions, social gatherings, and feasts. However, drunkenness in public places and during working hours is frowned upon. In a remarkable story by Marek Hlasko (1976) "Pijany w samo poludnie" (Drunk in Broad Daylight), a crowd is outraged by the sight of a drunken man on one of Warsaw's main streets, not because of the state he was in, but the hour of the day: "Son of a bitch. Got drunk in broad daylight. What can you do about the bastard?"

DRINKING-RELATED PROBLEMS: SOCIETAL DEFINITIONS AND REACTIONS TO DRINKING PROBLEMS

"Drunkenness has dark and bright sides to it. The drink can drown you in a gutter, head over ears, if you are weak-headed, but over a bottle you can also have a good time with a woman, chatting with chums on this or that, get yourself a better job . . ." In his story "Przyjecie na dziesieć osób plus trzy" (A Party for Ten Plus Three), author Jan Himilsbach (1976) succeeds in grasping an ambivalence of Polish attitudes toward alcohol, the use and abuse of which, on the one hand, is met with extreme disapproval, and, on the other, depending on the context, total acceptance. Despite the overall approving attitude toward alcohol, there is widespread sentiment about the necessity to reduce the consequences of drinking. Almost 90% of those studied by Janik (1976) think that "something should be done to make people in Poland drink less" and more than one-third see an urgent need to initiate some action in this field. Among alcohol-related problems, most often mentioned are the effects suffered by the family (67%) and alcohol-related accidents (27%).

In view of the relative permissiveness of Poles toward alcohol, and the general public attitude toward alcohol-related problems, the state's propaganda should focus primarily on the negative consequences of drinking. Instead, slogans have been directed, with few exceptions, against alcohol as such or, (in recent years) aimed at eliminating alcohol from leisure activities (have a good party without alcohol, holiday without alcohol, etc.). This strategy has not been effective. The often used slogan "Alcohol your enemy" has entered the drinking culture and is now functioning as a toast: "Alcohol your enemy — let's finish with it." Another anti-alcohol poster — "Alcohol kills slowly" — is often supplemented with anonymous handwritten remarks such as, "Kills slowly? I'm not in a hurry."

Control and Treatment Facilities

The Permanent Government Commission for Alcohol Problems deals with all alcohol-related problems on the central level. Composed of vice-ministers of various branches it is responsible for the coordination and initiation of actions aimed at alcohol control on the national scale, the framing of programmes in this field, and drafting of appropriate legal provisions. Affiliated with the Commission is the Experts Committee, gathering people of various academic disciplines (e.g. physicians, jurists, economists, and sociologists). The activity of the Commission has not been very efficient. Its members, for obvious reasons, have only a part-time interest in alcohol issues and primarily defended the interests of their own agencies. It has no specific administrative apparatus, and its powers are not well defined (Wald et al., 1981).

Treatment for alcoholism and rehabilitation of alcoholics, as well as assistance to their families, are entrusted to the Ministry of Health and Welfare. The treatment of alcohol-dependent persons is provided by outpatient clinics (counselling centres), intermediate units, and inpatient clinics (hospital wards). The first 88 outpatient alcoholism clinics were opened in Poland in 1956 and the first specialized alcoholism treatment unit was started two years later (Table 1).

In 1975, there were 431 outpatient alcoholism clinics in Poland employing physicians mostly on a part-time basis. Only 29 physicians

TABLE 1   *Alcoholic Treatment Institutions and Sobering-Up Stations*

Years	Outpatient Clinics for Alcoholics		Inpatient Clinics of Hospital Type**		Sobering-Up Stations	
	Number	Physician employment in terms of full-time posts*	Number	Beds	Number	Beds
1956	88	18.3	0	0	1	82
1957	122	21.0	0	0	8	260
1958	201	41.3	1	78	13	398
1959	231	N.A.	2	112	5	514
1960	289	N.A.	2	138	16	522
1961	344	N.A.	4	258	21	672
1962	357	81.4	6	398	22	741
1963	364	N.A.	5	350	22	728
1964	359	104.3	6	375	22	831
1965	365	101.9	6	375	22	940
1966	375	96.7	6	375	22	963
1967	385	99.1	6	375	23	1008
1968	404	107.1	7	475	24	1035
1969	406	115.9	7	490	26	1131
1970	415	116.9	7	535	27	1178
1971	431	127.5	8	530	27	1181
1972	426	123.6	8	535	28	1206
1973	428	123.0	10	746	30	1295
1974	N.A.	105.5	10	781	33	1421
1975	431	102.1	8	675	35	1517

Sources: Data of the Psychoneurological Institute
Data of the Ministry of Home Affairs

* Number of full-time is seven-hour posts plus overtime measured as full-time where one full-time post is 2,100 working hours per year.
** Treatment wards at psychiatric hospitals excluded.

worked full-time. With most employed on a part-time basis, the total number of physicians was the equivalent of only 102.1 full-time positions. The shortage, not only of physicians, but also of nurses, psychologists, and social workers, is a serious obstacle to treatment effectiveness. The only help the majority of patients can expect is disulfiram tablets.

Residential treatment is provided in specialized alcoholism treatment units or alcoholism treatment wards run within mental hospitals. In 1975, there were eight units with 675 beds and 36 hospital wards with 1,559 beds for alcoholics. Residential treatment facilities admit some 13,000 patients annually, 3,000 of them going to specialized alcoholism treatment units. In some local jurisdictions (voivodships), alcoholics directed by courts for compulsory treatment have to wait several years for admission. The number of personnel in these units is insufficient and some employ only one physician. The three intermediate units operating in bigger cities (night or day centres), which allow patients everyday contact with their community, have approximately 110 beds.

Prisoners also undergo alcoholism treatment: 3,000 were attended to in 1975, 30% of them in alcoholism treatment wards of prison hospitals. Social aid rendered to the families of alcoholics is not sufficient, though it uses up some 25% of local anti-alcohol funds. Particularly hard are conditions of the families of those alcoholics who have no permanent job and undergo hospital treatment. The allowance granted to such families is generally many times lower than the average pay.

The Polish alcohol treatment system has been dominated by provision of compulsory treatment. In the 1970s, about 40% of hospitalized alcoholics entered the system involuntarily. It is estimated that one-fourth of them are not "real alcoholics," i.e. are not dependent on alcohol in a medical sense. So-called compulsory patients often have no motivation to accept medical care and, according to many physicians, "they make a lot of mess in the hospital wards." An early discharge of those who are not dependent is rare because, as one of the doctors stated, "It is very complicated, and one has to do many formalities (questioning court decisions, filling out a lot of papers, and so on)." It seems that compulsory treatment grasps not only patients, but medical staff as well. It has had many adverse consequences, centred mainly around social perceptions. An alcoholic is perceived neither as an ill person, nor a criminal, but rather as a mad troublemaker. This influences the perception of the alcohol treatment system, and has a lot to do with the low status of the treatment staff.

Much of the alcohol control is exercised by the Ministry of Home Affairs which deals with the prevention of crimes and offences committed under the influence of alcohol. The Ministry supervises detoxification centres — called sobering-up stations — which have the right to detain for 24 hours those under the influence of alcohol who behave indecently in public. The stations perform not only public order-keeping but also medical, diagnostic, and preventive functions. The first sobering-up station was established in 1956. In 1975, there were 35 of them in Poland with 1,517 beds and 300,000 admissions (see Table 1). There are not, however, enough of these stations and many potential patients are detained in militia stations to sober up.

Several other ministeries are involved in alcohol-related problems. The Ministry of Wages, Labour, and Welfare is particularly concerned with preventing drunkenness in workplaces. In 1974, a programme to help deal with this was launched. A similar programme for transportation workers was organized under the Ministry of Transport. The Ministry of Justice is responsible for the organization of alcoholism treatment in penitentiary institutions and conducts training of prison personnel on treatment and prevention of alcoholism. Unfortunately, no statistical data on the effectiveness of these programmes are available.

Prevalence of Drinking-Related Problems

Polish statistics on consequences of alcohol abuse and drinking problems are shaped by frequent changes in data collecting systems, rule enforcement activity, and the capacity and availability of health services.

Some medical statistics, particularly data on alcohol psychoses, describe the reality relatively well. According to Wald and Jaroszewski (1978), the number of first admissions to hospitals for alcohol psychoses is highly correlated with the consumption of spirits. Correlation with the consumption of other alcoholic beverages is less strong. Thus, the prevalence of alcohol psychosis appears to be more a consequence of the widespread use of spirits in Poland than of high alcohol consumption. Between 1956 and 1975, the ratio of first hospital admissions for alcohol psychoses to 100,000 inhabitants rose more than threefold (see Table 2), whereas consumption of spirits grew a little more than twofold. This suggests that the proportion of heavy drinkers — from among whom alcohol psychotics mainly come — is growing faster than the level of alcohol consumption. By 1975, the coefficient of first hospital admissions for alcohol psychoses amounted to 7.2 admissions per 100,000 inhabitants: 13.9 for men and only 0.9 for women. The marked difference in coefficients for the two sexes reflects differences between male and female drinking patterns and shows a large consumption concentration among men. Similar trends regarding the rates of psychoses for men and women in the years 1956 and 1975 allows us to think that the male pattern of heavy drinking has thus far been adopted by a relatively small group of women. Similar conclusions may be drawn from data on deaths caused by acute alcohol poisoning. While the death rate among men remains much higher than that of the female population, between 1951 and 1975 the number of deaths caused by alcohol poisoning grew at approximately the same rate among both men and women.

First hospital admissions for alcoholism do not reveal the scale of alcoholism in Poland. They do reveal, however, capacity of the health service system. Between 1950 and 1955, prior to the enactment of the first anti-alcohol law regulating compulsory alcoholism treatment, no separate statistics on alcohol treatment were available. Six hundred and ninety-nine first hospital admissions were recorded in 1956; and 5,713 in 1975. A marked growth in the number of admissions took place in 1957 and in the early sixties following the introduction of two anti-alcohol laws, as well as in 1972 when the Council of Ministers' made voivodes (persons in charge of intermediate administrative organs) responsible for construction of

TABLE 2   Rates of Selected Alcohol-Related Problems

Years	First hospital admissions per 100,000 inhabitants		Deaths per 100,000 inhabitants		Detentions to sober up per 100,000 inhabitants			Cases of drunk driving per 1,000 motor vehicles	Road accidents involving alcohol per 1,000 motor vehicles
	Alcoholism	Alcohol psychosis	Alcohol poisoning	Liver cirrhosis	Sobering-up stations	Arrests	Total		
1951	N.A.	N.A.	1.0	5.9	0	N.A.	N.A.	N.A.	N.A.
1952	N.A.	N.A.	1.0	6.7	0	N.A.	N.A.	N.A.	N.A.
1953	N.A.	N.A.	1.0	6.8	0	N.A.	N.A.	N.A.	N.A.
1954	N.A.	N.A.	0.9	6.6	0	N.A.	N.A.	N.A.	5.8
1955	N.A.	N.A.	1.0	6.8	0	N.A.	N.A.	N.A.	5.7
1956	2.5	2.3	0.9	6.6	27	N.A.	N.A.	N.A.	5.3
1957	4.0	1.9	1.2	7.2	140	N.A.	N.A.	N.A.	5.7
1958	4.7	1.9	1.2	6.8	288	N.A.	N.A.	N.A.	4.2
1959	6.5	2.3	0.2	3.0	312	983	1295	N.A.	3.9
1960	7.4	2.0	0.4	3.4	343	891	1234	N.A.	4.2
1961	8.4	2.3	0.7	3.9	377	798	1175	N.A.	3.5
1962	9.9	2.3	0.9	4.8	388	642	1030	26.2	2.8
1963	9.2	2.5	0.9	5.8	395	691	1086	34.7	2.3
1964	9.7	2.0	0.9	5.9	413	612	1025	40.2	1.8
1965	10.7	3.2	1.2	6.0	457	483	940	43.2	1.5
1966	11.8	3.6	1.4	6.6	495	302	797	45.3	1.6
1967	11.9	3.8	1.4	7.1	534	279	813	43.4	1.7
1968	10.2	3.6	2.0	7.5	532	287	819	40.6	1.8
1969	11.5	4.2	2.1	8.1	565	273	838	N.A.	1.8
1970	13.1	4.7	2.0	8.3	656	280	936	N.A.	1.8
1971	13.9	5.1	2.3	9.0	680	445	1125	N.A.	2.0
1972	14.1	5.9	2.4	9.4	719	445	1164	39.4	2.1
1973	15.4	6.5	2.6	9.7	793	484	1223	41.6	2.0
1974	16.6	6.1	2.5	9.6	730	403	1133	33.6	1.8
1975	16.7	7.2	2.7	10.2	854	398	1252	N.A.	2.2[a]

Sources: Data on Hospital Admissions — Psychoneurological Institute; Data on Deaths — Central Statistical Office; Data on Detentions — Militia HQ, "Walka z Alkoholizmem" / Monthly Report of Polish National Anti-alcoholic Committee, 1962 no. 1; Data on Drunk Driving — Militia HQ, "Central Statistical Office, "Walka z Alkoholizmem" 1963 nos. 9-10.

[a] Data for 1975 — uncomparable.

alcoholism treatment institutions. Over the whole period, excluding the years 1956-59, the relation between the number of admissions and the number of beds for alcoholics has been more or less stable.

Polish statistics on deaths due to liver cirrhosis are not very useful because they do not separate alcohol-related deaths from the alcohol study perspective. Deaths caused by liver cirrhosis in the age group 65 and over account for more than 50% of the total number of deaths due to this condition.

Statistics on those kept in militia stations and sobering-up stations, though affected by the militia's changing policy toward insobriety, are considered a good indicator of public drunkenness. From 1959 to 1975, the number of alcohol-related detentions in militia stations decreased two-fold, while the number in sobering-up stations rose more than three times (cf. J. Morawski, 1980). These changes had no significant impact on the overall index of detention. In 1959, 1,295 persons per 100,000 inhabitants were detained to sober up in militia stations and sobering-up stations; in 1975, 1,252 persons per 100,000 inhabitants were detained. The stabilization of the rates of detention, in spite of the considerable growth in alcohol consumption, can partly be attributed to the decrease in public drinking. One may also risk a hypothesis that drinking in Poland is becoming more "civilized" and is leading to intoxication less frequently than previously. This can be partially verified by looking at alcohol misdemeanours. From 1953 to 1975, the number of adjudged "alcohol misdemeanours" (mainly public order disturbance under the influence of alcohol) dropped from 229,000 to 186,000, and the ratio to 1,000 litres of alcohol consumed dropped from 2.8 to 0.8 (cf. J. Morawski, 1980).

The reduction of drunk driving has for years been a major goal of the militia, as well as an important aspect of temperance publicity. This activity has been fairly effective. In spite of the threefold rise in the number of cars and the considerable growth in alcohol consumption from 1962 to 1975, the number of recorded cases of drunk driving per 1,000 registered vehicles or per 10,000 litres of alcohol consumed has decreased recently after a rise in the mid-1960s. However, drunk driving still remains widespread, and in 1974 militia stopped over 125,000 persons driving under the influence of alcohol (cf. J. Morawski, 1980). The ratio of road accidents involving alcohol per 1,000 motor vehicles decreased threefold during the decade following 1954, and remained at the same level in the following 10 years. Also the number of accidents involving alcohol grew at a slower pace than the total number of road accidents.

CONTROL SYSTEM

The first important alcohol-related laws were passed in Poland towards the end of the 15th century, giving noblemen the privilege to sell alcohol. In the course of time this developed into the noblemen's monopoly over the production and distribution of alcoholic beverages. Alcohol became one of the legal tenders — peasants were given alcohol for their work. With the spread of cheap and effective technology for spirits production from potatoes in the beginning of the 19th century, there was increased drunkenness among Polish peasants. Confronted with the rapid deterioration of health in the population, and particularly among military recruits, the authorities of the Tsars of Russia introduced a number of restrictions concerning the sale of alcohol, and abolished the noblemen's privileges (Wald et al., 1981). Those control measures and the appearance of the temperance movement partly explains an almost fivefold drop in alcohol consumption during the second part of the 19th century. In the inter-war period, several anti-alcohol laws were passed. Although relatively liberal as compared to the then existing prohibition tendencies, these laws were generally tougher than those introduced after World War II. Pre-war acts were formally in force until 1956, although in practice their provisions were not enforced. And yet the average alcohol consumption from 1950 to 1956, low by international standards, rose at a very slow pace, supposedly due to four alcohol price increases — alcohol prices rose much faster than the nominal income of the population.

Important Actors and Level of Decision-Making

There are many actors in the alcohol scene in Poland, and the overall effect of their involvement could be described as a collective compromise. It is difficult, however, to identify all the relevant forces. Nevertheless, the main visible actors in the alcohol control systems are undoubtedly the Sejm (Diet), People's Councils (local representative bodies), central administration, organs of local administration, the Polish National Anti-Alcoholic Committee, and the Church.

The Sejm. Since World War II, the Sejm passed a number of laws concerning the production of spirits. As early as 1944, a decree issued on illicit distillation levied severe penalties for persons who violated its provisions (e.g. up to 15 years imprisonment). The severity of penalties was motivated by the necessity to protect food resources during the war.

It was not until 1953 that the decree gave way to a more liberal law. In April 1959, the Sejm passed the current law against the illicit production of spirits. Like previous measures, this law authorized a state monopoly over spirits production, and defined penalties for illegal manufacture, storage of stills, and sale and purchase of illicitly distilled spirits.

The law governing the production of wines, wine musts, and meads, passed in 1948, pays particular attention to the quality of wines. For example, there are a dozen or so substances whose use in the production of wine is forbidden. According to the law, wine may be produced with appropriate permission by state-owned, cooperative, and private enterprises. In 1958, the private sector was deprived of this right by the Sejm. Wines for makers' use can be manufactured without permission but the quantity cannot exceed 100 litres per year, including current stocks.

Two laws governing the sale of alcohol, alcoholism treatment regulations, and drunk driving were introduced in 1956 and 1959. The latter measure contains a long list of restrictions concerning sales of alcohol. This law forbids the sale of alcoholic beverages to intoxicated persons, to persons on pledge, and the sale of liquors of more than 4.5% alcohol content to persons under 18. The law also specifies about 20 places and circumstances in which alcohol sales, service, and consumption are prohibited. Relatively, spirits are subject to the strictest control and beverages with less than 4.5% alcohol the mildest. Other important regulations in the 1959 law include the decriminalization of public drunkenness, introduction of sobering-up stations, introduction of compulsory treatment of alcoholics, and legal protection of their families.

The introduction of these acts between 1956 and 1959 promoted a wide public discussion and created a certain social climate around the "alcohol issue," which largely influenced the stabilization of alcohol consumption in the late 1950s and 1960s.

Local representative bodies.   These have the authority to impose further limitations on the sale of alcohol. People's councils, in consultation with appropriate organizations, may introduce the complete prohibition of sales and service of alcohol in a given area. However, in the study period, local representative bodies used these powers very rarely. The only exception worth mentioning is a resolution of the People's Council of Wolow (a small district town in the Southwest of Poland) introducing a ban on alcohol sale in the 1960s. The ban was in force for only a few years.

Central administration.   Many resolutions connected with alcohol control have been taken by the Council of Ministers. Two examples of the 1970s may be mentioned: one in 1972 made voivodes responsible for construction of alcoholism treatment institutions; another, in 1973, set up the anti-alcohol fund designed for prevention, publicity, and research activities. The Council of Ministers has the power to impose periodical bans on sales of alcohol beverages throughout the country (e.g. on election days). In 1971, the Chairman of the Council of Ministers appointed the Permanent Government Commission on Alcohol Problems. The Commission's duties cover initiation and coordination of activities connected with alcohol control. Central administration is also able to grant permission for the production of spirits and wines. General principles of issuing off-licences and on-licences, as well as the ratio of shops to the number of inhabitants, are set up by appropriate ministers.

Organs of local administration.   Local administrative governments grant licences for sales and services of spirits and wines, thus determining the actual density of the alcohol distribution network. A considerable hierarchical "distance" between those who set up general rules concerning the density of alcohol distribution networks (the Ministry of Domestic Trade and Services) and those who grant licences seems to be a factor responsible for a discrepancy between the prescribed density of outlets and the actual number of such outlets.

Polish National Anti-Alcoholic Committee.   The Polish Anti-Alcoholic Committee set up in 1948 had more than 120,000 members in 1975. Its statutory objectives include publicity for sobriety, cooperation in this field with other social bodies, and the carrying out of research on the observance of temperance legislation. The Committee published two monthlies, and has the power to submit legislative initiatives on alcohol control, to issue opinions on decisions of local authorities regarding alcohol sales, and to distribute voivodship funds earmarked for alcohol control. It seems that the Committee, on its central level, has failed to act as a pressure group representing the social temperance movement. But at the local level, members of the Polish National Anti-Alcoholic Committee have had more influence on alcohol control policies.

The Church.   The Church alcohol-related activity represents a moral rather than a public health perspective. In sermons there are frequent appeals for sobriety. Alcohol abuse is often condemned. Special action is taken during Lent: every year the Church sends a special pastoral letter calling for sobriety. Some actions have been recently taken at the community level to prevent illicit distilling and sale of alcohol. There is an Episcopal Commission for Sobriety and the dioceses appoint special clerics working in this field. Much educational effort has been directed towards priests as well as laymen.

The role of certain other actors, typically influential in a free market economy, is negligible. No formal limitations affect alcohol advertising in Poland. Yet alcoholic beverages are, in effect, not publicized by the mass media and a relatively weak advertising industry cannot act as a pressure group in this respect. Foreign trade also exerts little impact on alcohol control policy. Although there are no legal restrictions, alcoholic beverages are not a significant item in Polish foreign turnover. Only the consumption of grape wines, which is almost totally dependent on imports, has been limited by the amount of currency at the disposal of foreign trade.

Rule Enforcement and Observance of Alcohol-Related Regulations

No specialized agency in Poland monitors the observance of alcohol control regulations. Absence of studies makes it impossible to say authoritatively to what extent existing regulations are observed. However, everyday experience shows that alcohol control systems operate unsatisfactorily. Bans on sales of alcoholic beverages to intoxicated persons and persons under 18 are commonly violated. Legal provisions concerning localization of alcohol outlets are often violated or evaded. For example, the easy way to evade the ban on the sale of spirits in rest houses (recreational resorts for the workers of various trades and occupations) is to give them a name other than the "rest house." Legislation aimed at restricting the accessibility of alcohol provides a good example of how ineffective very detailed legal acts may be. Often the spirit of the law is violated without any formal deviation from its letter.

The enforcement of local regulations for on-premise outlets which limit the serving of alcoholic beverages without food often creates humorous situations. For instance, doughnuts forced with beer remain untouched and are only a table-dressing. Limitations on the network of wine-and-vodka-selling stores set up by the Minister of Internal Trade and Services are not observed. Legally, since 1964 there should only be one such store per 4,000-5,000 inhabitants in towns and one to three stores for each commune in rural areas. Accordingly, one would expect to have one store selling wine and vodka for approximately 3,000 inhabitants throughout the country, whereas, in fact, there was one retail outlet to 839 inhabitants in 1970.

Compared to the enforcement of regulations pertaining to outlets, greater efforts have been made to protect the state monopoly over the production of spirits, as well as to eliminate drunk driving. From 1950 to 1969, between 1,000 and 2,000 instances of illicit distillation were detected (Galarski, 1976). In the 1970s, after initiating awards for assistance in detecting such offences, the number of recorded offences doubled within a year.

A reduction of the rate of drunk driving may be considered a success. Polish laws in this respect are relatively tight. Driving with a blood alcohol content of over 0.02% is prohibited. Despite the fact that in 1974 the militia charged 125,000 drivers with violating the law, the share of accidents caused by drivers under the influence of alcohol does not exceed 5% of the total number of road accidents. However, drunk cyclists, motorcyclists, cart drivers, and pedestrians are still a problem.

Drunk driving is disapproved of socially. To be a driver is a good excuse not to drink during the party. The social disapproval of drunk driving may be a result of the strict laws concerning blood alcohol concentration, as well as frequent road controls, severe punishments, and selective propaganda against drunk driving rather than against alcohol as such.

Prices

Prices of alcoholic beverages are centrally determined by the State Prices Commission according to government recommendations. Price increases are introduced every few years. Each increase reduced the rate of growth of alcohol consumption for one year and most led to a slight drop in consumption.

Although this indicates the importance of prices in shaping alcohol consumption in Poland, the disadvantages of a restrictive alcohol price policy should be discussed as well. Radical price increases have been introduced every few years in order to reduce the consumption of heavy drinkers and yet these people are the least responsive to increases in alcohol prices as they are less able to control the level of their alcohol consumption. Sharp increases in prices necessarily affects their families' budgets. In many cases, this dramatic lowering of the living standard, which is a problem in itself, gives rise to many other alcohol-related problems. Thus, price increases aimed at limiting alcohol problems, may, in fact, make them more difficult.

Temporary stabilization of alcohol consumption following each price increase is a result of a rapid rise in relative alcohol prices. After two or three years, however, other prices tend to increase and the relative price of alcohol decreases, stimulating the consumption of alcohol. Furthermore, periodic rumours regarding possible price increases result in a stockpiling of alcohol, which is often consumed well before a price incease is actually introduced.

ALCOHOL IN THE POST-1975 PERIOD

In the period following 1975, there were substantial changes in the alcohol scene in Poland. In 1976 and 1977, there was a rapid growth in alcohol consumption, which was unprecedented in this country (from 6.9 litres in 1975 to 7.8 litres of 100% alcohol per capita in 1976 and 8.3 litres in 1977). This may be partly explained by a sudden drop in relative alcohol prices due to inflation and to the rise in nominal income of the population. Alcohol prices had been stable since 1974.

The year 1978 saw a sharp increase in alcohol prices (38% for spirits, 20% for wine, and 32% for beer) and the stabilization of consumption at 8 litres per capita. Consumption in 1979 remained at the same level. In 1978, the Council of Ministers passed a resolution aimed at limiting the growth of alcohol consumption. The resolution stimulated alcohol control activities at the local level. In 1979 and 1980, many regional representative bodies and administrative organs passed various resolutions limiting the accessibility of alcohol. There were, for example, prohibitions against the off-premise sale of alcohol on special days, such as Saturdays, Sundays, paydays, and market days; a reduction of off-premise outlets; and limitations of selling hours of alcohol in off-premises outlets. Currently, alcohol beverages are usually sold between 10 a.m. and 8 p.m. or between 11 a.m. and 8 p.m.; previously, one could buy alcohol at any time in certain food shops.

Since the strike wave of August 1980, alcohol has become an important political issue. During the first days of the strikes in the Gdansk region, strike committees decided to prohibit alcohol in many factories (e.g. the oil refinery and shipyards). A few days later, local authorities introduced a regional ban on the sale of alcohol. The rationale was "to avoid an open, violent conflict as in 1970 and in 1976" as stated unanimously by both workers and local authorities. Both sides claimed to initiate the idea. The desire of the protagonists to be "the first" in advocating restrictive measures underscores the significance of the decision and clearly reflects the will of both sides to be perceived as agents of social peace or non-violence (Bielewicz and Moskalewicz, 1981).

Since that time, the new trade union, Solidarity, has entered the alcohol control stage as one of the most important and hard-line actors. Bans on alcohol sales, which were introduced several times, both regionally and countrywide, have become a symbolic gesture emphasizing "the seriousness" of the situation. Both Solidarity and the government are in favour of strict control measures and speedy actions aimed mainly against alcohol accessibility and drinking in the workplace. An example of this is Solidarity's demand to reduce the alcohol retail network to one outlet per 30,000 inhabitants which would result in a dramatic decrease from about 35,000 shops to 1,200.

The 10-point programme of the new government, which has been referred to as "the government of the last chance," includes "the fight against alcoholism." Alcoholism is often perceived as a pathology and rarely as a manifestation of a complex social and cultural process. In March 1981, prices were increased 50% for vodka, 15% for wine, and 10% for beer. Shortly before these price increases, the supply of spirits was cut down by some 20% and vodka joined a great variety of products (such as meat and butter) which people searched for. Long lines in alcohol shops became common in Poland. This new status for vodka did not change after the recent price increase, as supplies remain limited.

CONCLUSION

The new forces seeking to influence the Polish alcohol control system make the state responsible for the growth in alcohol consumption and the increase in problems. The accusation was explicitly formulated in a document entitled, "Demands to counteract the further pushing of alcohol," which was used as a starting point of a Solidarity working group negotiating alcohol issues with the government. The belief in the possibilities of restrictive government action appears to be justified. Even though in the past, the state did not implement effective control measures to prevent the growth of alcohol consumption, and its interests were primarily of fiscal and economic character.

The social changes which have characterized Poland since World War II are more than the backdrop on the alcohol control stage. Unprecedented horizontal and vertical mobility of the society resulted in a cumulation and homogenization of cultural patterns. Various drinking practices and alcohol uses which previously existed exclusively in specific cultural circles and reflected the diversity of pre-war society became nationwide.

The process of adaptation to new drinking practices was facilitated by the disruption of traditional methods of social control. Weak social controls can explain, to some extent, both an increase in consumption by former drinkers as well as the appearance of new drinkers. Some success has been noted in controlling those drinking comportments which were not very well established (e.g. drunk driving) and in alleviating some drinking-related problems (e.g. medical alcohol problems). Nevertheless, compared to the effects of fundamental social change, alcohol policy probably has had a minor influence on the alcohol scene.

REFERENCES

Bielewicz, A. & Sikorska, C., 1979, *Efektywność stacjonarnego lecznictwa odwykowego (Effectiveness of Treatment of Alcoholism)*. Working report from research project now in progress. Psychoneurological Institute.

Bielewicz, A. & Moskalewicz, J., 1981, *Doświadczenia gdańskie — sierpien 1980 (Gdańsk Experiences — August 1980)*. Working report from research project now in progress. Psychoneurological Institute.

Dodziuk-Lityńska, A. & Markowska, D., 1971. *Rodzina w miastach polskich (The Family in Polish Towns)*. Warszawa, Poland.

Galarski, S., 1976, *Kryminologiczne i prawne aspekty nielegalnego gorzelnictwa (Criminological and Legal Aspects of Illicit Distilling)* Wydawnictwa Prawnicze, Warszawa, Poland.

Himilsbach, J., 1976, *Monidlo*. Przepychanka Panstowowy Instytut Wydawniczy, Warszawa, Poland.

Hłasko, M., 1976, *Opowiadania (Short Stories)*. Czytelnik, Warszawa, Poland.

Janik, J., 1976, *Problemy alkoholizmu w Polsce — wybrane zagadnienia z uwzglednieniem badan empirycznych (Problems of Alcoholism in Poland — Selected Problems and Empirical Findings)*. Public Opinion Research Centre at Polish Radio and Television, Warszawa, Poland.

Morawski, J., 1980, *A Note about Statistics on Alcohol-Related Problems in Poland in the Years 1950 - 1975*. Paper presented at the ISACE Third Working Meeting Serock, Poland.

Podgórecki, A., 1968, *Zarys socjotechniki (An Outline of Sociotechnics)* Wiedza Powszechna, Warszawa, Poland.

Stocka, I. et al., 1975, *Postawy mieszkanców jednej z dzielnic Warsawy wobec niektórych problemów alkoholizmu (Attitudes of Inhabitants of One Warsaw District to Some Alcohol-Related Problems)*. Psychoneurological Institute Warszawa, Poland.

Świecicki, A., 1963, *Struktura spożycia napojów alkoholowych w Polsce na podstawie badań ankietowych (Alcohol Consumption Pattern from Survey)* Polish National Anti-alcoholic Committee, Warszawa, Poland.

Wald, I. et al., 1981, *Raport o problemach polityki w zakresie alkoholu (Report on Alcohol Policy)*, Psychoneurological Institute, Warszawa, Poland.

Wald, I. & Jaroszewski, Z., 1978, *Possibilities of Using Statistics of Alcohol Psychosis for Measurement of Prevalence of Heavy Drinking*. Paper presented at the ISACE First Working Meeting. Helsinki, Finland.

3. Drink in Finland: Increasing Alcohol Availability in a Monopoly State

K. Mäkelä, E. Österberg, and P. Sulkunen*

INTRODUCTION

This report is an attempt to analyze the social dynamics of alcohol in Finland since World War II. It presents a conceptually structured description of a set of historical processes in one country in the course of a given period of time. We shall therefore begin by briefly characterizing the country and the period.

Finland is a sparsely populated and culturally homogeneous country with 4.7 million inhabitants in 1975. Over 90% of Finns belong, albeit formally, to the Lutheran church. The Swedish-speaking minority (7% in 1970) is culturally very similar to the Finnish-speaking majority. Regional variations in culture are also small despite an uneven economic development and an east-west division in traditional culture. These differences have further decreased as a result of migration to the cities and a rapid expansion of popular mass communication media, especially television.

Finland is a highly politicized society, and political cleavages are usually described as deep. Occupational status is a better predictor of voting behaviour than in many other capitalist countries (Uusitalo, 1975). The main parties are the conservative party, the agrarian centre party, the social democratic party, and the communist party. Since 1966, government power has been in the hands of a remarkably stable coalition of parties of the left and the centre. Finland is also an industrialized country with a relatively high standard of living. Its industrialization is, however, of recent origin, and the country moved rapidly from an agrarian economy to a ser-

---

*The Finnish ISACE project was a joint undertaking of the Finnish Foundation for Alcohol Studies and the Social Research Institute of Alcohol Studies, and over the years all members of these two organizations have participated in the production of this report. Tuula Muhonen served as project secretary for the Finnish aspect of ISACE.

31

vice economy, partly bypassing the intermediate stage of manufacturing (Alestalo, 1980). Economic change was accompanied by similarly exceptional internal migration from rural to urban areas. Another important dimension of change was the expansion of the educational system.

Economically and socially, Finland underwent rapid changes in the post-war period which undercut (but certainly did not eliminate) traditional moral attitudes and ideologies. The concern with moral order and social control which characterized the late 1940s gradually gave way to more liberal attitudes about daily life in general and drinking behaviour in particular.

This report deals with the period between 1950 and 1975. Immediately after World War II, the consumption of alcohol was higher than in 1950, and public disturbance related to drinking was also at a high level. Alcohol policies in the early 1950s can in some respects be viewed as a continuation of the post-war period and as the last years of a successful effort to restore order in public behaviour. During the study period, new and less restrictive alcohol legislation came into force at the beginning of 1969. The years after 1975 differ in many respects from the preceding decades, especially as the continuous increase in alcohol consumption has come to a standstill since 1974. Data on 1976-1980 are referred to only when necessary for an understanding of the special historical characteristics of the study period.

CONSUMPTION OF ALCOHOLIC BEVERAGES

In Finland, the historically dominant use of alcohol has been its use as an intoxicant, and the cultural acceptance of drunkenness is still widespread. In his drinking group experiments, Kettil Bruun (1959) documented the existence of the following norm: "It is manly and prestigious to drink a great deal whenever one drinks." In two surveys, a sizeable proportion of the respondents preferred occasional intoxication to regular moderate drinking (Allardt, 1957; Allardt et al., 1962). Immediately after World War II, drinking was infrequent and separated from everyday life. In 1946, only 50% of the men and 12% of the women had drunk more recently than one month before, but the amounts consumed at one sitting were quite high (Kuusi, 1948). In 1976, as many as 80% of the men and 60% of the women had drunk within the previous month (Sulkunen, 1979). The frequency of light drinking had greatly increased but the fundament of heavy drinking occasions was still intact, even if drinking had become less isolated from other social activities (Simpura, 1978a, b).

After the liberalizing legislation of 1969, it was expected that the subsequent increase in aggregate consumption would be accompanied by a growing share of moderate drinking occasions, and this was precisely what happened during 1969 compared to 1968. The new legislation thus brought about an increase in consumption and created new drinking practices. At the same time, however, the absolute frequency of heavy drinking occasions also increased (Mäkelä, 1975a). Surprisingly enough, the share of heavy drinking occasions in total consumption increased again from 1969 to 1976 (Simpura; 1978a). The Finns thus seemed to return to less restrained patterns of drinking soon after the legislative reform.

The share of total alcohol consumption accounted for by women increased from 13% in 1968 to 17% in 1969 and 21% in 1976 (Mäkelä, 1971; Simpura, 1978a). The distribution of drinking occasions according to the age and sex composition of the company, however, was very similar in 1969 and 1976. The contribution of all-female parties to total drinking occasions may have increased somewhat, whereas the share of all-male parties tended to decrease. Both changes reflect the increased acceptance of female drinking. For both sexes the great majority of drinking occasions continued to occur in private surroundings rather than in restaurants (Simpura, 1978b). It is also generally known that drinking spread to a wide array of new social situations, even if survey data are not detailed enough to give a full picture of this diversification of drinking occasions.

Aggregate Consumption

In 1950, the recorded consumption of alcohol in Finland was at a very low level by international comparisons (1.7 litres of 100% alcohol per capita). By 1975, this level had risen by more than threefold but still remained at a comparatively moderate level (6.2 litres). In the 1950s, the consumption level remained quite stable (Figure 1). From 1959 onwards, a steady increase occurred, culminating in a 46% jump in 1969, the year of the great alcohol reform. This growth continued in the early 1970s, but since 1974 the consumption has remained stable (Österberg, 1980). The years 1959-1974 therefore appear as a distinct period of growth in alcohol consumption. It is possible that stable consumption levels after 1974 signify an end to a long wave of rising consumption.

The beverage structure of consumption greatly fluctuated (Figure 2), often in response to changes in relative prices or in the control system. As in many other countries, consumption growth was accompanied by the diversification of beverage structure. Beer became especially popular, and Finland changed from a spirits country to a spirits and beer country. The share of distilled beverages fell from 80% in 1950 to under 40% in 1969. The tenacity of Finnish beverage preferences is, however, evident in the rise of the share of distilled beverages again to 45% in 1975. Although price policies supported wines as a source of relatively cheap alcohol, their popularity remained low (Österberg, 1979a).

FIGURE 1   *Consumption of Alcoholic Beverages by Type of*
                       Outlet in Litres of 100% Alcohol Per Capita,
                       1950-1975

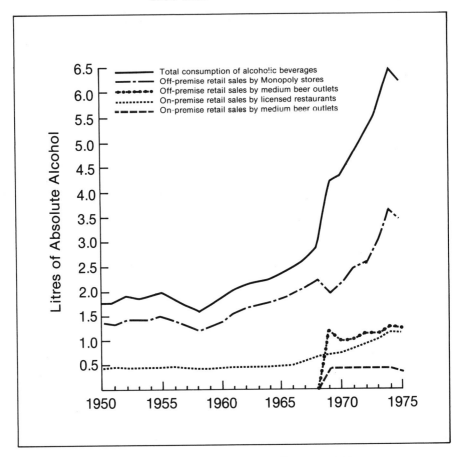

Sources: Alkon vuosikirja 1950-1975; Österberg, 1979a

In the 1950s, the assortment of wines sold consisted almost exclusively of domestic fortified wines. The consumption of wines fluctuated from year to year inversely with the consumption of distilled spirits, indicating that both groups were rather close substitutes for each other. Later on, the wine group included a growing share of light wines, which probably indicates a differentiation of wines from spirits (Österberg, 1979a and 1981). With the exception of wines and spirits in the 1950s, changes in the beverage structure did not involve substitution effects. On the contrary, the introduction of medium beer into grocery stores and other liberalization measures instituted in 1969 were followed by a rapid increase in spirits drinking as well.

FIGURE 2   *Consumption of Alcoholic Beverages by Beverage Class, in Litres of 100% Alcohol Per Capita, 1950-1975*

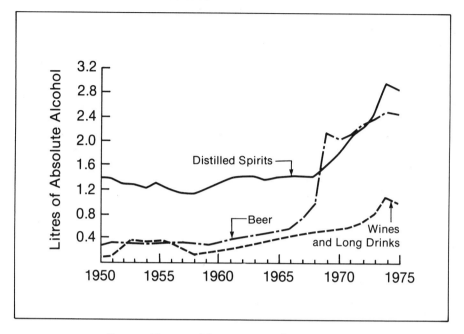

Sources: Alkon vuosikirja 1950-1975; Österberg, 1979a

       The structure of consumption by type of outlet remained stable throughout the period. The share of on-premises consumption in total alcohol sales remained at about one-quarter, although the on / off-licence price ratio rose from 1.6 to 2.1 (Mäkelä, 1980a). One contributing factor to the persisting importance of restaurants is their diversification and this ability to draw new types of customers (Simpura, 1976; Koskikallio, 1979). The overall level, beverage structure, and sales composition by distribution outlet developed along the same lines and at a similar pace in all regions of the country (Ahlström-Laakso and Österberg, 1978).

       Unrecorded consumption remained at the same level throughout the period. Contrary to expectations, it was not substituted for by the large increase in recorded consumption. The ratio of unrecorded consumption to recorded consumption declined from about one-quarter to below 10%. The structure of unrecorded consumption underwent radical changes. Most of the illicit segments decreased and non-beverage alcohol for human use practically disappeared in the 1970s. Instead, travelers' imports grew to be the biggest element of unrecorded consumption and an interesting medium of cultural influence from other countries (Mäkelä, 1979).

Drinkers and Abstainers

In the beginning of the study period, women constituted a large abstaining segment. In 1946, 31% of women and 5% of men had never in their lives consumed alcohol. The corresponding figures were 9% and 4% in 1976 (Sulkunen, 1979). If the last 12 months are used as a criterion, the rate of abstinence among women was 43% in 1968, 35% in 1969, and 20% in 1976. The respective figures for males were 13, 9, and 9% (Mäkelä, 1969; Simpura, 1978a). A considerable number of former abstainers became drinkers during the first year of the new legislation, but the recruitment of new drinkers among the women continued into the 1970s.

In 1946, important differences existed in the abstinence rates between occupational groups and between rural and urban areas. Within these groups, abstinence rates did not vary according to age. In 1976, differences between occupational and residential groups had levelled off, and among the youngest age groups even sex differences had almost disappeared. On the other hand, age differences in abstinence rates were quite considerable. In 1946, abstinence was related to work and living conditions, and in 1976 to age (Sulkunen, 1979).

The older and younger generations reacted differently to the profound structural transformation of the 1950s and 1960s. The cohorts born before 1925 did not change much. Of these 17% had never consumed alcohol in 1946, and 14% continued to be lifelong abstainers in 1976. Among these cohorts, occupational and other demographic differences also persisted in 1976. In contrast, the younger cohorts were internally very homogeneous in respect to abstinence. Generational differences also appear in the sequence of decreasing abstinence rates. The younger generation had already by 1969 reached the low point in their abstinence. Older people, especially women, continued to become drinkers into the 1970s, often very late in their life cycle (Sulkunen, 1979).

It thus seems that the structural transformation of Finnish society, together with the expansion of the educational system, created a cultural gap between generations. The internal homogeneity of the younger generation also suggests that the increase in drinking was not directly related to changes in individual living conditions but was a reflection of an overall change in cultural attitudes towards drinking, which only later permeated the older generation as well. The pervasiveness of this cultural rupture is also manifested by the manner in which these changes in aggregate drinking occurred uniformly and at a similar pace in various regions.

The considerable expansion of the drinking population has not had a great direct effect on the overall consumption level. From 1968 to 1976, when most of the increase in per capita consumption occurred, the increase was from 3.8 litres to 8.0 litres, or 4.2 litres of absolute alcohol per adult. Assuming that the new drinkers in 1976 were consuming at the average rate of the total population in 1968, their contribution to the increase was 0.6 litres or about 15%. Since the new drinkers were mostly women, the assumption on which this estimate is based may exaggerate their contribution (Sulkunen, 1979).

CONSEQUENCES OF DRINKING

In modern societies, three principal ways of formulating "the social liquor question" can be distinguished (Mäkelä and Viikari, 1977). The consequences of drinking can be viewed primarily as a question of public order and security, as a problem of productivity, or as a question of public health. Possible changes in cultural conceptualizations exert an influence both on the experiences of individual drinkers and on official statistics on alcohol problems. It is difficult to deal separately with the "objective" consequences of drinking and the cultural perceptions of and social reactions to drinking problems. By carefully analyzing various sources of error and through the simultaneous use of several complementary statistical series it is possible to generalize about the realities behind the statistics. Therefore, we shall begin by discussing trends in various indicators of consequences of drinking. Only then shall we proceed to an assessment of changes in the overall mixture of problems and in cultural perceptions of the "social liquor question."

Trends

The dramatic increase in aggregate alcohol consumption has been accompanied by a substantial increase in the adverse consequences of drinking. Table 1 presents an overview of the magnitude of this increase. The rate of arrests for drunkenness increased by 60% from 1950 to 1975. The violent crime rate increased by some 85%. In 1951, the number of cases of drunk driving known to the police was about 2,000, and in 1975 about 18,000. In 1975, the number of road accidents classified as alcohol-related was more than threefold compared to the early 1950s.

Three times as many deaths resulted from alcohol poisoning or alcoholism in 1975 as in 1951. Deaths caused by liver cirrhosis and alcohol psychosis similarly trebled between 1951 and 1975. From 1969 to 1975, hospital admission rates for alcoholism, alcohol psychosis, and pancreatitis increased markedly. In 1975, the admission rate in the male population for alcoholism was 1.7-fold, the rate for pancreatitis twofold, and that for alcohol psychosis 2.1-fold compared to 1969. The rate for liver cirrhosis increased only slightly, and there was no change in the admission rate for alcohol poisoning. The increase in alcohol-related admissions seems not to be explained by changes in the number of hospital beds available, admission policies, or diagnostic practices (Poikolainen, 1980).

TABLE 1   *Recorded Consequences of Drinking in Finland in
                                  1950, 1960, 1968, and 1975*

	1950	1960	1968	1975
Arrests for drunkenness per 100,000 inhabitants	3,668.0	2,964.0	3,185.0	5,842.0
Crimes of violence per 100,000 inhabitants	153.0	129.0	157.0	283.0
Alcohol-related road traffic accidents per 100,000 inhabitants	20.0	28.5	44.9	75.1
Cases of drunk driving per 100,000 inhabitants	37.5[1]	96.0	147.2	379.0
Deaths from liver cirrhosis per 100,000 inhabitants	2.3[1]	3.3	3.6	6.3
Fatal alcohol poisonings per 100,000 inhabitants[2]	2.2[1]	2.4	5.2	4.3
Deaths from alcoholism per 100,000 inhabitants[2]	0.2[1]	0.2	0.8	2.3
Deaths from alcohol psychosis per 100,000 inhabitants	0.1[1]	0.1	0.1	0.2
Arrests for drunkenness per 1,000 litres of alcohol	16.4	13.1	8.4	8.2
Crimes of violence per 10,000 litres of alcohol	8.9	7.0	5.5	4.6
Alcohol-related road traffic accidents in % in all road traffic accidents	9.4	5.8	7.3	12.9
Cases of drunk driving per 1,000 registered motor vehicles	17.0[1]	11.8	9.3	15.1

[1] 1951

[2] Alcohol poisoning and alcoholism should be dealt with in combination, since according to the office processing statistics these diagnoses are used interchangeably in identical cases of death. More specifically, since 1968 the diagnosis of alcoholism has been used in many cases that earlier would have been classified as fatal alcohol poisonings.

Source: Österberg, 1979b

    Survey data corroborate this picture. From 1968 to 1976, the proportion of male drinkers reporting that they had stayed off the job because of alcohol increased from 10 to 18%, and the percentage who had had to change jobs because of drinking doubled from 1.1% to 2.4% (Table 2).

    The second general finding is that the increase in most adverse consequences was less than proportionate to the growth in consumption. Consequences thus decreased in relation to units of alcohol consumed. This trend is visible for most consequences, but in Table 1 arrests for drunkenness and violent crime have been chosen as examples. Of all indicators available these are most closely related to behaviour in single drinking occasions and may therefore be used to depict changes in drunken comportment.

TABLE 2 *Adverse Consequences of Drinking Reported by Survey Respondents in 1968 and 1976*

Percentage of 15–69-year-old male drinkers reporting who have ever	1968	1976
been arrested for drunkenness	15.4	19.3
had to stay away from work because of alcohol use	10.0	17.8
had to change jobs because of alcohol use	1.1	2.4

Sampling procedures and questions were identical in both surveys. The questions refer to lifetime experience of each consequence of drinking.
Sources: Mäkelä, 1975b; Simpura, 1978a

A closer analysis (Österberg, 1979b) shows that, with the exception of the early 1970s, the ratio of most drinking problems to consumption had decreased steadily over the entire period. This can be interpreted as a reflection of changes in patterns of drinking and drunken comportment. Common sense indeed tells us that harmful consequences should increase less than in proportion to consumption, and the 1950s and 1960s satisfy this expectation. Therefore, it is all the more surprising to observe that in 1970-1975, adverse consequences increased in pace with average consumption. The trend towards less conflict-prone patterns of drinking was apparently interrupted suddenly after the legislative reform of 1969. It is still too early to judge whether this is merely an isolated episode or a more permanent change in trends. It seems, though, that from 1975 to 1979, the ratio of recorded problems to the level of consumption again started to decrease (Österberg, 1980).

The third main observation is that the rate of increase from 1950 to 1975 varied from one type of consequences to another. Health consequences related to prolonged drinking (e.g. liver cirrhosis) showed a steeper increase than did social conflicts related to single drinking occasions (e.g. arrests for drunkenness and violent crime). This is all the more significant as the number of deaths from liver cirrhosis not related to alcohol probably remained fairly stable, so that the rate of increase in alcohol cirrhosis may be considerably higher than the rate for all cases of cirrhosis. It is easily understandable that the most dramatic increase occurred in drunk driving, since the number of motor vehicles increased more than tenfold between 1950 and 1975. Because of improved general traffic safety, alcohol-related road accidents did not rise in step with drunk driving, but their share in all road accidents grew markedly.

The fourth point is that certain important consequences of drinking reflect sizeable fluctuations that are unrelated to the average level of consumption. The rate of fatal alcohol poisonings reached its peak in the late 1960s, not because of the increase in overall consumption but because of the epidemic use of a newly introduced brand of potent surrogate alcohol. Because of its widespread use as an intoxicant, the production of this brand was discontinued and it was replaced by a more strongly denatured compound (Mäkelä, 1975b: 58).

Changes in Problem Mixture and Cultural Perceptions of Consequences

In 1950, the level of alcohol consumption was very low and chronic ailments related to drinking were uncommon, as illustrated by the low rate of cirrhosis mortality. On the other hand, the average amounts consumed per drinking occasion tended to be substantial, and social conflicts related to drunken comportment were highly visible. As a reflection of these objective circumstances, alcohol problems were culturally structured as events related to single drinking occurrences and viewed from the perspective of public order rather than as symptoms of dependence or from the public health perspective. This cultural perspective is readily seen in Finnish alcohol research. A comparative content analysis of Finnish, French, and American alcohol studies (Mäkelä, 1978) indicates that the two topics of crime and drunkenness were much more commonly discussed in the Finnish and American literature, whereas the French studies more frequently dealt with mortality and somatic diseases. Alcoholism or alcohol addiction was most frequently discussed in the American literature with French studies not far behind, whereas it was much less commonly treated in Finnish studies. A study of the terms used to designate deviant drinkers similarly shows how slowly the concept of alcoholism spread into common usage in Finland (Taipale, 1979).

Over the study period, the prevailing view of "the social liquor question" was altered in many respects. First of all, there was increased tolerance of drunken comportment. Not only was public drunkenness decriminalized in 1969, but it is also evident that police arrest practices became much more liberal than in the early 1950s (Ahlström and Österberg, 1981). The proportion of involuntary inmates in all heavy drinkers receiving inpatient treatment under social welfare legislation decreased radically (Mäkinen, 1979: 78). The diminishing reliance on individualized control of drinking is also manifest in the gradual abolition of the system of individual sales control. It is also symptomatic that no public outcry arose in response to research reports in the mid-1970s showing that a sizeable proportion of girls and boys under 15 years old attending public dances were perceptibly drunk (Keski-Suomen lääninhallitus, 1975; Mäkelä, 1978). All in all, there was less social stigmatization of heavy drinking in the 1970s than in the 1950s.

One type of behaviour related to single drinking occasions, namely drunk driving, has, however, steadily gained in importance. The bulk of the increase in drunk driving may well be explained by the growing volume of traffic, but it nevertheless became more and more prominent from the standpoint of the workload of authorities responsible for the management of alcohol problems. Drunk driving also became more important as a criterion for mandatory individual measures. In 1975, 45% of imprisonment sentences (including suspended sentences) were for drunk driving as opposed to only 14% in 1950 (Official Statistics of Finland, XXIII:88 and XXIII B:111).

At the same time that attitudes towards drunken comportment became more tolerant, public health aspects of the social liquor question received increased consideration. A content analysis of medical journals in the early 1950s and early 1970s showed that alcohol problems were discussed much more frequently during the latter period, and in the 1970s alcohol received more attention in resolutions by medical organizations (Mäkelä, 1978). The division of labour between different authorities in the handling of alcohol problems underwent dramatic changes. In 1960, prisons and cells in police stations accounted for 74% of the total number of daily shelterings related to alcohol use, whereas social institutions and mental hospitals accounted for 20% and 5%, respectively. In 1970, prisons and police stations provided only 23% of the total number of shelterings. Institutions run by social authorities accounted for 55% and mental hospitals 22%. Comparable data on general hospitals are not available, but it is known that the number of patients with explicit alcohol diagnoses has greatly increased (Mäkelä and Säilä, 1976). The growing medicalization of alcohol problems was also manifested in the vast expansion of therapeutically oriented services in the 1960s and 1970s (Mäkinen, 1979).

Alcohol was also increasingly emphasized as a factor threatening productivity and employed problem drinkers, and an interest in occupational treatment programmes gained impetus in 1974 because of the temporary scarcity of labour (Mäkelä, 1978). Data from surveys indicate that the relative importance of productivity problems as compared to issues of public order was increasing, as the number of respondents reporting work-related consequences increased much more steeply than the number of men admitting arrest for drunkenness (Table 2). The Finnish peculiarity of more people reporting arrests than days off because of drinking did not, however, disappear.

Viewed from an international perspective, consequences related to single drinking occasions are still the most obvious feature of the Finnish scene, and this should not be buried under the growing public emphasis of the somatic consequences of prolonged drinking. Until very recently, alcohol poisoning killed more people than did cirrhosis of the liver. Nevertheless, it is very probable that the public health aspects of the social liquor question will be accentuated in the future. Health consequences already display a steeper increase than do social conflicts related to drinking. Moreover, many health ailments have a rather long incubation time.

The importance of alcohol as a public health problem is accented by the fiscal crisis of the state. Because of the vast expansion in health expenditure during the last decades it was relatively easy to provide services suited to alcohol-related conditions. In the future, a more strained financial situation will mean that alcohol-related public health expenditure will be closely watched.

CONTROL POLICIES

As a counterreaction to disruptive drinking patterns, Finland has a long tradition of alcohol control legislation with a period of prohibition in 1919-1932. Since the 1932 Alcohol Act, the production, import, export, distribution, and pricing of alcoholic beverages have been awarded as a monopoly to a state corporation, the State Alcohol Monopoly. The Monopoly is supervised by the Ministry of Social Affairs and Health but has extensive powers of its own. Its board is appointed by the state council so as to represent the parliamentary strength of political parties.

The 1968 Alcohol Act did not alter the basic organizational structure of alcohol control and actually strengthened the position of the State Alcohol Monopoly. It is true that new and more detailed mechanisms were stipulated to ensure parliamentary and governmental control of the Monopoly. At the same time, however, new tasks and more extensive authority were delegated to the Monopoly (Bruun, 1972).

Over this period, the Monopoly has been moderated by regulations under which the State Alcohol Monopoly can entrust the production and on-premise retail sales of alcoholic beverages to private persons or corporations. Since 1969, private corporations have been engaged in off-premise as well as on-premise retail sales, as the 1968 Medium Beer Act entitles grocery stores to obtain licences from the Monopoly to sell medium beer (maximum alcohol content 3.7% by weight). Municipal consent is still separately required for both on-premise and off-premise sales of alcohol in the community, although some details in the new legislation have been amended.

The Monopoly has multiple tasks. It operates distilleries and bottling factories as well as liquor stores and, through two subsidiaries, restaurant chains. It sets the prices of alcoholic beverages as well as the recompensation paid to private producers and distributors and supervises production and distribution costs. It has extensive administrative responsibilities to interpret and enforce alcohol legislation. It sponsors research and carries out educational programs.

At the turn of the century, the temperance movement was one of the strongest popular movements in Finland, and in the beginning of the study period it still was very influential. Despite shrinking popular support, the temperance movement continued throughout the study period to be the most important political actor supporting restrictive alcohol legislation.

Monopoly Stores

Under the 1932 Alcohol Act, liquor stores were not permitted in rural areas. As early as 1950, the Monopoly had at least one store in practically every urban community. With the exception of new establishments in localities already having at least one store, the density of the off-licence network grew mainly at the pace at which municipalities gained city rights. Rural quasi-prohibition was repealed in 1969, and liquor stores were established in 29 municipalities, whereas from 1950 to 1968 only 16 new municipalities obtained stores. From 1970 to 1975, liquor stores were opened in 30 more communities. The total number of stores more than doubled from 1950 to 1975 (Ahlström-Laakso and Österberg, 1976).

Licensed Restaurants

In 1950, 70% of the rather few licensed restaurants were entitled to serve all alcoholic beverages. Beer restaurants had been strongly attacked by the temperance movement in the 1930s, and they were not revived after the war-time suspension of beer production. In the 1950s, the increase in the number of restaurants was in the main due to fully licensed establishments. The expansion of the on-premise network accelerated in the 1960s, but about half of new establishments received beer or wine licences in line with the general policy favouring beverages with a low alcohol content.

Under the 1932 Alcohol Act, on-premise licences could be granted to rural communities in very exceptional circumstances only, but with time the interpretation of the law grew more liberal. The new alcohol legislation coming into force in 1969 made no legal distinction between urban and rural communities. Another important change was that most former beer restaurants were granted licences to serve all beverage types. The total number of licensed restaurants increased from 1968 to 1969 by one-fifth and fully licensed establishments by 60%. The growth in the number of restaurants continued into the 1970s, and in 1975 there were more than four times as many licensed establishments as in 1950 (see Table 3). Alongside these quantitative changes important qualitative changes occurred. Especially in the 1970s, new and specialized types of restaurants appeared and opening hours were extended. Moreover, the general climate in restaurants became less tightly controlled. Restaurants have legal rights to choose their customers, and, for example, to apply rigid dress codes. For a long time, it was almost impossible for unaccompanied women or female parties to enter restaurants. Abandonment of restrictions of this nature was mainly related to general cultural change but also to a more permissive line adopted by the Monopoly (Ahlström-Laakso and Österberg, 1976).

TABLE 3   *Retail Outlets for Alcoholic Beverages, 1950-1975*

	1950	1960	1968	1969	1970	1975
Total number of liquor stores	83	108	132	161	167	194
Number of municipalities with a liquor store	59	67	75	104	111	134
Number of licensed restaurants	348	464	911	1,086	1,170	1,470
Off-premise outlets for medium beer only	—	—	—	17,431	16,736	11,968
On-premise outlets for medium beer only	—	—	—	2,716	3,299	3,078

Sources: Alkon vuosikirja 1950-1975; Österberg, 1979a

Distribution Network for Medium Beer

Until 1968, medium beer could be bought only in liquor stores and licensed restaurants. The Medium Beer Act authorized the Monopoly to grant grocery stores and cafeterias permits respectively to sell or serve medium beer. The Monopoly granted permits fairly liberally to almost all applicants fulfilling the minimum requirements set by law, and in 1969 medium beer outlets accounted for 37% of the total consumption of alcohol (Figure 1). Since then, their number contracted somewhat, mainly because of a decrease in the number of grocery stores and cafeterias in general (Ahlström-Laakso and Österberg, 1976).

Prices

Within very narrow limits, the average real prices of alcoholic beverages remained at the same level during the whole study period. Since the implementation of centralized income policies in the late 1960s, however, government attempts to regulate the general cost of living and the pace of inflation have made it increasingly difficult to maintain the real price level (Mäkelä, 1980a).

Price relationships between various beverage groups showed considerable fluctuation. Starting from the mid-1950s up to the mid-1960s the prices of distilled beverages tended to increase at a faster pace than wine and beer prices. From 1954 to 1957, wine prices were kept at a relatively high level, but this may be regarded as an isolated episode. Price policy was directed against fortified wines, which had become popular among heavy drinkers (Österberg, 1981). In relation to the average price index for all alcoholic beverages, the index for malt beverages fell to its lowest point in 1962, and the index for wines hit its nadir in 1965. In the 1970s, relative price increases tended to be greater for wines and beer than for distilled beverages (Mäkelä, 1980a).

Buyer Restrictions

In 1950-1968, the legal age limit was 21 in liquor stores and 18 in restaurants. The 1968 Alcohol Act lowered the off-premises age limits to 18 years for light beverages and 20 for distilled beverages. Up to 1968, maximum allowable quantities per purchase were prescribed by law. In 1969, the Monopoly used the powers delegated to it by the new legislation to substantially relax these restrictions (Ahlström-Laakso and Österberg, 1976).

In 1950, a special certificate issued by the Monopoly was required for purchases of fortified wines and distilled beverages. In 1952, the certificate requirement was waived for fortified wines, only to be reimposed in 1958. In the 1950s, the certificate was used as a tool for an extensive system of individualized sales control. During its heyday, individual sales control engaged a considerable number of Monopoly officials working in close collaboration with the police and social authorities, and in 1955, more than 15,000 persons had their certificates revoked. Individual sales control was gradually abolished, and the certificate system was discontinued in 1971 (Ahlström-Laakso and Österberg, 1976).

Trends in Alcohol Control

In 25 years, Finland moved from a tightly regulated system with rural prohibition to a much more liberal system, in which alcohol is readily and nearly universally available. Liberalization was cautiously begun in the 1950s, in the guise of a policy favouring wines and beer. Policy was mainly based on the differential treatment of various groups of beverages within a strict system, and overall consumption did not increase to any marked extent.

From the late 1950s onward, beer policies became more expansive (Österberg, 1974). In the 1950s, each brewery had its own sales area as a regional monopoly and in the 1960s this system was gradually abandoned. These measures did not immediately affect the availability of beer, but they forced breweries to compete and contributed to the expansion of the brewing industry. Marketing and advertising became both a means of increasing sales and a condition for the survival of individual breweries. The Monopoly established a subsidiary company to operate beer restaurants, including several in formerly dry rural communities. This measure had great impact on breaking down traditional cultural barriers against alcohol in the countryside (Mäkelä, 1978). Other sectors of the restaurant industry also expanded rapidly in the 1960s.

The new legislation in 1968 was thus the dramatic climax of the process of liberalization. Rural communities obtained liquor stores, the number of fully licensed restaurants grew by 60% and medium beer became available everywhere. The liberalization of the control system was not the only factor affecting availability, however. Migration from rural to urban areas, for example, actually increased the availability of alcohol to a greater extent than did the establishment of new liquor stores (Ahlström-Laakso and Österberg, 1976).

Within the new legal framework, the liberal policy continued well into the 1970s, when the first signs of a more restrictive policy became visible. A number of municipalities revoked the permission for distributing medium beer in the community. In 1977, a new law came into force prohibiting all public advertisement of alcoholic beverages. Since 1978, the Monopoly has experimented with closing its stores on Saturdays during part of the year. Medium beer outlets have been more closely supervised, and restaurants have not been granted extended hours as freely as in the early 1970s (Alkon hallintoneuvoston kertomus, 1969-1979).

ALCOHOL PRODUCTION AND TRADE

Alcohol production and trade are of minor significance to the Finnish national economy in terms of the value of production or the number of persons employed — 0.8% in 1950, and 1.9% in 1975 (Mäkelä, 1980c). In 1977, the production cost value of alcoholic beverages was estimated to be around 1% of the gross value of industrial production (Kasurinen, 1979). Due to the spreading network of Monopoly stores, less restricted retail sales of medium beer since 1969, and the increase in licensed restaurants, the number of persons employed in the distribution of alcohol grew at a faster pace than the size of the labour force working in the production of alcoholic beverages. Of all employees in the alcohol branch in 1975, more than 80% were working in the distribution sector (Mäkelä, 1980c).

Alcoholic beverages had little bearing on the trade balance of Finland. The value of alcohol imports in relation to all imports was only

.2% in 1975, and the value of exports of alcoholic beverages corresponded to 35% of the value of alcohol imports in 1975. The role of imports is small compared to domestic production (Mäkelä, 1980c).

The production of alcoholic beverages is carried out partly by the State Alcohol Monopoly itself and partly by private companies working under close Monopoly supervision. The economic significance of home production for private use is negligible. Almost all distilled beverages are produced by the Monopoly, but there is considerable private production of liqueurs, aperitifs, bitters, and wines from fruits and berries, and all breweries are privately owned. The market shares of the Monopoly and the private sector were thus closely related to the beverage structure of consumption and fluctuated considerably. The relative share of private production reached its peak in 1969, but throughout the 1970s the share of the Monopoly in domestic production remained on a lower level than in the 1950s and early 1960s. Also, the share of private production of wines and distilled beverages continued to increase in the early 1970s (Mäkelä, 1980c).

As in most other countries, the degree of concentration of alcohol production and especially brewing was increasing (Österberg, 1974). The capital intensity also grew more rapidly than in industry on the average.

The relative importance of various types of outlets in the retail sale of alcoholic beverages is shown in Figure 1. Up to 1969, Monopoly stores were responsible for all off-licence sales of alcohol. Since 1969, medium beer has been sold in grocery stores as well, and their share of total off-licence retail sales in terms of 100% ethanol was 37% in the peak year 1969 but decreased to 27% in 1975 (Österberg, 1979a).

Licensed restaurants are mainly privately owned even if the Monopoly has some hold on this sector through its two subsidiary companies operating restaurant chains. The concentration of the restaurant sector has also grown as private and cooperative chains have increased their market shares (Koskikallio, 1977). Alcoholic beverages were of considerable importance to the restaurant industry, as the share of drinks was nearly 60% of the total turnover of restaurants over the whole study period (Mäkelä and Österberg, 1976).

The fiscal significance of alcoholic beverages was considerable. Despite the expansion of the state budget, alcohol revenue fluctuated between 7% and 10% of all state revenue (Mäkelä, 1980c). State alcohol revenue enters into the regular budget, and only a tiny fraction of it is earmarked for purposes of prevention and treatment of problem drinking (Pekkala, 1970).

Another important economic feature was the high share of spending on alcohol in total private expenditure (Österberg, 1981). Especially in the 1970s, alcohol prices had a considerable impact on the cost-of-living index, and their political importance was augmented by the symbolic value in popular thinking of the price of a bottle of vodka and the high visibility of price decisions related to alcoholic beverages (Mäkelä, 1980a).

All in all, the economic significance of alcohol in general, and more specifically of private profit motives, increased during the study period. From the perspective of the national economy it still is of minor importance, and alcohol industries are under strict Monopoly control. More important than the quantitative changes described above is perhaps that alcohol policy measures have begun to have a bearing on more and more multifarious interests and to at least marginally affect the economic conditions of increasingly diversified population groups. The various aspects of the economies of alcohol have therefore tended to diminish the leeway for alcohol policy.

DETERMINANTS OF CONTROL POLICIES

The liberalizing alcohol control legislation was an expression of a metamorphosis of alcohol attitudes, especially in Finland, where drinking used to be a moral issue intimately linked to basic cultural perceptions. Changing living conditions and increasing buying power undoubtedly affected people's actual drinking behaviour and, consequently, their attitudes. More importantly, economic change and migration to the cities put the whole prevailing value system under strain, and alcohol attitudes were reshaped as one aspect of an ideological process, rather than because of any specific social factors of remolding peoples' attitudes toward drinking. Amidst the general cultural rupture in the 1960s, interests and arguments more immediately related to alcohol also gained ground. There were, on the one hand, interests and doctrines of social policy and, on the other hand, economic interests related to alcohol.

One of the adverse side-effects of the restrictive legislation was the widespread use of illicit and non-beverage alcohol, especially in rural areas. This use was not a mechanical consequence of strict legislation but rather had social dynamics of its own. In any case, it was a social reality in the beginning of the 1950s and provided ammunition for criticism of restrictions (Mäkelä, 1979).

More important than arguments related to illicit consumption was the conviction that the "social liquor question" could be solved by modifying the style of drinking and the tight restrictions, in fact, provoked immoderate drinking patterns (Kuusi, 1952). The first expression of attempts to alter drinking patterns appeared in a policy adopted by the Monopoly in the 1950s in favour of wines at the expense of distilled beverages. Later on, this policy was expanded to include beer, and step by step it was developed into a doctrine which sought to promote integrated drinking even if it implied increasing average consumption (Bruun, 1972).

The policy adopted by the Monopoly was based on genuinely socio-political considerations and was not a disguise for hidden fiscal or private economic interests. Nevertheless, the policy of promoting beer and easing the regulation of brewery sales areas stimulated competition and expansion in the industry. International trade policies also played a role in this process. The abolition of sales area restrictions was in preparation for the agreement between Finland and the European Free Trade Association (EFTA), which stipulated the EFTA breweries should have the right to compete with domestic products throughout the country. The increased competition spurred the concentration of the brewing industry and strengthened its position in relation to the Monopoly (Österberg, 1974).

The most important economic force pushing towards a more liberal system was the growing significance of tourism and leisure industries in general, not so much because of its inherent weight than because of its pervasive ramifications. In Finland, the tourist trade stimulated state and municipal interests in the restaurant industry as a means of attracting travelers and contributed to break down the temperance tradition in the countryside (Mäkelä, 1978).

Increased costs of marketing and distribution gnawed the state revenue per consumption unit. Change in the beverage structure similarly narrowed the fiscal margin of alcohol sales, as production costs of alcohol are higher for beer and wine than distilled beverages. As a consequence, the share of state revenue in the value of private consumption expenditure on alcohol decreased from 73% in 1950 to 58% in 1975 (Mäkelä, 1980c). Nevertheless, the liberal policy in no way collided with fiscal interests, as the consumption increase more than compensated for the lower revenue percentage (Mäkelä, 1978).

The tide of liberalism in alcohol policy was part of the general transformation of the moral and ideological climate in the 1960s. The change in popular opinion was remarkably sudden. Polls indicate that support for the unrestricted distribution of medium beer remained essentially on the same low level into the 1960s. Then came the landslide: support for the unrestricted sale of medium beer grew by 50 percentage points from 1964 to 1969. The abruptness of this change is also reflected in the consecutive bills prepared within the administrative machinery. Legislation passed in 1968 was considerably more liberal than an earlier bill submitted to parliament (Mäkelä, 1978).

The cultural metamorphosis reflected overall structural changes, but it was formulated and carried out especially by the cohorts coming of age amidst the heavy migration to the cities, the very same cohorts which we have shown to have broken the tradition of abstinence (Sulkunen, 1979). With slight exaggeration we could say that these cohorts enacted their values into law in 1968 but that the new legal framework then displayed important cultural repercussions.

One primary function of the restrictive legislation was to safeguard public order, and public order was mainly threatened by drunks from the lower strata. The parliament elected in 1966 not only had a socialist majority but also the turnover of members of parliament was exceptionally great in all political groups (Noponen, 1972). The vote on the new legislation split all parties, but the new parliament as a body had a new outlook on moral issues. Even if this metamorphosis transgressed traditional political divisions, it may have been related to the changing structural position and the increased strength of the lower social strata.

After the 1969 reform, the increase of both consumption and the adverse consequences of drinking surpassed all forecasts. Alcohol consumption reached its peak in 1974, when real prices of alcoholic beverages were at their lowest since the war. The year 1974 also was a time of temporary labour scarcity which brought drinking problems to the factories and to the attention of labour market organizations (Mäkelä, 1978). Alcohol policies became slightly more restrictive, a vocal debate called for a ban on unrestricted medium beer and a Parliamentary Alcohol Committee was appointed in 1976 (Alkoholikomitea, 1978). At the same time retail trade struggled with severe difficulties caused by supermarkets and internal migration, and the number of stores rapidly diminished. Medium beer accounted only for a small portion of the total turnover in retail trade, but it may have affected the marginal profitability of neighbourhood stores under the threat of closure. It is symptomatic that the sales commission on medium beer has been increased to subsidize the increased wage cost to the retail trade (Mäkelä and Österberg, 1975).

The growing significance of licensed restaurants to the economy of cooperative enterprises (Koskikallio, 1977) may have had political implications, as the two main cooperative groups have close ties with Centre Party and labour parties, respectively.

The late 1970s witnessed a very high level of unemployment. In such circumstances, any measures that may adversely affect employment in the alcohol sector encounter strong opposition, despite the relatively small magnitude of that sector.

From the perspective of Finnish agriculture in general, the malting barley and fruits and berries used by the alcohol industry are of minor importance. Nevertheless, the state of alcohol production affects the livelihood of a number of specialized farmers, whose interests are articulated by the Central Organization of Agricultural Producers in a similar fashion as the special interests of brewery workers strongly affect the opinion of the Central Organization of Labour Unions. Typically, these two organizations were outspokenly critical of the report submitted by the Parliamentary Alcohol Committee in 1978, whereas the political parties supported by roughly the same population groups, the Centre Party and the two labour parties, stated quite favourable opinions of the restrictive measures proposed by the Committee. It thus seems that the special interests related to the economy of alcohol do not have much influence in general political platforms where social considerations receive more emphasis, whereas they have considerable impact on the policy of corporate organizations and thereby on actual decision-making.

This conflict creates symbolic issues through which temperance-minded members of parliament may express their commitment without having to shoulder the responsibility for strict measures and the short-term economic consequences. The debate concerning the role of alcoholic beverages in measuring the cost of living is offered as an example. On the technical level, political opposition to increasing alcohol prices is bound to the impact on the cost-of-living index. Therefore, the temperance movement has advocated the simple solution of eliminating alcoholic beverages from the index, and this proposal received strong minority support within the Parliamentary Alcohol Committee (Alkoholikomitea, 1978: 201). The proposal would have little impact on actual wage negotiations, as unions would immediately compute a new index including alcoholic beverages (cf. Kuusi, 1974).

EFFECTS OF CONTROL POLICIES

From a *historical perspective*, the effects of control policies should not be dealt with separately from other, more fundamental factors affecting both drinking and its control. From a *policy-making perspective* it is essential to assess whether changes in control measures can be shown to have had an autonomous impact on drinking. This section first presents data on the effects of control measures on total consumption, beverages structure, and unrecorded consumption. The section is concluded by a discussion of the after-effects of the 1968 alcohol legislation on the cultural climate.

It is apparent that when other factors remain unchanged, changes in disposable income and in real prices affect the consumption of alcoholic beverages as well as the consumption of other commodities. Nyberg (1967) has shown that the values of the price- and income-elasticities of alcoholic beverages in Finland are approximately one. Elasticity values are not, however, inherent attributes of alcoholic beverages but change from one set of historical circumstances to another. For example, in Finland the growth in the share of alcohol expenditure implies that in the late 1960s and early 1970s important changes occurred that are not taken into account in econometric models. The share of alcohol in total private consumption expenditure grew exceptionally fast from 1964 (4.2%) to 1972 (7.3%), with a sudden jump in 1969 (Österberg, 1981). As the real prices of alcohol remained stable throughout the study period, and as the income elasticity was about one, an increase in real income fails to explain why expenditure on alcohol grew much faster than total private consumption expenditure.

Changes in control policies are part of overall social change. It is often difficult to unmask the effects of marginal or gradual changes in control on consumption. The research task is complicated even more when the effects of alcohol policy measures on consumption are indirect and mediated through the cultural climate. Nevertheless, existing studies have demonstrated the effects of quite small changes.

For instance, the introduction of strong beer in the mid-1950s increased the annual consumption of beer by 7%. Similarly, the introduction of a new brand of vodka (Koskenkorva) in 1953 increased the consumption of distilled spirits by 5%. Waiving the certificate requirement for fortified wines in 1952 and its partial reimposition in 1958, as well as other marginal readjustments of the system of individual sales control, also influenced the overall consumption in a measurable fashion (Nyberg, 1967).

When Lehtonen (1978) analyzed the demand for alcoholic beverages in restaurants, he had to estimate an elasticity for supply factors besides income- and price-elasticities. Half of the increase in on-premise sales in 1962-1977 is explained by the increase in the number of restaurants. The restrictive policy was thus able to dam up the demand for alcohol for a long time so that it was realized only as a response to the increase in restaurant capacity.

In addition to the use of econometric models, other means exist to control confounding efforts. In a field experiment with panel data and matched control communities, Kuusi (1957) studied the effects of opening a liquor store in formerly dry municipalities. Overall consumption increased markedly, whereas the share of illegally produced or non-beverage alcohol clearly diminished. The 1968 alcohol legislation provides the most impressive example of the impact of availability on consumption (Bruun et al., 1975; Ahlström-Laakso, 1975). When it came into force in 1969, consumption of alcohol increased by 46%, the bulk of this increase represented by medium beer which rose by about 240%, while the consumption of distilled spirits increased by one-tenth (Österberg, 1979a).

It can thus be shown that increase in the availability of alcoholic beverages was one of the factors which increased the consumption of alcohol. This should not be understood as saying that it would have been possible to maintain the system as it stood in 1950 or that the consumption would not have increased irrespective of the control system. In any case, the dramatic effects of the enactment of the 1968 alcohol legislation indicate that strict alcohol legislation has been able to squeeze potential demand. Most of the more recent changes in alcohol control measures have increased the availability of alcoholic beverages. Therefore, it is of special interest to present examples of the effects of the decreasing availability of alcohol.

In the mid-1970s, a number of municipalities withdrew their consent for retail sales of medium beer. Beverages obtained through other channels of distribution replaced approximately 70% of the alcohol consumed earlier in the form of medium beer, but the overall consumption was nevertheless reduced by 8% (Mäkinen, 1978). In 1977, the Monopoly closed its liquor stores on Saturdays during the summer in one part of Finland. Even this marginal restriction caused a measurable drop in the alcohol consumption in the experimental region compared to a control region. There were no signs of an increase in the consumption of non-beverage or illicit alcohol (Kaski, 1978; Säilä, 1978).

In the spring of 1972, a strike broke out in Monopoly liquor stores. Restaurants and medium beer outlets were not affected by the strike. It can be estimated that the aggregate consumption was some 30% less than what it would have been without the strike (Mäkelä, 1980b).

There are ample examples of the autonomous impact of policy changes on the overall level of consumption. Even more evident is the impact of control systems on the beverage structure of consumption. Pricing policy favoured wines and beer especially in the late 1950s and early 1960s. In the 1970s, the real prices of distilled spirits decreased in relation to the prices of beverages with a low alcohol content. These changes in price relations were distinctly reflected in the structure of alcohol consumption (Figure 2). Along with price policy, wines and beer were gradually made more available, and this clearly contributed to the increase in the share of beer in the 1960s (Österberg, 1981).

The impact of more specific measures is exemplified by the individual sales control in the 1950s. Waiving the certificate requirement for fortified wines led to an increase in the consumption of fortified wines and a decrease in distilled spirits (Österberg, 1981). The barriers against legal beverages in the rural regions were important in contributing to the widespread use of non-beverage alcohol in the 1950s. Nevertheless, both smuggling and the use of non-beverage alcohol were curbed by specific control measures well before the tide of liberalization, and the revival of the use of surrogate alcohol in the late 1960s was also not related to the availability of legal beverages (Mäkelä, 1979).

We have already suggested that the new legislation was a codification of the cultural break in the 1960s, but it also had important secondary effects on the cultural climate. Not only did the overall consumption dramatically increase after the new legislation but drinking habits became more unrestrained. It was as if loosening of the legal strait-jacket freed the Finns to give full expression to their basic cultural patterns.

Another interesting feature was the reaction of the youngest age groups to the new legislation. Survey results show that the age at first drink tended to fall during the 1960s. What happened in the early 1970s was not, however, simply a continuation of this trend. The available surveys indicate that the aftermath of the legal reform created a historically unique situation in which several cohorts were simultaneously recruited to become drinkers. This furthermore seems to have been a true cohort effect, as the age at first drink has been higher among those reaching their early teens in the late 1970s (Ahlström, 1979).

Another cultural side-effect was the spread of illicit distillation in the early 1970s. Survey results indicate that the drinking of illicit liquor was twice as common in 1974 as it was in 1972. Moreover, it was especially popular in urban areas. Small and cheap factory-made stills were mostly used in making illicit spirits. The cheapness of moonshine does not alone suffice to explain that home distilling expanded despite the increased availability of legal alcohol, as the real prices were actually falling in 1972-1974. Cheap stills were also not inventions of the 1970s, but in the atmosphere created by the liberalized alcohol legislation they were marketed more actively than before. Liberalization also had its effect on the attitudes of ordinary citizens. In the 1960s, a middle class family man of established financial standing would have looked down on brewing liquor at home. In the early 1970s distilling spirits evolved into a popular indoor hobby (Mäkelä, 1980b).

The return to less restrained patterns of drinking, the simultaneous recruitment of several cohorts into the drinking population, and the spread of illicit distillation together provide a reminder of the complexity of the interplay between legislation and the cultural climate.

CONCLUDING REMARKS

One noteworthy feature of the Finnish scene is the persistence of beverage preferences and patterns of drinking. To be sure, new ways of drinking have emerged and alcohol has permeated an increasing variety of social situations. Our analysis of the consequences of drinking in relation to overall consumption further indicated a continuous trend towards less conflict-prone drunken comportment, a trend that was only temporarily interrupted by the enactment of the new legislation. Nevertheless, changes in ways of drinking have been additive rather than substitutive, and the core pattern of single heavy drinking occasions still remains intact. This does not exclude the possibility that intoxication has a number of different social meanings, which also have altered in response to changes in living conditions. It is very likely that, for example, alcohol is increasingly used as an adhesive in social interaction, impersonalized as a result of the breakup of organic social networks and as a result of increasingly instrumental work relationships (Sulkunen, 1980). In any case, control measures have had demonstrable effects on the level of consumption, but all attempts to remold basic patterns of drinking have more or less failed.

From a historical perspective, the role of control measures in regard to aggregate consumption is also problematic. In the foregoing, we have occasionally spoken about secular trends and said that strict control policies have been able to reduce the demand for alcoholic beverages. It would be tempting to proceed along this path of interpretation. Structural transformations and changes in living conditions led to an increased demand for alcoholic beverages and reshaped the social meanings of alcohol. The tenacity of control structures, erected in a very dissimilar historical situation, impeded the realization of this new demand. When control legislation finally broke down under social pressures, the aftermath brought about a temporary interruption in the administration and enforcement of controls and a loosening of cultural restrictions on drinking. Continuing this line of thought, it could further be speculated that the end of the consumption increase in the late 1970s signified a spontaneous saturation point and that a state of equilibrium was reached once the legal impediments were swept away.

There is much to support this interpretation. The position of the state is very strong in Finland, the political structures may well delay their adaptation to changes that have already taken place in society. Finland also is a very legalistic society, where laws are both enforced and obeyed. Legislation consequently plays an important role as the instrument of change or retention. Tempting as this interpretation may be, it is incomplete and conceptually inadequate. The state is not a shell of society. Society is not the body of a hermit crab that continues to grow until it has to replace its shell. There is continuous interplay, mediated by political processes, between social currents and state policies. In describing the social history of drinking, this interplay has always to be borne in mind.

The present stabilization of alcohol consumption probably cannot be described as a spontaneous state of equilibrium. As a reaction to rapidly increasing alcohol problems, both public opinion and state policies took a turn in a more restrictive direction. Moreover, the standstill may well be an interlude related to economic recession. The consumption level of alcohol is still not determined solely by market forces. If the control system were further stripped, for instance by introducing wines into grocery stores, it may well be that consumption would again climb to a qualitatively new level. Consumption is thus also regulated by state policies, which again depend on whether the problem level stemming from a certain level of consumption is to be politically tolerated or not.

The tide of temperance and control legislation before and after the turn of the century can be viewed as an attempt to regulate alcohol problems bound up in the Finnish way of drinking. As time went by, the rationale of the restrictions was culturally forgotten, and they began to be seen as remnants of bureaucratic narrow-mindedness. The more restrictive climate of opinion in the late 1970s may then be considered as a new counter-reaction to the increase in alcohol problems.

The less restrictive control policies have not signified a general decrease in state activities in regard to alcohol problems, but part of the emphasis has shifted from prevention to treatment and problem management. Contemporaneously, there has been a redefinition of the "social liquor question" as a public health issue rather than as a problem of public order. This restructuring of the liquor question was concomitant with a general expansion of social and health services, and it signified a shift from repressive to integrative control of deviant drinking.

The fiscal crisis of the state and the diminishing resources available for the social and health sector in the future may well have a fundamental impact on the nature of the control of deviant drinking. In the American context, a redefinition of the division of responsibility for public health has already been suggested: "I believe the idea of a 'right' to health should be replaced by the idea of an individual moral obligation to preserve one's own health — a public duty if you will" (John H. Knowles, 1977: 59). Such a definition of public health in terms of individual responsibility may well be extended to smoking and drinking. Thus, one returns to a way of speaking about alcohol problems in terms of moral responsibility and, perhaps, in terms of decent behaviour and public order.

REFERENCES

Ahlström, S., 1979, *Trends in Drinking Habits among Finnish Youth from the Beginning of the 1960s to the Late 1970s.* Reports from the Social Research Institute of Alcohol Studies, Helsinki.

Ahlström, S. & Österberg, E., 1981, *Juopumuspidätystiedot alkoholihaittojen ja juomatapojen kehityksen kuvaajina Suomessa vuosina 1960-1978, (Arrests for Drunkenness as Indicators of Alcohol Problems and Patterns of Drinking in Finland in 1960-1978).* Reports from the Social Research Institute of Alcohol Studies, Helsinki.

Ahlström-Laakso, S., 1975, *Drinking Habits among Alcoholics.* Forssa: The Finnish Foundation for Alcohol Studies.

Ahlström-Laakso, S. & Österberg, E., 1976, Alcohol Policy and the Consumption of Alcohol Beverages in Finland in 1951-1975. *The Bank of Finland Monthly Bulletin,* L(7):20-28.

Ahlström-Laakso, S. & Österberg, E., 1978, *Alkoholin kulutus Suomessa vuosina 1960-1976, (Consumption of Alcohol in Finland, 1960-1976).* Reports from the Social Research Institute of Alcohol Studies, Helsinki.

Alestalo, M., 1980, Yhteiskuntaluokat ja sosiaaliset kerrostumat toisen maailmansodan jälkeen, (Social Classes and Social Strata After World War II). In *Suomalaiset* (The Finns), pp. 102-221. Tapani Valkonen *et al.*, (Eds). WSOY, Juva.

Alkoholikomitean mietintö, (Report of the Parliamentary Alcohol Committee), 1978. Committee Reports 1978:33.

Alkon hallintoneuvoston kertomus, (Report of the Board of the State Alcohol Monopoly), 1969-1979.

Alkon vuosikirja, (Statistical Yearbook of the State Alcohol Monopoly), 1950-1975.

Allardt, E., 1957, *Drinking Norms and Drinking Habits.* Helsinki: The Finnish Foundation for Alcohol Studies.

Allardt, E., Myllyniemi, O. & Piepponen, P., 1962, *Alkoholiasenteista (On Alcohol Attitudes).* Reports from the Institute of Sociology, University of Helsinki.

Bruun, K., 1959, *Drinking Behaviour in Small Groups.* Helsinki: The Finnish Foundation for Alcohol Studies.

Bruun, K., 1972, *Alkoholi: käyttö, vaikutukset ja kontrolli (Alcohol: Its Use, Effects, and Control).* Tammi, Helsinki.

Bruun, K., Edwards, G., Lumio, M., Mäkelä, K., Pan, L., Popham, R.E., Room, R., Schmidt, W., Skog, O-J., Sulkunen, P. & Österberg, E., 1975, *Alcohol Control Policies in Public Health Perspective.* Forssa: The Finnish Foundation for Alcohol Studies.

Kaski, I., 1978, Alkon myymälöiden lauantaisulkemiskokeilusta (A Trial Closure of Alko Retail Shops on Saturdays). *Alkoholipolitiikka,* XL111:87-90.

Kasurinen, V., 1979, *Alkoholitalousprojektin väliraportti, kesakuu 1979 (Interim Report of the Project on the Economics of Alcohol, June 1979).*

Keski-Suomen lääninhallitus ja Jyväskylän yliopiston yhteiskuntapolitiikan laitos (The Government of the Province of Keski-Suomi & the Institute of Social Policy of Jyväskylä University), 1975. Raportti päihteiden käytöstä huvitilaisuuksissa Keski-Suomen läänissä (Use of Intoxicants at Public Dances in the Province of Keski-Suomi). Mimeograph.

Knowles, J.H., 1977, The Responsibility of the Individual. In *Doing Better and Feeling Worse: Health in the United States.* J.H. Knowles (Ed.). New York: W.W. Norton & Comp.

Koskikallio, I., 1977, *Suomen anniskeluravintoloiden kehitys vuosina 1967-1975 (The Trend of Development for Licensed Restaurants in Finland from 1967-1975).* Reports from the Social Research Institute of Alcohol Studies, Helsinki.

Koskikallio, I., 1979, Socio-Economic Functions of Finnish Restaurants. *British Journal of Addiction* LXXIV:67-78.

Kuusi, P., 1948, *Suomen viinapulma gallup-tutkimuksen valossa (Liquor in Finland in the Light of a Gallup Poll)*. Otava, Helsinki.

Kuusi, P., 1952, Väkijuomakysymys (The Liquor Question). Helsinki: Otava.

Kussi, P., 1957, *Alcohol Sales Experiment in Rural Finland*. Helsinki: The Finnish Foundation for Alcohol Studies.

Kuusi, P., 1974, Hintapäätöksen jälkeen (After the Price Decision). *Alkoholipolitiikka,* XXXIX:217-218.

Lehtonen, P., 1978, Anniskeluravintolaelinkeinon kehityspiirtcitä ja-näkymiä 1962-1980 (Development and Prospects of the Restaurant Industry, 1962-1980). *Alkoholipolitiikka,* XL111:290-298.

Mäkelä, K., 1969, Raittiit (Abstainers). *Alkoholikysymys,* XXXVII:45-53.

Mäkelä, K., 1971, Concentration of Alcohol Consumption. *Scandinavian Studies in Criminology,* III:77-88. Halden: Universitetsforlaget.

Mäkelä, K., 1975a, Consumption Level and Cultural Drinking Patterns as Determinants of Alcohol Problems. *Journal of Drug Issues,* V:344-357.

Mäkelä, K., 1975b, *Notes on the Relationships between Alcohol Problems.* Reports from the Social Research Institute of Alcohol Studies, Helsinki.

Mäkelä, K., 1978, Alkoholipoliittisen mielipideilmaston vaihtelut Suomessa 1960- ja 70-luvulla (Fluctuations in the Climate of Opinion Concerning Alcohol Control Measures in Finland in the 60's and 70's). *Yearbook of the Society for Social Policy 1977,* 11:35-82.

Mäkelä, K., 1979, *Unrecorded Consumption of Alcohol in Finland, 1950-1975.* Reports from the Social Research Institute of Alcohol Studies, Helsinki.

Mäkelä, K., 1980a, *Prices of Alcoholic Beverages in Finland, 1950-1975.* Reports from the Social Research Institute of Alcohol Studies, Helsinki.

Mäkelä, K., 1980b, Differential Effects of Restricting the Supply of Alcohol: Studies of a Strike in Finnish Liquor Stores. *Journal of Drug Issues,* X:131-144.

Mäkelä, K., 1980c, Tables on the Economic Significance of Alcoholic Beverages in Finland, 1950-1975. ISACE, Third Working Meeting, Serock, Poland, April 1980.

Mäkelä, K. & Österberg, E., 1975, Olut viinamaassa (Beer in a Spirits Country). *Alkoholipolitiikka,* XL:255-267.

Mäkelä, K. & Österberg E., 1976, Alcohol Consumption and Policy in Finland and Sweden, 1951. *The Drinking and Drug Practices Surveyor,* 12, December 1976, pp. 4-7 & 37-45.

Mäkelä, K. & Säilä, S-L., 1976, *Alkoholiehtoisten majoitusten jakautuminen eri viranomaisten kesken (The Distribution of Shelterings Related to Alcohol Use between Different Authorities in Finland in 1960 and 1970).* Reports from the Social Research Institute of Alcohol Studies, Helsinki.

Mäkelä, K. & Viikari, M., 1977, Notes on Alcohol and the State. *Acta Sociologica,* XX:155-179.

Mäkinen, H., 1978, Kunnallisten keskiolutkieltojen vaikutuksista (Effects of Local Prohibition of Medium Beer). *Alkoholipolitiikka,* XL111:246-254.

Mäkinen, H., 1979, Treatment Facilities and Programs for Deviate Drinkers in Finland, 1950-1975. ISACE, Second Working Meeting Pacific Grove, California, April 1979.

Mäkinen, T., 1979, *Suljettujen laitosten laitospopulaatioiden kehitys* (The Population of Closed Institutions). Reports from the Research Institute of Legal Policy, Helsinki.

Noponen, M., 1972, Eduskunnan jäsenistön uusiutuminen (Turnover among Members of Parliament). In *Protestivaalit, nuorisovaalit (The Protest Elections, the Youth Elections),* pp. 286-315. P. Pesonen (Ed.). Tampere: Ylioppilastuki.

Nyberg, A., 1967, *Alkoholijuomien kulutus ja hinnat* (Consumption and Prices of Alcoholic Beverages). Helsinki: The Finnish Foundation for Alcohol Studies.

Official Statistics of Finland: XX111: 88 and XX111 B:111 (Criminality).

Österberg, E., 1974, *Alkon panimopolitiikka vuosina 1948-1972* (The Brewery Policy of the State Alcohol Monopoly in the Years 1948-1972. Reports from the Social Research Institute of Alcohol Studies, Helsinki.

Österberg, E., 1979a, *Recorded Consumption of Alcohol in Finland, 1950-1975.* Reports from the Social Research Institute of Alcohol Studies, Helsinki.

Österberg, E., 1979b, Indicators of Damage and Development of Alcohol Conditions in Finland During the Years 1950-1975. ISACE, Second Working Meeting Pacific Grove, California, April 1979.

Österberg E., 1980, Recent Trends in Alcohol Consumption, the Consequences of Drinking and Alcohol Control in Finland. ISACE, Third Working Meeting Serock, Poland, April 1980.

Österberg, E., 1981, Alcohol Policy Measures and the Consumption of Alcoholic Beverages in Finland, 1950-1975. *Drug and Alcohol Dependence,* V11:87-99.

Pekkala, J., 1970, *Uusi alkoholilainsäädäntö (The New Alcohol Legislation).* Helsinki: Kansanvalta.

Poikolainen, K., 1980, Increase in Alcohol-Related Hospitalizations in Finland 1969-1975. *British Journal of Addiction,* LXXV:281:291.

Säilä, S-L., 1978, Lauantaisulkemiskokeilu ja juopumushäiriöt (A Trial Closure of Alko Retail Shops on Saturdays and Disturbances Caused by Intoxication). Alkoholipolitiikka, XL111:91-99.

Simpura, J., 1976, *Ravintolassa käymisen tiheys Suomessa vuosina 1968, 1969, ja 1974 (The Frequency of Restaurant Visits in Finland in 1968, 1969, and 1974).* Reports from the Social Research Institute of Alcohol Studies, Helsinki.

Simpura, J., 1978a, *Suomalaisten juomatavat vuosina 1969 ja 1976. Kulutetut alkoholimäärät ja alkoholin ongelmakäyttö (Finnish Drinking Habits in 1969 and 1976. Alcohol Consumption and Alcohol Problems in Demographic Groups).* Reports from the Social Research Institute of Alcohol Studies, Helsinki.

Simpura, J., 1978b, *Suomalaisten juomatavat vuosina 1969 ja 1976. Juomiskertojen lukumäärä ja ominaisuudet (Finnish Drinking Habits in 1969 and 1976. The Number and Attributes of Drinking Occasions).* Reports from the Social Research Institute of Alcohol Studies, Helsinki.

Sulkunen, P., 1979, *Abstainers in Finland 1946-1976. A Study in Social and Cultural Transition.* Reports from the Social Research Institute of Alcohol Studies, Helsinki.

Sulkunen, P., 1980, Alkoholin kulutus ja elinolojen muutos toisen maailmansodan jälkeen (Consumption of Alcohol and Changes in Conditions of Living After World War II). *Yearbook of the Society for Social Policy 1980,* V:129-169.

Taipale, I., 1979, *Terms Applied to Deviant Drinkers in Finland.* Reports from the Social Research Institute of Alcohol Studies, Helsinki.

Uusitalo, H., 1975, *Class Structure and Party Choice: A Scandinavian Comparison.* Reports from the Research Group for Comparative Sociology, University of Helsinki.

4. Alcohol Control Policy in Switzerland: An Overview of Political Compromise

Monique Cahannes and Richard Mueller*

GEOGRAPHIC, SOCIOECONOMIC, AND POLITICAL BACKGROUND

Situated in the centre of Europe, Switzerland is geographically, economically, and culturally quite diversified. Geographically, it has some flat country, the Jura region, and the Alps, the latter representing almost one-fourth of the country's surface. Three-quarters of the native population are German speaking, 20% French, 4% Italian, and 1% Romanche, each living in clearly distinct geographical areas. This linguistic division of the Swiss population has remained very stable in recent years: German is still dominant, but French, Italian, and Romanche-speaking minorities have not lost any ground.

With respect to religious affiliation, the country has changed from a majority of Protestants in the 1950s to an equal division between Catholics and Protestants in the 70s. One important reason for this change is the post-war immigration from Catholic countries such as Italy and Spain. Between 1950 and 1970, the foreign population, largely made up of workers from Italy and Spain, increased from 6 to 17% of the total population. With the economic recession in the mid-1970s, this percentage decreased to 15% by 1979. Without any doubt, this immigration of workers from traditional wine countries has some influence on alcohol consumption patterns in Switzerland, even though their stay in the country is short-term.

A substantial proportion of the six million people in Switzerland still live in rural areas. And unlike in many other countries, even relatively important cities have not grown into large metropolitan centres. This

*Swiss Institute for the Prevention of Alcoholism, Lausanne

predominance of a semi-rural habitat is probably an important factor in social control and may explain the relatively low crime rate and low incidence of deviant subcultures.

Switzerland is, nonetheless, a highly industrialized country with substantial textile, chemical, and tool-making industries. Also, many services have expanded rapidly, especially transportation, trade, banking, and, most particularly, tourism. Since 1950, the number of persons occupied in the agrarian sector has declined while those employed in the service sector has increased from 37% of the workforce in 1950 to more than 50% in 1979. In Switzerland, girls and boys are told at an early age that their country is one of the wealthiest in the world. The lofty economic position in relation to other countries may, in part, explain the traditional conservative attitudes of the Swiss.

Real disposable income more than doubled between 1950 and 1977. During this period, a lower proportion of income was spent on food, and more was spent on education, leisure activities, and travel (Almanach der Schweiz, 1978). The relative percentage of the average consumer's expenditures for goods and services allocated to the purchase of alcoholic beverages has remained quite stable, oscillating between about 5.5% and 5.8%.

Politically, Switzerland is a plebiscitary democracy with a federal structure. Its 20 cantons and six half-cantons have considerable autonomy on the legislative as well as on the executive level. For example, education and health care fall under the cantonal authority. On the federal level, the executive power is exerted by seven ministeries. Since 1959, the composition of the federal government has not changed, with a conservative majority plus two socialists. The legislative power is bicameral, consisting of the Council of the States, where each canton has two representatives, and the 200-seat National Council, where the representation for each canton is proportionate to its population.

The most outstanding feature of Switzerland's political system is not its federal structure, which emphasizes the rights of linguistic and regional minorities, but its particular tradition of "amicable consent," always trying to compromise without articulating conflict and overt disagreement. Thus, all the important parties form the federal government and no powerful opposition exists. In addition, the executive power is exerted by mutual agreement between all members of the government (on the federal as well as on the cantonal level). This tradition of democratic concordance or "amicable consent" should not be viewed as a political ideal, but rather as the consequence of overlapping structural and cultural factors which hinder the outbreak of clear-cut conflicts between the different linguistic, religious, regional, and even socioeconomic groups. Swiss alcohol policy is an excellent example of this type of political culture, bringing together rather different political and economic interests.

THE SWISS ALCOHOL LEGISLATION

In Switzerland, as in other countries, the 19th century witnessed the beginning of industrialization. The federal government enacted several laws to enable growing industries to expand, including the increasingly popular distilling industry. The cantons allowed full freedom in the exercise of trades, including the right to operate "public houses" and this led to an enormous growth of on-premise outlets (Jellinek, 1976). In some regions there was one outlet selling alcohol for less than 50 people. But heavy spirit consumption, especially among the working class, ran counter to the requisite of industrial production for a disciplined and attentive worker. In 1830, the formation of a temperance society which demanded abstinence from distilled spirits but approved the moderate use of beer and wine found wide public support.

In 1885, a constitutional amendment was passed, giving the confederation the right to legislate matters concerning distilled spirits. The main aim of the Alcohol Act of 1885 was to channel the consumption of spirits distilled from potatoes to fermented beverages. This practice gave an advantage to medium-sized distilleries over small and large distilleries. The distillation from grape wine and from fruit cider was exempted from legislation as these seemed an unimportant source of brandies in comparison with large-scale potato distillation. In subsequent legislative acts, a production monopoly was granted to the federal government, who did not exert this right but, in turn, granted distilling concessions. Besides the production monopoly, an import monopoly for spirits was established. Again with some exceptions, import concessions, in turn, were granted to private companies. Finally, the sale of spirits was to be free for quantities of 40 litres and more (wholesale), while for smaller quantities (retail) a licence was required. All spirits distilled from potatoes, however, had to be delivered to the Alcohol Administration, who fixed the prices and became the sole seller of potato spirits. In addition, the Alcohol Act stipulated the replacement of various cantonal taxes by a uniform federal tax. Cantons were explicitly not allowed to tax fermented beverages. The net proceeds of the Alcohol Administration were allotted to the cantons who were obliged to use 10% of this amount to fight alcoholism (alcohol tithe).

The alcohol legislation of 1885 may be viewed as a result of balanced interests. Public health concern was taken into consideration by the attempt to reduce distilled spirit consumption and by introducing the alcohol tithe. Agricultural concern was evident by the demand that fermented beverages be made out of fruits, thus protecting the Swiss grape and fruit growers. Finally, political and fiscal concerns were also taken into account by returning the benefits of the Alcohol Monopoly to the cantons in order to compensate their loss of tax revenues from alcoholic beverages.

The main effect hoped for was obtained. The per capita consumption of spirits fell from 4.8 litres of pure alcohol during 1880-84 to 2.9 litres during the period 1893-1902. But during the same period, the consumption of fermented beverages rose from 9.6 litres of pure alcohol to 12.9 litres. However, the substitutive effect of the price policy of the Alcohol Administration did not last very long. The high price of potato spirits was an incentive for the distillation of fruits exempted from the control of the Alcohol Administration and, after a few years, the consumption of fruit spirits nearly reached the former level of potato spirits.

It is somewhat surprising that Switzerland, with its federal structure and liberal political ideology, chose the state monopoly in order to regulate the distilled spirits market. But first, it is noteworthy that the Swiss Monopoly is a much more limited system than, for instance, the Finnish, Swedish, or Polish Monopolies. Secondly, one should take into account public concern with alcohol problems in the late 19th century. Alcohol was commonly blamed as the root of all evil, not only in Switzerland but all over Europe and even, to some extent, in France. The prohibition of absinthe at the beginning of the 20th century offers a good example. A multiple manslaughter committed by an absinthe-addict led to a Swiss social movement which, in a very short time, resulted in a popular initiative to prohibit absinthe. And even though the federal government was against prohibition and preferred a special tax on this beverage, and even though the approval of such an initiative is very rare in Swiss political life, the initiative was accepted by popular vote. It is of interest that the prohibition of absinthe in France had exactly the same trigger as in Switzerland. Furthermore, in both countries the prohibition was facilitated by the fact that absinthe competed with white wine, and the prohibition therefore had been supported by wine growers.

The contemporary law on alcohol dates from 1932. The principal modification of the law of 1885 was the enlargement of the Monopoly to include fruit and wine distillation. But the acceptance of this modification had to be reached by concessions which resulted in the creation of vested rights for the peasantry. Home distillers who distill for their own consumption from produce of their own orchard or vineyards or from gathered wild products are exempted from the law. The same applies to "contract-giving distillers," i.e. persons who give, for their personal use, their homegrown or gathered wild materials for distillation to professional distillers. Home distillers as well as contract-giving distillers must obtain a licence which is free of charge (Table 1).

After the amendment of the law in 1932, the alcohol administration continued to not exercise the right of fabrication but to instead grant concessions to third persons. In order to decrease consumption, the law stipulated that the Alcohol Administration reduce the number of stills by purchase and promote the utilization of raw products for purposes other than distillation. The latter resulted in subsidizing the renewal of orchards with fruits of better quality and higher prices. This demonstrated again how important agricultural concerns in Swiss alcohol policy are.

TABLE 1 *Concessions Granted by Alcohol Monopoly*

Types of Concessions	Characteristics
Professional distillers with delivery obligation	Obliged to deliver their production to the Federal Alcohol Monopoly. Fully liable to taxation.
Professional distillers without delivery obligation	May produce and distribute "specialty" spirits, i.e. kirsch, prune, brandy, etc. Fully liable to taxation.
Home distillers	Allowed to have their own stills. Not taxed on production for own use.
Contract-giving distillers	Allowed to have their spirits produced by others. Not taxed on production for own use.

In the post-war period, few legislative changes concerning distilled spirits occurred. In 1966, the electorate and the cantons rejected by a large majority a national initiative demanding a more effective fight against alcoholism by taxing all alcoholic beverages according to their alcohol content. In 1968, an amendment authorized the federal government to subsidize national and intercantonal organizations devoted to the prevention of alcoholism. In February 1979, approximately 60% of the electorate decided against an initiative proposed by the Swiss Good Templer Youth who advocated a total prohibition of publicity for alcoholic beverages and tobacco. The federal government recommended its rejection, arguing that it would be possible, by revising the alcohol law, to attain the same goal, i.e. a reduction in consumption.

Though public health is clearly one of the concerns of the law on distilled spirits, this cannot be said about the law governing the production of wine. On the contrary, the production of wine is much encouraged by subsidies and protected against foreign competition. At the end of the 19th century, the first law concerning agriculture included a section concerning viticulture. At this time, only sporadic measures were foreseen, like the fight against vine illnesses. Later a more systematic intervention in viticulture took place as its position became increasingly weak (Gugelberg 1950). Thus, in 1936, subsidies for replanting vines of better quality were granted and wholesalers were obliged to buy domestic wines. The payment of these subsidies was, and still is, insured by a tax levied on wine imports (the vine fund).

The law now in force, the "Federal Law on the Improvement of Agriculture and the Maintenance of a Rural Population," dates from

1951. It stipulates that viticulture must be adapted to the needs of the home market, not only quantitatively but also from the point of view of the kind of wines. Thus, the over-specialization in white wines had to be changed in favour of more red wines whose consumption is now far more important. As in the past, the subsidies come from a "vine fund." For example, from 1969 to 1975, the confederation was spending 1.8 million Swiss francs per year to promote home-grown wines and 4.5 million per year for the encouragement of new plantations or the restoration of existing ones.

Not surprisingly, the production of beer and fermented cider is subject only to quality regulations laid down in the legislation concerning food. In Switzerland, it has always been the distilled beverages, first that of potatoes, then of absinthe, that have been stigmatized as being at the root of alcohol problems. It is, therefore, with respect to these beverages that there exist legal statutes in the Constitution. This is based on an underlying concept of differential danger of the various alcoholic beverages: hard liquor represents evil, whereas wine is the noble drink.

The most salient feature of the production of alcoholic beverages in Switzerland, excluding beer, is the almost archaic mode of production. For instance, the average vineyard in 1975 was only 57 acres. More than 179,000 distilling licences existed (or one licence per 26 persons aged 20 years or older). This fragmented structure of the production of alcoholic beverages is even more astonishing considering that Switzerland is a highly industrialized country. The dissimilarity between the structure of the production of alcoholic beverages and the structure of production of other goods can be explained by the fact that agriculture occupies a very protected position which is reinforced by the political structure which gives small agricultural cantons a disproportionate weight in political decision-making. Further, the development of large agricultural estates was hindered by geographical characteristics of the country.

As elsewhere, however, some concentration of alcohol production has occurred. The number of licence holders for spirit distillation has decreased by 17% between 1951 and 1975 while the number of tax-free distillers decreased by 47% during this time. The number of agricultural estates producing wine has fallen by 47% from 1955 to 1975 (from about 38,000 to 20,000) while the viticultural acreage has increased slightly. Fermented cider production became totally negligible by 1975, while beer production, on the other hand, became highly concentrated (from 423 breweries in 1883 to 47 in 1975).

Trends in Production

Even though the number of distillers has been reduced between 1950-1975, the overall production of distilled spirits has increased slightly. Although the area for wine-growing remained about the same, the yield has risen by nearly 23%, due to technical improvements and the use of pesticides. Domestic production now amounts to nearly one million hecto-litres per year and covers about one-third of the demand. The production of cider has become insignificant while the production of beer has increased by 150% since 1950, amounting to more than four million hecto-litres in 1975.

Illicit or Undeclared Production

Home distillers must fill out a distillation sheet declaring the quantity produced. Accuracy is difficult to determine, but it could be that a substantial part of the production remains undeclared. Illicit production is not as widespread as partially undeclared production. Indeed, the possibility to distill legally, without close supervision, is the reason behind federal Monopoly emphasis on buying up stills, whose number has declined by 30% between 1951 and 1975, with approximately 17,000 stills still operating.

In the case of wine, cider, or beer, private production is not illicit. For wine, cultivating up to 10 acres is not even declarable. Cider production is entirely free and the agricultural production is therefore only estimated. The low price of beer renders home-brewing unattractive and is, in fact, almost non-existant.

Political, Economic, and Fiscal Significance

The economic significance of the production of alcoholic beverages, relative to the overall production of goods, is unimportant. The value of this production in relation to the G.N.P. was approximately 0.6% for 1971-75. The agricultural production of alcoholic beverages accounted for little more than 4% of the value of the total agricultural production. Only 0.6% of the employees in the industrial sector are occupied with production of alcoholic beverages and about 5% in the agricultural sector. Since fermented cider and distilled spirits production is never the only activity at a farm, it is difficult to calculate employment figures.

From a political point of view, however, it is important in that more than 80% of wine is produced in the French part of the country, and in one canton of French-Switzerland as much as 50% of the value of agricultural production is derived from viticulture. As a consequence, every decision against viticulture is interpreted as a sign of aggression from the German-speaking majority towards the French.

The fiscal revenues from alcoholic beverages (consumption taxes and taxes on revenues) account for less than 5% of total fiscal income of the federation in 1975 (7% in 1950). But one has to keep in mind that the federal state levies only about one-third of all taxes; the remaining two-thirds are levied directly by the cantons and the communes.

THE DISTRIBUTION OF ALCOHOLIC BEVERAGES

Imports and Exports

As in the case of production, the confederation does not exercise its importation monopoly for spirits with the exception of potable alcohol and proof spirits. Thus, any private person is authorized to import distilled spirits, under 150-proof, against payment of the monopoly duties. In the past 25 years, imports increased by more than 600%, accounting for one-third of total distilled consumption. At the same time, much diversification has occurred. Imports of whisky, gin, and vodka grew tremendously, and the integration of these drinks in existing drinking patterns was helped along by mass media and by tourism.

Legally the importation of one litre of distilled spirits (more than 25% of volume) is duty free. Because of the much lower prices for these beverages in the neighbouring countries and their relatively small geographical distance, it can be assumed that duty free imports of distilled spirits are substantial.

The 1951 law on agriculture permits the limitation of the volume of imported products if they compromise the sale of indigenous products. By decree, this has been the case for wine imports since 1931. The volume of red wine imports is fixed according to quotas and re-examined every three years in order to allow an adaptation to market situations. To protect the indigenous white wine production, the imports of white wines in barrels are forbidden, but white wines in bottles up to one litre can be imported. As a result, wine imports consist mainly of red and sparkling wines. At the present time, they account for two-thirds of total wine consumption, and this proportion has remained quite stable since 1950. In comparison, beer imports are negligible, accounting for about 5% of total beer consumption. Brewers themselves control most of these imports.

Retail Trade

The federal constitution provides the cantons with the right to restrict the number of outlets to the existing demand if the existence of trade is threatened by excessive competition. Public interest must be taken into account when fixing the number of establishments. In addition, the peddling of alcoholic beverages is prohibited. Again the constitution mixes public health interests with trade and industrial policy interests and it is hard to say which interest predominates.

Most cantons make use of the right to limit the number of outlets, adapting ratios for on-premise outlets varying from 1:100 to 1:600 inhabitants and for off-premise outlets from 1:300 to 1:1,600. These prescribed ratios, however, are at best only a guide for granting new licences. The real density of alcohol outlets is generally much higher than the prescribed number. Nonetheless, the ratio of outlets selling alcoholic beverages per inhabitant has decreased from 1:309 in 1955 to 1:440 in 1975 for on-premise establishments, and from 1:245 in 1955 to 1:522 in 1975 for off-premise outlets. As a result, properties in which businesses are located have increased their market value. The rents for the establishments are correspondingly high and, in turn, have forced up the prices of alcoholic beverages.

The granting of a licence for on-premise sale of alcohol is not only tied to a proficiency certificate to be held by the restaurateur but also to the moral qualifications of the individual and even of the family. For example, a good reputation, citizenship rights, and lack of debts are generally required. In most cantons, fully licensed on-premise outlets are permitted to sell alcoholic beverages for off-premise consumption but only in quantities below two litres. These "'across-the-street" sales play probably a greater role in Switzerland than in many other countries and certainly affect the availability of alcoholic beverages.

For the off-premise sale of alcoholic beverages in stores, the goods must be "naturally connected" to other merchandise sold. Stores are usually open between 7 a.m. and 7 p.m. But as interests of tourism are taken so seriously in Switzerland, a great number of exceptions exists not only for opening hours but also regarding the maximum density of on-premise outlets. One special regulation is the morning ban on spirits. In several cantons, sale of spirits is forbidden before 9 a.m. The origin of this measure was presumably not to prevent alcoholism among workers but to maintain their labour productivity during the day. The legal drinking age is usually 16 years, in some cantons 14, in others 17 or 18 (for distilled spirits). But this only pertains to minors not accompanied by adults. It is also forbidden to serve anyone who is already drunk. These laws are not enforced and hardly respected. Nowhere does the law stipulate an obligation on the part of the server or the seller to assure the client's age and there is no penalty for not knowing the client's age.

In sum, it can be stated that due to the changes in the structure of the retail market, the physical, economic, and psychological accessibility of alcohol has increased despite the fact that the number of outlets selling alcohol has decreased. The main changes for on-premise establishments has been that small traditional restaurants have been replaced by large ones, where modern management pushes for greater turnover. This has been accompanied by the opening of numerous dancing clubs, closing much later than midnight. For off-premise outlets, the emergence of supermarkets and self-service stores in the sixties has been a major change. This rationalization of the retail trade has permitted the selling of alcoholic beverages at lower prices than before. The closing down of small stores and consequent lower density of outlets has been compensated by higher sales volume. Alcoholic beverages are even sold through vending machines. Thus, alcohol is one of the most accessible consumer goods in Switzerland, considering that they can be obtained almost everywhere, at almost any hour.

CONSUMPTION OF ALCOHOLIC BEVERAGES

Alcohol consumption in Switzerland has been at a fairly high level for centuries. For example, in 1880-1884, average consumption was more than 14 litres of absolute alcohol per capita and during the next five years the average was almost 16 litres, the highest consumption rate ever reported. Subsequently, a decrease in consumption took place, with the lowest per capita consumption occurring in the years 1939-1945 (less than 8

FIGURE 1   *Consumption of Alcoholic Beverages by Beverage Class, in Litres of 100% Alcohol Per Capita, 1950-1978*

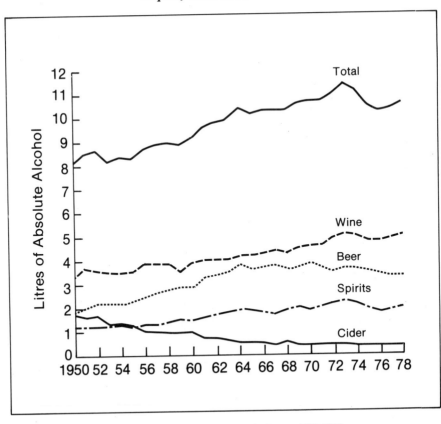

Source: Régie fédérale des alcools, Berne, 1950-1978.

litres at 100%). A decline in alcohol consumption at the end of the 19th century until the first half of the 20th century was reported not only for Switzerland but also for several other countries. Factors accounting for this drop in consumption are numerous. Among others, it is probable that in the first phase of rising consumerism, income was absorbed by more basic goods than alcohol.

The increase in consumption, calculated in litres of pure alcohol per capita, rose by 30% from 1950 to 1975. Distilled spirits consumption rose by 74% (1.2 to 2.1 litres at 100%); beer consumption increased by 68% (2.1 to 3.6 litres), and wine by 37% (3.5 to 4.9 litres). The consumption of fermented cider, however, decreased by 73% (1.3 to 0.4 litres).

The apparent replacement of cider by beer is the most outstanding feature in changing beverage preferences. In 1950, both beer and fermented cider accounted for about a fifth of total alcohol consumption, and in 1975, beer accounted for more than a third of total consumption, whereas cider's share dropped to less than 3%. This substitution process was due to the decline of the agricultural sector in general and to the aggressive marketing of brewers. Beer has been portrayed not only as a popular working-class drink, but also as a light all-purpose drink. In addition, its on-premise price has been lower than that of any non-alcoholic drink, which certainly has contributed to its growing importance.

During the same period, consumer tastes became more diversified. There were increases in the consumption of sparkling wine as well as of distilled spirits such as whisky, gin, rum, and vodka. Thus the substitutive process by which beer almost totally replaced cider was overlapped by an additive one, whereby new drinks, symbolizing a modern way of living, were adopted.

Switzerland is, in general, typified as a wine country, and as a matter of fact, wine consumption accounted for 46% of total alcohol consumption in 1975. The remainder of consumption was divided as follows: 33% beer, 18% distilled spirits, and 3% fermented cider. Regional differences in the preference of alcoholic beverages, however, are important. The label "wine country" attributed to Switzerland is mainly due to the fact that the Latin minorities drink large amounts of wine. This casts some doubt on the usefulness of drinking typologies in cases where large regional differences exist.

Patterns of Consumption

It has only been in the last few years that epidemiological studies of alcohol consumption have been conducted. Only one study representative for all of Switzerland has been undertaken so far (in 1975). These data have shown that the Swiss are extremely permissive towards alcohol. Alcohol is legitimately consumed during an almost infinite number of occasions and situations. At the age of 12 years, an overwhelming portion of boys and girls have already had their first drink. This occurs usually within the family, particularly on the occasion of a festivity, thus fostering the positive values attributed to alcohol in this country (Müller, 1979a).

Regular consumption of alcohol starts at an early age. A study of male recruits for military service indicated that 30% of those 15 years of age or younger consume alcohol regularly (Battegay, 1977). Due to its low price, youngsters start regular consumption with beer. As they grow older, they switch to wine. As elsewhere, Swiss women have much more restrictive attitudes then men toward alcohol consumption in certain situations, as their consumption usually occurs at home with meals.

Within this context, it is important to mention the role of functional equivalents to the consuming of alcohol. Although cultural norms inhibit women from using alcohol as a means of reducing tension, this is not the case for medications. Whereas chronic alcoholism is the principal cause of hospitalization in the medical wards of general hospitals for men between the ages of 25 and 39, for women this cause ranks thirteenth for the age group 30-34 and fourteenth for the age group 35-39. On the other hand, for women between the ages of 20 and 24, the abuse of psychoactive drugs is the second leading cause of hospitalization and the abuse of sleeping pills and sedatives ranks fourth (Meyrat et al., 1977).

The quantities consumed per drinking event proved to be very stable. Estimations obtained from survey data suggest that a total of 4.4% of the population consumes 80 grams or more pure alcohol per day: 8.1% of the men and 0.7% of women drink this amount daily (Wüthrich and Hausheer, 1979). Since excessive drinkers have a tendency to minimize their consumption and to be over-represented in the category of non-response, the actual proportion of such drinkers is probably higher.

Twelve percent of the population are abstinent (no alcohol intake within a period of at least one year), but this percentage is much lower in younger age groups. Other variables such as sex, level of income, and place of residence (rural vs. urban) also influence the adherence to the abstinent group. It is interesting to note that there is little variance in the rate of abstinence among the linguistic regions of Switzerland, although these regions differ greatly as to the quantities consumed and as to the patterns of consumption.

A study carried out at the end of 1979 demonstrated that little change has taken place since 1975 in the number of abstainers and the frequency of consumption (Müller, 1980).

Cultural Diversities

As mentioned previously, Switzerland is divided into three main linguistic regions: German, French, and Italian. The Swiss-Italian drinking pattern is characterized by a high average consumption per inhabitant, especially wine. The Swiss-French drinking pattern is also characterized by a high consumption rate of wine per inhabitant. It is interesting to note that the consumption of beer does not show much difference according to linguistic regions, and its consumption appears to be the most equally distributed in Switzerland. In the mountainous regions of the German part of Switzerland, relatively more distilled spirits are consumed.

TABLE 2   *Quantity-Frequency-Variability-Typology by Sex, Age, Economic Level, and Linguistic Region (Survey Data, 1975)*

	I (high) %	II %	TYPE III %	IV (abstinent) %	V %	n(= 100%)
Grand total	13	15	53	7	12	926
Men	23	19	47	3	7	428
Women	4	10	60	11	15	498
Men age 15-24	17	13	44	9	17	64
25-34	23	28	44	2	3	114
35-44	31	19	43	4	3	82
45-54	26	23	44	2	5	61
55-64	17	9	63	0	11	54
65-74	24	10	52	5	9	53
Women 15-24	4	10	51	12	23	59
age 25-34	6	14	66	6	8	108
35-44	5	12	69	8	6	96
45-54	4	7	57	16	16	79
55-64	4	11	54	15	16	76
65-74	1	5	58	10	26	80
Linguistic region						
French	15	19	52	3	11	417
Italian	30	25	31	4	11	366
German	12	13	55	9	12	668
Income less than 1,000						
sfr. a month	13	8	40	12	27	76
1,000. to 1,999.	13	11	54	9	14	185
2,000. to 2,999.	12	18	55	6	8	327
3,000. to 3,999.	14	17	54	6	9	124
4,000. up	18	16	58	6	3	83

Sources: P. Wüthrich and Hausheer, 1979; and calculations from the raw data; see Knupfer (1967) for a description of the drinking typology.

The distribution of consumption also differs by linguistic regions. Thus, in the Swiss-German part, 10% of the population drink 52% of the total quantity consumed; in the Swiss-French part, 10% of the population drink 42% of the total quantity consumed; and in the Swiss-Italian part, 38% is consumed by 10% of the population (Wuthrich and Hausheer, 1979). Functionally, the significance of the consumption of alcohol in the Swiss-German part can be defined as socio-ceremonial and restitutive, in the Swiss-French part to have a more convivial meaning with characteristics of autogratification, whereas in the Swiss-Italian part it combines both cultural traits. A related difference pertains to social context. In the Swiss-French and Swiss-German areas, the family is the predominant social context, whereas in the Swiss-Italian part, friends and acquaintances form the major context for alcohol consumption.

Finally, regional comparisons have shown a relatively high tolerance of the Swiss-Italians towards alcoholics and much intolerance in relation to abstinent behaviour. The Swiss-French also display a relatively high intolerance towards abstinent behaviour. But the image of the alcoholic in both the German and French regions is decidedly negative.

The Temperance Movement

Unlike other countries with a high wine consumption, Switzerland has a long history of abstinent movements. Interestingly enough, the idea of total abstinence did not emerge in German but in wine-drinking French-Switzerland, a fact which might explain the different attitudes of Italian and French-speaking Swiss towards alcoholism. L.L. Rochat, the founder of the Blue Cross, who owned a vineyard himself but was deeply rooted in Calvinism and French Pietism, became concerned with "salvaging the inebriate." According to Jellinek (1976), the temperance movement started rather slowly, but gained momentum after the abstinence volunteers became established as a profession.

It seems that the Swiss temperance organizations have succeeded in avoiding too much antagonism between themselves and the wider public. This is reflected in the financial subsidies granted to them by the cantons (Jellinek, 1976). The influence of the abstinence movement on the political level has certainly declined. Nevertheless, more than 4% of all constitutional amendments submitted for referendums in the past 100 years concerned alcohol and were lobbied for by the temperance movement. The last of these submissions occurred, as already mentioned, in 1979 and although defeated, it created considerable pressure to change existing alcohol laws.

Prices and Expenditures For Alcoholic Beverages

The price of distilled spirits is strongly influenced by the rate of taxes fixed by the federal government. Monopoly taxes and duties were raised in 1959, 1963, 1965, 1969, 1970, 1973, and 1975 but there was little effect on the consumption of distilled spirits. There is no special taxation for cider and indigenous wine. Beer, however, is subject to special taxation, fixed by the Constitution to 17.7% of the wholesale prices of barrels.

From 1939 to 1966, the share of alcoholic drinks in the overall consumer price index amounted to 1.3%, divided into 0.7% for wine and 0.6% for beer. From 1966 to 1977, it amounted to 1.75%: 0.75% for wine, 0.75% for beer, and 0.25% for distilled spirits. Expenditures for alcoholic beverages as a proportion of all expenditures for goods and services remained relatively stable, ranging from 5.5 to 5.8% between 1950 and 1975.

ALCOHOL-RELATED PROBLEMS

The consequences of alcoholic beverage consumption are assigned a certain reality and value only within a given social perception. One only has to consider the changes in attitude towards the conception of alcoholism seen in the course of history. Another illustration is the phenomenon of "public drunkenness." Whereas in Anglo-Saxon and Northern European countries "public drunkenness" is a frequently reported form of deviant behaviour and has accordingly been given a good deal of research attention, it does not exist in Switzerland as an official problem category. Despite these differences in problem awareness, there do exist some cross-cultural similarities, particulary with regard to organic dysfunction.

Mortality

Liver cirrhosis mortality increased from 1950 to the beginning of the seventies by approximately 50%, but from 1970 to 1978 a slight decrease was noted. The relative importance of this cause of death is shown when compared to the total figure of all deaths. Whereas at the beginning of the fifties about 1% of all deaths was due to liver cirrhosis, in 1970-71 this figure amounted to 1.7%, and from 1975 to 1978, it was 1.5% (Figure 2).

Until the beginning of the 1970s, 1.5% to 2.5% of all deaths in Switzerland was attributed to alcohol psychoses. In the 1970s, however, mortality due to alcohol psychoses decreased, and disappeared almost completely towards the end of the decade. This tendency is mainly due to treating delirium tremens by drugs. Alcohol psychoses is a highly sex-specific cause of death: male mortality is 10 to 30 times higher than the rate for females. The crude mortality rate from alcohol psychoses shows no covariation with the average per capita consumption of alcoholic beverages.

FIGURE 2   *Alcohol Consumption and Mortality Rates Per 100,000 Population of Liver Cirrhosis, Alcohol Psychosis, and Alcoholism, 1950-1978*

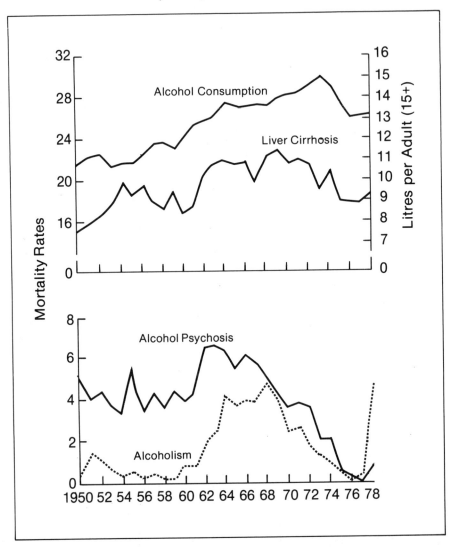

Sources: Régie fédérale des alcools, Berne; office fédéral de statistiques, Berne en annuaires statistiques de la Suisse, Berne, corresponding years.

Although in the case of alcohol psychoses the symptoms that characterize the syndrome are more or less defined, this is hardly the case for "alcoholism." Thus, the large fluctuations in the crude alcoholism mortality rate show no covariation with consumption rates. This may be due to the fact that physicians are differently disposed in diagnosis, or in their awareness of alcoholism as the primary or secondary cause of death on death certificates. In .1978, a sudden increase in alcoholism mortality rate occurred, perhaps caused by the greater problem awareness in the general public and in the medical professions. This greater awareness of alcohol-related problems was reflected by increased mass media and medical review coverage.

Acute alcohol poisoning is generally regarded as being linked directly to alcohol intake. This cause of death is very rare in Switzerland and the corresponding mortality rate seems totally independent of average consumption. Indeed, the total number of deaths due to alcohol poisoning has fluctuated during the study period at around 30 per year.

Morbidity

It is well known that the first admission rate or the number of users of psychiatric institutions does not correspond to the incidence or prevalence of morbidity in a given society. Socioeconomical, attitudinal, as well as administrative factors significantly determine the utilization of such institutions. Indeed, first admission rates into mental hospitals due to alcoholism or alcohol psychoses have been surprisingly stable for the time interval 1950-70 and do not, in any way, reflect the increase in average consumption (Figure 3). If male and female first admission rates are considered separately, an increase in the rates can be seen for women, whereas the rates for men decreased. Similarly, the specialized in-patient treatment centres for addicts show a similar trend for first admissions: a decreasing trend for males and an increasing one for females.

During the period observed, the age structure for first admission patients changed: the percentage of patients below the age of 39 increased. This change in the age structure is also reflected in the marital status of first admissions: the portion of single men increased in the period 1950-1976.

Road Traffic Accidents

Prior to 1964, article 31 of the federal law on road traffic only stated that "Anyone who has been drinking, is overworked, or for other reasons incapable to drive a vehicle, is obliged to refrain from doing so," without stipulating exactly the limit of blood alcohol concentration. In 1964, this was changed by a decree of the federal court, fixing the maximum non-punishable blood alcohol content of a driver at 0.8 mg/100 ml.

As in other countries with a high density of motor vehicle traffic, the number of road accidents in Switzerland increased from 1963 to 1977 by approximately 20%. Alcohol-related road accidents nearly doubled in the same period. The number of persons injured in alcohol-related road accidents increased by nearly 100% for the period 1963-1977 but fatalities did not, however, rise substantially (Figure 4).

FIGURE 3   *Alcohol Consumption and First Admission Rates to Treatment Institutions*

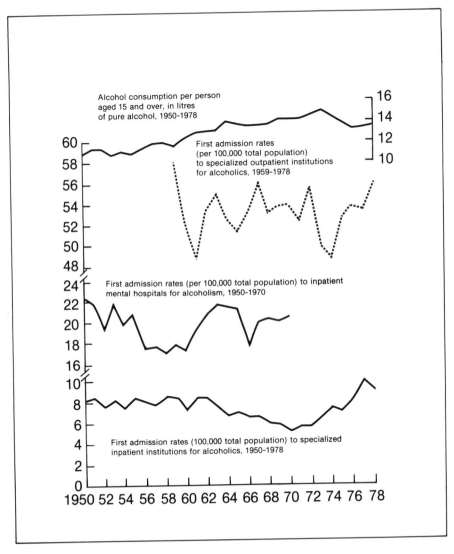

Sources: Annuaires statistiques de la Suisse, Berne, corresponding years and statistique des services médico-sociaux et des maisons d'accueil pour alcooliques, Berne, corresponding years.

FIGURE 4 *Alcohol-Related Road Traffic Accidents and Withdrawals of Driving Licences*

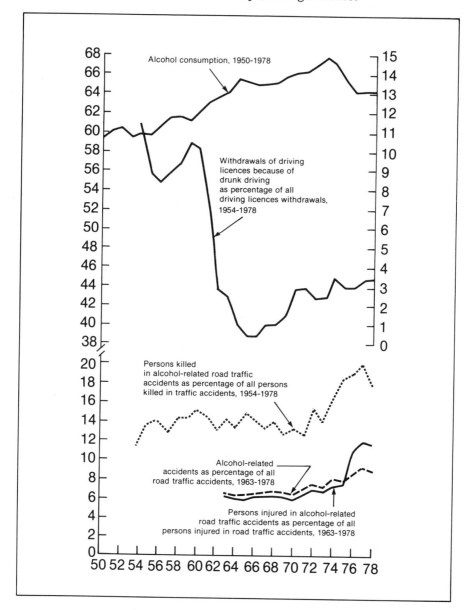

The rate of drivers convicted for driving while intoxicated is not only dependent on the average consumption of alcoholic beverages but also on the preventive effects of control measures by the police. Although the withdrawals of drivers' licences more than tripled from 1954 to 1977, withdrawals for driving while intoxicated decreased in relation to the total number of withdrawals from 60 to 45%. Together with the clearly disproportionate increase of alcohol-related traffic accidents, this is an indication of the decreasing determination of the Swiss police to enforce the laws related to drunk driving.

Other Alcohol-Related Problems

Besides road traffic accidents, no other accident statistics exist listing "alcohol-induced" as a special category. In a study investigating the reasons for hospitalization of accident victims by Kielholz et al. (1973), it was determined that 19% of working accidents, 8% of sport accidents, and 46% of the remaining non-traffic accidents were alcohol-related. These percentages cannot, however, be considered to be an indicator of frequency of working and non-working accidents. They merely serve as very rough indicators of the role of alcohol in accidents.

The relationship between alcohol dependency and suicide has been well-documented in the literature. Compared to other countries, Switzerland has high suicide rates. It is not possible, however, to establish a definite relationship between consumption rates and the number of suicides.

Future Developments

Swiss alcohol consumption has proved to be relatively sensitive to recession, even though the economic slump of 1974/75 just scratched the surface of wealth. Probably the drop in alcohol consumption during these years was due not only to reduced purchasing power and the expulsion of foreign workers, but also to the disciplinarian effect of the threat of job losses. The Swiss economy is not an especially dynamic one and its strength lies much more in its accumulated wealth. The forecasts for the near future indicate more or less stagnating economic growth with an increasing labour force shortage. Presumably, alcohol consumption will increase somewhat. Due in part to rising public problem awareness, indices of alcohol-related problems will probably increase even faster than consumption.

THE TREATMENT SYSTEM

The health care system in Switzerland is under the jurisdiction of the cantons. Approximately half of their laws concerning treatment were enacted before 1950. The principal difference between older and more recent laws consists of different concepts of alcoholism. In the more recent ones, alcoholism is considered as an illness, alleviating the individual from responsibility. In the older laws, alcoholism is still seen as a personal moral failure. But, independently of the underlying conception of alcoholism, the major criterion for intervention in most cases is not medical, but economic and moral. The laws state that a "person who, because of his drinking endangers himself and his family economically and/or morally, must be given care."

Preliminary measures consist of warnings, assignment to outpatient treatment centres, alcohol purchase and tavern interdiction, wage management, and compulsory membership in an abstinence group. If these measures are not successful and the person is considered to be curable, treatment in a specialized inpatient institution is prescribed. If this fails or if the person is considered to be incurable, but capable to work, he is sent to a working institution for an indefinite length of time. Interestingly, the conceptualization of alcoholism as a weakness of personal character is still very visible in the laws on illnesses, accidents, and infirmities. In these laws it is stated that all allowances can be reduced if the illness, the accident, or the infirmity results from a severe personal failure. This disposition is often applied in the case of alcoholism or acute alcohol intoxication.

The Management of Treatment Alternatives

An important indication of how the concept of alcoholism has changed in the past decade in Swiss society is obtained by analyzing referrals to treatment centres. Whereas in 1970 the authorities referred the greatest number of female patients, in 1977 women were mostly sent by medical institutions. In the case of men, the authorities still refer the greatest number but welfare institutions have gained in importance as assigning agents. Self-referral has become increasingly common for both sexes. This is indicative of the spread in the medicalization of alcoholism, for contacting a specialized alcohol institution by the patient himself requires a certain degree of deculpabilization (an important notion of the medicalization of alcoholism), even though many of these self-referrals are undoubtedly influenced by strong social control mechanisms. The differential trends in the rates of referral for men and women to alcohol treatment centres does not necessarily indicate differences in the development of male or female alcoholism, but could just as well indicate a change in the social visibility of alcohol problems.

Analogous to the number of first admissions to mental hospitals and to specialized inpatient treatment centres, the rate of female first admissions to outpatient treatment centres for alcoholics has also increased by more than 100% from 1960 to 1977. The rate of male first admissions has remained more or less constant.

In the outpatient sector, new alcohol and drug treatment centres have been established that are specifically directed towards adolescents and young adults, but those centres are not accounted for in the statistics.

The clientele of the outpatient treatment centres, contrary to the specialized inpatient centres, showed an increase in liberal professions and non-skilled workers, and a decrease in skilled workers. This tendency may have been the result of the professionalization of these services which took place in the last 10 years, making them acceptable for the higher social classes as well as the lower, as well as a consequence of the economic recession which led to lower consumption on the part of the middle classes.

Types of Treatment Institutions for Alcohol Addicts

The treatment system in Switzerland is characterized by a great variety of institutions, based not only on the federal structure of the health care system, but also on the historical development of the perception of alcohol problems.

Three main characteristics distinguish the different types of existing institutions. The first is whether those institutions address themselves to alcohol addicts only, or if they have a broader range of clients. The second is related to the aim of the institution, i.e. if it intends to "cure" the patient, or if it serves punitive or guarding functions. Finally, there is the distinction between inpatient and outpatient treatment centres, halfway houses being an intermediate category. The total number of beds occupied by alcohol addicts in all inpatient treatment institutions amounted to about 3,700 in 1978/79.

Specialized institutions and mental hospitals provide most of the inpatient treatment services. During the period studied, the number of specialized institutions rose from eight to 13, with 500 available beds. Two major trends can be observed with regard to these institutions. First, the newer ones have extended their clientele to include women and young adults. The broadening of the clientele brought about an enlargement of the concept of addiction to include other legal and illegal drugs. The second important change was the "medicalization" of those institutions. Whereas the management of those institutions was previously overwhelmingly laic, they now have medical and/or psychiatric management (Müller, and Tecklenburg, 1978). Partly as a consequence of this medicalization, the mean duration of stay has decreased.

Mental hospitals are still the most important setting for the inpatient treatment of alcohol addicts, accounting for 60% of all beds available. For patients whose primary diagnosis was alcohol psychosis or alcoholism, the mean duration of stay was 107 days in 1978. Between 1950 and 1970, short-term stays (up to three months) have increased slightly. Changes in treatment practices are mainly responsible for this decrease in the average length of stay in mental hospitals. However, during the same time period, there was a strong increase in re-admissions, while first admissions have remained quite constant; thus, the "revolving door" phenomenon set in.

There exists only one special ward for alcohol addicts in a general hospital. It serves as a detoxification centre for a short period, two to three weeks, after which the patient is transferred to another institution, according to the medical and/or social prognosis.

A third type of inpatient institution is formed by the so-called "working institutions," which serve exclusively penal functions. They are intended for those alcoholics who are considered incurable, as well as for socially difficult or mentally handicapped persons who are nevertheless capable of work. Depending on the economic situation, they work outside the institution to help provide for their residence costs.

Halfway houses are few, and often not listed as a separate category when they are part of an inpatient treatment centre. Those institutions are intended as a passage between an inpatient treatment centre and the patient's own home.

The most important aspect of the Swiss treatment system for alcohol addicts is the outpatient treatment. At the beginning of the century, outpatient treatment centres included the informal care activities by members of abstinence and temperance organizations. After the passage of the cantonal welfare and treatment laws, formerly private treatment centres became more and more public, subsidized by governmental funds. Between 1950 and 1977, their estimated number grew from 90 to 130, about one-fifth run by abstinence organizations. The estimated number of persons treated in those institutions doubled in the same period (from 15,000 to 30,000). As in the case of inpatient treatment centres, a professionalization of those outpatient centres has taken place. Abstinence is no longer a sufficient criterion for employment in these institutions; one must have professional training, usually in the field of social work. Medicalization is also reflected in the changing characteristics of such institutions as social-medical centres, as well as in the increased use of medical or psychiatric management consulting.

SUMMARY

Alcohol has been a political issue in Switzerland since the Middle Ages. With few exceptions, alcohol has always been conceptualized as a special commodity. However, the underlying rationale of this conceptualization has changed markedly. Even though the cantons had discovered very quickly the fiscal benefits of alcohol taxation, the ultimate aim of alcohol regulations was, until the end of the 18th century, to maintain public order. There is some historical evidence that in those days alcohol problems consisted mainly of damage due to occasional excess (Jellinek 1976). But after transportation advances and the change from the field system to crop rotation made it possible to produce and distribute alcoholic beverages efficiently on a large scale, alcohol problems became much more evident in large segments of the population. It is to the credit of the temperance movement that health concerns as well as the hygiene argument were given consideration, even though most temperance and abstinence movements in Switzerland never questioned the social conditions of widespread excessive alcohol consumption in the country. Alcohol itself, and distilled spirits in particular, were deemed the root of all evil and served as a scapegoat for the sins of capitalist society. By thus legitimizing state and society, the claims of the temperance movement had to be taken seriously into account.

Alcohol policy in Switzerland at the end of the 19th and beginning of the 20th century involved agricultural, trade and industrial, and public health interests and the bureaucracy's own interests, the latter fostered by the abstinence movement. One has to bear in mind the federal political structure of the country, particularly the cultural antagonisms in the meaning of "alcoholic beverages" and the regional differences in the economic importance of wine-growing. Fiscal interests were important but not prevailing. Within this frame of divergent interests, the political system acted as a catalyst, translating all the different pressures as well as the bureaucracy's own interests into legislation which is an elaborated piece of Switzerland's system of checks and balances.

In Switzerland too, the rise of the welfare state after World War II rendered obsolete the legitimizing function of the abstinence movement. Concern about public interest and public health belongs to the built-in mechanisms of the modern welfare state. Interestingly enough, since the end of the 1970s, a revitalization of the influence of the abstinence movement can be observed. Probably this has to be seen against the background of the limits on the growth of the welfare system in general and the medical care system in particular. Part of the attempt to overcome these limits is the tendency to individualize alcohol problems. The effort in the last few years by many cantons to implement alcohol education (in a rather superficial manner) in the school curricula may be seen as such an attempt. In the long run, this may well result in re-culpabilizing the individual and in de-culpabilizing the welfare system. This tendency is enhanced by a return to traditional values and a tendency among the general population toward a backlash against youth, females, and drug and alcohol addicts.

In sum, the alcohol question, whether seen from the perspective of production, consumption, or alcohol problems, remains a very sensitive issue in the political life of Switzerland. Production is closely linked with minorities, specifically the French and Italian parts of Switzerland and the agricultural population. Consumption is strongly related to diversities in the cultural significance of alcohol. On the political level, the past 10 years have been marked by a renewal of preoccupation concerning alcohol-related problems, and it seems that the heyday of the conceptualization of alcoholism as an illness is coming to an end. Due in part to the "costs explosion" of the health care system, an increasing moralization and individualization of alcohol problems in public health debates can be observed. The proper responsibility for one's own health is stressed and, therefore, the notion of individual failure may be revitalized.

REFERENCES

Almanach der Schweiz, 1978, *Soziologisches Institut der Universität Zürich*. Lang, Berne.

Angst, J., Bendel, H., & Binder, J., 1980, Unterschiedliche Entwicklung des Suchtmittelkonsums bei jungen Zürcherinnen — ein Vergleich 1971/78. *Schweizerische Aerztezeitung*, 61, 447-450.

Battegay, R., Mühlemann, R., Hell, D., Zehnder, R., Hoch, P., & Dillinger, A., 1977, *Alkohol und Tabak im Leben des jungen Mannes*. Basel: Karger.

Cahannes, M., 1979, *General social structure and demographic composition*. ISACE Second Conference, Asilomar.

Cahannes, M., 1979, *Aggregate statistics on alcohol consumption*. ISACE Second Conference, Asilomar.

Dietrich, W. & Cahannes, M., 1980, The treatment system for alcohol addicts in Switzerland. Paper prepared for ISACE Third Conference, Warsaw.

Gugelberg, A.V., 1950, *Der Staatsinterventionismus in der schweizerischen Weinwirtschaft*, Bischofsberger. Chur.

Jellinek, O., *Working Papers on Drinking Patterns and Alcohol Problems*. R.E. Popham (Ed.), Addiction Research Foundation, Substudy 804, Toronto, 1976.

Kielholz, P., Battegay, R., & Mühlemann, R., 1973, Alcool et circulation, Tiré à part du supplément B, no 2/1973 du "Bulletin du Service fédéral de l'hygiène publique."

Knupfer, G., 1967, The Epidemiology of Drinking Problems. *Am. J. Publ. Hlth*, 57: 973-986.

Ledermann, S., 1956, *Alcool, Alcoolisme, Alcoolisation*, Donnés scientifiques de caractère physiologique, économique et social. P.U.F. Paris.

Leu, R. & Lutz, P., 1977, *Oekonomische Aspekte des Alkoholkonsums in der Schweiz*. Zürich.

Meyrat, P., Abelin, T., Stutz, J., & Ehrengruber, H., 1977, Die häufigsten Spitaldiagnosen nach Alter und Geschlecht. *Schweizerische Aerztezeitung*, 15, 595-598.

Müller, R., 1979a, Drinking Populations, Institutions, and Patterns. ISACE Second Conference, Asilomar.

Müller, R., 1979b, Gesamtschweizerische Repräsentativuntersuchung über den Alkohol-konsum der Schüler des 6., 7. and 8. Schuljahres, Lausanne.

Müller, R., 1979c, The Swiss Control System. ISACE Second Conference, Asilomar.

Müller, R., 1980, Alcohol-related problems in Switzerland, 1950-1977. Paper prepared for the Third ISACE Conference, Warsaw.

Müller, R., 1981, Zur Entwicklung der Rauch — und Trinkgewohnheiten. In der Schweiz 1975-1979, Lausanne.

Müller, R. & Tecklenburg, U., 1978, La médicalisation de l'alcoolisme. *Drogalcool,* no 2/78, Lausanne.

Wüthrich, P., & Hausheer, H., 1979, *Alkohol in der Schweiz.* Huber, Frauenfeld.

Zurbrügg, C., 1976, *Die schweizerische Alkoholpolitik.* Haupt, Berne.

5. Anti-Drink Propaganda and Alcohol Control Measures: A Report on the Dutch Experience

Jan de Lint*

The Kingdom of the Netherlands is one of the most densely populated countries in the world with more than 400 inhabitants per square kilometre. The main language and culture is Dutch, although in recent years many newcomers of Turkish, Moroccan, and Surinam origin have settled in the large urban areas. Approximately 30% of the 14 million Dutch residents are Roman Catholic, 30% Protestant, while 40% have a different or no religious affiliation.

Since the end of the Second World War, the political scene in the Netherlands has been dominated by left to centre political parties which — among other things — has resulted in a so-called "guided" economy, with wage and price controls, extensive social welfare legislation, and a wide variety of governmental assistance programs for farm and industry. Contrary to what many expected, the Dutch have, to date, survived the loss of their great empire (East Indies, New Guinea, Surinam) rather well and are now enjoying one of the highest living standards in Western Europe. And while becoming more affluent, the Dutch also have become more urban.

Concurrent with many socioeconomic changes, the overall pattern of consumption has changed much since the 1950s. Not too long ago Gadourek (1965) found the average Dutchman to be essentially "non-indulgent" but this description is no longer applicable. Indeed, expenditures on luxury items such as cars, foreign travel, and second homes (cottages or caravans) have risen rapidly, whereas the proportion of disposable income going into savings has gradually been reduced (C.B.S. 1951-1976).

The consumption of alcoholic beverages has also changed significantly during the post-war period. For many, alcohol use is now a daily habit and questions pertaining to the possible effects of repeated

*The author gratefully acknowledges the support of the Alcohol Fund and the assistance of colleagues at the Dutch Foundation for the Scientific Study of Alcohol and Drug Use.

87

alcohol consumption on the health of the consumer and to the type of measures needed to stabilize the current trend and minimize the damages have been receiving considerable public attention in recent years.

Many years ago, anti-drink propagandists were very active but relatively little alcohol control legislation resulted from their efforts. The dramatic increase in the consumption of alcoholic beverages in recent years can therefore not be explained in the context of a relaxation of alcohol control measures. And as to the consequences to public health, it will probably take some time before the higher prevalence of excessive use leads to a higher prevalence of alcohol-related health problems.

Implementing restrictive measures at this time would be difficult. The anti-drink propagandists have aged, many alleged health consequences of increased consumption are not as yet in evidence, and previous experience with alcohol control legislation is very limited.

RECENT TRENDS IN ALCOHOL CONSUMPTION

In the Netherlands, there is a highly concentrated brewing and distilling industry with a sizeable export market. The Dutch have been brewing and distilling for many centuries but have not engaged, to any significant extent, in viticulture.

Statistics pertaining to the sale of alcoholic beverages have been routinely collected since the beginning of the 19th century. During this period, the lowest rate of consumption occurred during the war years 1916 to 1918 and again in 1942 to 1945 (Table 1). Since 1960 the use of alcoholic beverages has greatly increased.

On a per capita basis, wine consumption increased 12 times between 1950 and 1975, beer consumption seven times, and the use of distilled beverages has more than doubled (de Lint, 1980). During the same period, the percentage contribution of the use of wine, beer, and distilled beverages to total consumption changed from 5.1, 24.9, and 70.0 respectively in 1950 to 15.4, 45.5, and 39.1 respectively in 1975.

It is evident that changes of such magnitude cannot be attributed to small differences in the proportion of drinkers within the total drinking-age population. For 1958, this proportion of drinkers was estimated at 83%, for 1976 at 87% (Gadourek, 1963; Sijlbing, 1978). Rather, we must consider here the significant modifications in Dutch drinking behaviour that have recently occurred. Alcoholic beverages are now consumed on many occasions and the percentage of daily drinkers has risen from about 9% of all drinkers in 1958 to about 23% in 1976 (Gadourek, 1963; Sijlbing, 1978). Compared with the other member states in the European Community, such a rapid proliferation of alcohol use patterns is remarkable (Table 2).

TABLE 1   *Per Capita Consumption in the Netherlands:*
10-Year Averages in Litres of Absolute Alcohol,
1830-1979

	Wine	Beer[1]	Distilled	Total
1830-1839	0.37	0.70	5.25	6.32
1840-1849	0.33	0.80	3.92	5.05
1850-1859	0.32	1.00	3.81	5.13
1860-1869	0.30	1.20	3.89	5.39
1870-1879	0.29	1.43	4.51	6.23
1880-1889	0.27	1.66	4.64	6.57
1890-1999	0.23	1.98	4.34	6.55
1900-1909	0.21	2.00	3.80	6.01
1910-1919	0.15	1.49	2.42	4.06
1920-1929	0.22	1.24	1.30	2.76
1930-1939	0.14	0.93	0.88	1.95
1940-1949	0.07	0.78	0.86	1.71
1950-1959	0.13	0.77	1.18	2.08
1960-1969	0.39	1.81	1.52	3.72
1970-1979	1.16	3.38	2.68	7.22

Source: Produktschap voor Gedistilleerde Dranken, 1975-79.

[1] For the period 1830-1870, no data were available to indicate the average consumption of beer. It is reported however that beer use gradually increased during these years and on this basis the 10 year averages were estimated to be about 0.7, 0.8, 1.0 and 1.2 litres (absolute alcohol) respectively.

TABLE 2   *Alcohol Consumption in the European*
Community in 1975 (Alcohol Consumption in
1950 equals 100)

Belgium	137
Denmark	222
France	74
Italy	144
Netherlands	406
Luxembourg	162
United Kingdom	162
West Germany	380

Source: de Lint, 1980

During the same period, many other important changes in Dutch consumption patterns have occurred. Expenditures on housing, utilities, recreation, transportation, medical care, fish, meats, soft drinks, and chocolates have increased while expenditures on shoes, clothing, personal hygiene articles, some oils, fats, and bakery products have decreased (C.B.S., 1966 and 1979). Fewer households now have maids or cleaning help but more have colour T.V. and hi-fi sets.

Undoubtedly numerous socioeconomic factors are relevant in bringing about these changes in the uses of time and money: the influence of neighbouring countries, the decline of large and medium-sized families which used to absorb many resources, urbanization, technical innovation, a greater availability of some goods and services, more leisure, and more income.

It is difficult to determine the relative importance of each of these changes. For instance, much significance has often been attached to the availability of a good or service. However, in the Netherlands, the consumption of tea and milk has declined although in terms of their relative price and the number of places where they can be purchased they have become much more available. There are obvious limitations to the total consumptive capacities in terms of food calories, time available for consumption, and litres of fluids that can be drunk. Within these limitations, we find that certain usages of time and money have gradually been replaced by other ways of using time and money.

Thus, in attempting to explain the increased consumption of alcoholic beverages in the Netherlands it may well be relevant that the frequencies of some competing habits such as the drinking of tea and milk, of some competing uses of time such as being at work or taking care of a family, of some competing expenditures such as church donations or saving for old age, have been decreasing (de Lint, 1979). For drinking habits to proliferate it is not sufficient to have a greater availability of alcoholic beverages from year to year. It is also necessary that this behaviour be accommodated within the limits of total consumptive capacity which may have been relevant to the increase in alcohol consumption. Indeed, in retrospect, it is not difficult to identify and describe some of the relevant socioeconomic developments during the 1950s, 1960s, and 1970s. For instance, the Dutch birth rate has dropped from 24 per 1,000 in 1950 to 13 per 1,000 in 1975 permitting many alternate uses of time and money. Similarly, church attendance has significantly declined and much social legislation has been implemented, making unemployment more bearable and hard work less financially rewarding. It may be argued, however, that there are other countries where, since the war years, much more time and money have likewise become available for alcohol consumption, but where nevertheless very little change in drinking behaviour has occurred.

It should be noted that the level of alcohol consumption in the Netherlands compared to neighbouring countries was very low until the late 1950s when it began its dramatic rise. Since that time, there have been progressively more intimate cultural and economic exchanges between the member states of the Benelux and the European Community. It is certainly interesting to note that in the E.C. countries with the highest rate of use (France and Italy) the consumption of alcoholic beverages has been decreasing in recent years, while in the E.C. countries with the lowest rate of use (Denmark, Ireland, and the Netherlands) the consumption of alcoholic beverages has much increased. Indeed, within the European Community, it may be difficult to try to maintain a very deviant pattern of use. But the fact that the rapid increase in alcohol consumption in the Netherlands was in part attributable to the very low rate of use in the 1950s, raises another interesting question. Why was the level of alcohol consumption in the Netherlands so very low to begin with compared to the neighbouring countries? Did the Dutch have very stringent alcohol control laws or can we point to a different reason?

A HISTORICAL PERSPECTIVE

Throughout the 19th century the rate of consumption of alcoholic beverages and, in particular, of distilled spirits had certainly been rather high, ranging from 5 to 6.5 litres of absolute alcohol per capita (Don and Van der Woude, 1904). However, in the early 20th century it fell to a low of 1.7 litres in the 1940s (Produktschap voor Gedistilleerde Dranken, 1968).

The growing popularity of distilled spirits at the beginning of the 19th century and the increasing concern about drunkenness led to a wide assortment of temperance activities. The Society for the Abolition of Strong Beverages was founded in 1842 after a number of local temperance organizations instituted during the 1830s had failed to bring about a reduction in the rate of distilled beverage consumption. The Society had among its members many clergymen, medical doctors, and teachers. In one of its briefs to the government it made reference to the heathen Chinese emperor who had just decreed the prohibition of the use of opium while lamenting the fact that Christian governments were not willing to act in a similar way with respect to the use of distilled beverages. In the main, its activities were directed towards parliamentarians and cabinet ministers who, according to the Society, should use their prestige and legislative powers to prevent alcohol abuse. Specifically, it advocated a reduction in the number of outlets for the on-premise consumption of distilled beverages, the removal of the taxes on beer, and the prohibition of consumption of distilled beverages in prisons, on military bases, and in other governmental institutions.

Although the well-meaning liberal bourgeois members of the Society recognized the need to lessen the widespread poverty, little attention was paid to the terrible circumstances in which the working classes were living. They wanted to end poverty by creating more jobs in the agrarian sector of the economy and not by means of more fundamental social reforms (Proost, 1941; Maas, 1977).

Towards the end of the 19th century, several other organizations had joined the Society in its fight against alcohol abuse. One was the People's League against Alcohol Abuse (Volksbond gegen het Alcohol Misbruik), a temperance organization, which campaigned for a reduction of the number of liquor outlets and engaged in other initiatives, such as the establishment of so-called penny banks where one could deposit small amounts of money, housing corporations to facilitate home ownership, courses for working class housewives in cooking and other domestic skills, and public houses where only beer, coffee, milk, and soft drinks were served. It also lobbied for much cheaper beer than was available at that time which, it felt, should have an alcohol content of about 3%.

Surprisingly, the People's League did not seek higher taxes on distilled beverages as a means to discourage their consumption. Along with other temperance forces, it argued that the State was already too dependent on the liquor trade for its revenue (amounting to 23% of total State income at the time). It was particularly concerned that higher taxes would only make widespread poverty worse.

The People's League was indeed a remarkable organization. In the vicinity of large cities it helped to establish the so-called people's gardens (volkstuintjes), small plots of land which could be rented at little expense thus providing many with an opportunity to grow their own vegetables. Now almost 100 years later, these gardens have become part of the Dutch cityscape, while the People's League is still active as a catering organization running numerous alcohol-free canteens in factories and office buildings.

In the meantime, the Society for the Abolition of Strong Beverages had itself become more militant, now promoting total abstinence of all alcoholic beverages and enrolling many young people from the working classes. This new Society hotly debated with the People's League and the Socialist Worker's Party (the third major force in the battle against alcohol abuse) about what the best course of action would be.

Initially, the Socialists had a rather simple solution to the alcohol problem: since people were driven to abuse by conditions resulting from the capitalists' means of production, the defeat of capitalism would automatically lead to a significant reduction in the rate of alcohol abuse (Kautsky, 1890). To this argument the Abolitionists replied that in many countries of Europe during the 1870s and 1880s, the rate of alcohol use increased while the economic situation improved, while at other times when the economic situation was deteriorating, the rate of alcohol consumption decreased (Van der Woude, 1903).

Gradually, towards the early years of the 20th century many Socialists had recognized that the problems of alcohol abuse could not simply be attributed to poverty, long hours of work, and malnutrition. Although some leaders had been convinced that alcohol abuse was the result of a conspiracy between Kapitaal (capital), Kerk (church), and Kroeg (pub) aimed at keeping the working classes uninformed and powerless, they too began to promote abstinence and to campaign for effective legal restrictions on the availability of strong beverages.

The activities of the People's League, the Abolitionist Society, the Socialist Worker's Party, and numerous other groups finally led to further government action. Already in 1881 the so-called Maximum System had been introduced requiring licences for the sale of distilled beverages for on- and off-premise consumption to be obtained from the municipality. The number of licences to be issued was dependent on the size of the municipal population. However, the requirements for a licence were very easily met. After the Abolitionists and their allies had collected more than 100,000 signatures to a petition requesting new control measures, the government presented to parliament a new Alcohol Law, which passed in 1904. In this piece of legislation, the central government — and no longer the municipality — specified the requirements for a licence to sell distilled beverages. Licences to sell beer and wine for on-premise consumption also were needed although not subject to the maximum rule. As before, all licences had to be obtained from the municipal governments.

For the Abolitionists and their Social Reform allies this new alcohol law was a great disappointment. Specifically, they felt that too many outlets were still possible. For the sale of distilled beverages, it ranged from one outlet per 250 persons in rural areas to one outlet per 500 persons in large cities. For the on-premise sale of beer and wine a licence was required but no maximum rule pertained. For the sale of beer and wine for off-premise consumption, not even a licence was needed. Also, they had expected that the new law would recognize the right of local option which their petition had specifically asked for. Thus, they decided to continue to pressure the government and in 1912 almost 700,000 signatures were collected to demand the right of local option. This represented about 25% of the Dutch adult population. But World War I prevented the government from taking action and it wasn't until 1921 that a local option bill was finally introduced.

The local option bill passed the House of Commons but was rejected by one vote in the Senate. Two years later the same legislation was again passed by the House of Commons and again rejected by the Senate. The Prime Minister then promised a third introduction of local option legislation but when the new Alcohol Law was tabled in the House of Commons (1931) the provision for local option had been withdrawn. According to the government this drastic measure was no longer necessary because the consumption of distilled beverages had become relatively insignificant (Table 1) and little alcohol abuse was in evidence.

However, a new Alcohol Law of 1931 did set a ceiling for the number of licences to be issued for the on-premise sale of beer and wine. By 1931, the number of outlets of various kinds had already been decreasing so rapidly due to declining consumption that the maximum rule had become virtually meaningless as a restrictive measure. In most municipalities there were fewer outlets than were permitted under the maximum rule.

Thus, in the Netherlands, dry sentiment was widespread during the first half of the 20th century but only a few alcohol control measures were ever implemented. It follows that the low rates of alcohol consumption in the 1930s, 1940s, and 1950s may have been the result of the massive anti-drink propaganda during the early 20th century but they definitely were not brought about by restrictive legislation. Indeed, the Maximum System has been the only restrictive measure of any real significance throughout the alcohol-political history of the Dutch.

How then does one explain the low rates of alcohol use in the 1930s, 1940s, and 1950s? Can it be argued that dry sentiment which is not transformed into law is better sustained? And why did this sentiment quickly evaporate into thin air in the 1960s and 1970s, leaving a handful of aged abstainers wondering what had happened? A partial explanation at least is found by looking at the place of alcohol within 19th century social reform movements.

Whether or not alcohol abuse was indeed attributable to capitalist exploitation of the working classes was not as historically relevant as the belief on the side of many social reformers that there was in fact, an intimate connection between the two. Thus, what the liberal bourgeois Abolitionists of the 1850s and 1860s could not achieve, the rather mixed group of Christian and Socialist reformers of the 1880s and 1890s did bring about, namely to generate mass support for a temperant if not abstinent society.

In retrospect, it is perhaps significant that throughout the long alcohol-political history of the Dutch, attention was focused only on moral persuasion and a reduction of outlet frequency to combat alcohol abuse. Other preventive strategies, such as a rationing system of a state monopoly of production and/or distribution of alcoholic beverages, were never important issues, while drastic fiscal measures were, until recently, rejected by the anti-drink movement as a possible means to reduce the availability of alcohol.

And with respect to the many efforts to promote temperance or abstinence, it is noteworthy that already in 1846 the Dutch Teachers Association had begun to distribute to primary schools various reading books in which young people are warned about the dangers of drinking strong beverages. At the end of the 19th century, the government agreed to include alcohol studies in the curriculum of all teachers colleges. Their activities in the schools as well as the considerable influence of red (Socialists) and blue (Abolitionist) youth organizations did much to strengthen dry sentiment (Harmsen, 1961).

But by far the more significant factor in explaining the low level of consumption in the early 20th century would seem to have been the very close relationship between the anti-drink movement and the social reformers. Socialists and progressive Christians tried hard to persuade workers not to drink or at least to abstain from the use of distilled spirits. An alcoholic was no longer considered a sinner — as was the case in the early and middle 19th century — but a weakling who had failed to liberate himself from the drinking customs of a bourgeois society (Maas, 1977). According to the *Young Socialist* (*'De Jonge Socialist'*), a periodical from 1892, the fight against capitalism and against alcohol use were both aimed at "freeing mankind from centuries of physical and spiritual slavery" (Harmsen, 1961).

During the parliamentary debates about the Alcohol Laws of 1931 and 1964, government spokesmen paid tribute to the great achievements of the temperance and abolitionist groups. Indeed it used these successes to justify its own unwillingness to introduce a "local option" law (1931) or to continue with the Maximum System (1964). However, as noted earlier, Dutch dry sentiment was not sustained in the 1960s and 1970s.

THE CONTEMPORARY CONTROL SYSTEM

In 1954, the government established two commissions to evaluate the need for a new alcohol law. One commission was made up of members of the medical community and temperance interests; the other included representatives of alcohol beverage industries in the Netherlands. They met for 10 years but accomplished little. In 1964, the government proposed to abolish the Maximum System, making frequent references to the successes of the anti-drink propaganda. It was argued that the System was no longer needed now that the consumption of alcoholic beverages had apparently stabilized at a reasonable level. It also recognized that there had been a considerable improvement in the work situation, in housing, in the possibilities for recreation, and in the intellectual development of the working classes. Many members of parliament voted against the new law but to no avail. Valid arguments to retain it were difficult to find and in 1967 the Maximum System was officially abolished.

Since the repeal of the Maximum Law in 1967, the availability of alcoholic beverages did not substantially change. The total number of licensed outlets increased 14% from 33,064 in 1966 to 37,813 in 1976 (Table 3), while the population of drinking age increased 16% during that period. There may well have been a substantial increase in the number of places where beer and wine could be purchased for off-premise consumption. These outlets include snack bars, gas stations, grocery stores, and even vending machines which have always been outside the jurisdiction of the alcohol law and therefore there is little information on the extent of their proliferation.

TABLE 3   *Population (15 years and older), Alcohol Consumption in Hectolitres of Absolute Alcohol, Retail Stores for the Sale of Distilled Beverages, Public Houses, Licensed Restaurants, and Hotels, 1966 and 1976*

	1966	1976	% Increase
Population	8,900,000	10,300,000	16
Alcohol Consumption	483,700	1,117,400	131
Retail Stores	3,230	3,740	16
Public Houses	12,542	13,819	10
Restaurants and Hotels	6,871	6,032	−12
Other Outlets*	10,421	14,213	36

* Includes lunch bars, private clubs, ice cream parlours, coffee houses, vending machines, rooming houses.
Source: Produktschap voor Gedistilleerde Dranken, 1967 and 1977.

At present, there are few alcohol-specific controls left governing these on- and off-premise establishments (Smits and van Loon, 1979). In some areas both on- and off-premise establishments are open throughout the night. The federal regulations for obtaining a licence to sell distilled spirits concerns primarily the age and moral character of the applicant. The minimum age is 16 years for the purchase of beer and wine, and 18 years for distilled spirits. Municipal governments continue to issue licences for on-premise establishments and for the off-premise sale of distilled spirits. And indeed, for reasons of "social hygiene" they can refuse to issue such licences. In general, however, the regulations governing alcohol sales differ little from the requirements for the sale of other goods.

The advertising of alcohol beverages is regulated by the same laws which cover other commodities and production is governed by general regulations pertaining to food and health. Thus, in general, the control of alcoholic beverages is very much integrated into the elaborate mechanisms of control found in a highly regulated state with a planned economy.

ALCOHOL USE AND PUBLIC HEALTH

As has been illustrated before (Table 1), the per capita consumption of beverage alcohol is now higher than at any time during the 19th century. Admittedly, to document the public health effects of this increase in consumption is usually difficult. Indeed, the influence of alcohol use on morbidity and mortality has been investigated by a wide variety of methods for more than 100 years, but a satisfactory description of its etiological relevance viz à viz numerous other factors has yet to be produced.

The case of the Netherlands provides a good illustration of this difficulty. Not only has the use of alcoholic beverages much increased, but also, with respect to variables such as road traffic, atmospheric conditions, population density, dietary habits, medical services, birth rate, and family composition, significant developments have recently taken place (C.B.S. 1951-1976). It is thus not surprising that the risk of dying from a great many causes has not remained the same during the post-war period. For example, men aged 35 to 74 had a much higher rate of death from malignant neoplasms, cardiovascular diseases, and diseases of the respiratory system in 1975 than in 1950. Among women aged 35 to 74, mortality from accidents, poisonings, and violence increased between 1950 and 1975 but mortality from all disease categories decreased.

Many diseases and accidents have been found to cause death among alcoholics more often than expected (Ledermann, 1964; Sundby, 1967; Schmidt and de Lint, 1972; Bruun et al., 1975). But, as has often been remarked, the excess mortality from these causes should not only be attributed to the frequent use of alcoholic beverages. Alcoholics are often depressed, smoke heavily, neglect their diet and health care, and are much exposed to environmental hazards. Tuberculosis, for example, used to be an important cause of death among alcoholics (Sundby, 1967). But in the Netherlands, the incidence of this disease has much decreased among alcoholics and non-alcoholics alike, while the consumption of alcoholic beverages has much increased (de Lint, 1980).

The question of whether the chronic use of alcoholic beverages is relevant in the etiology of certain malignant neoplasms is of much current interest (Tuyns, 1978). Among patients in alcoholism clinics, malignant neoplasms of the upper digestive and respiratory tracts are rather common and there is also some evidence to suggest that mortality from esophageal neoplasm is higher in regions where more alcohol is consumed (Tuyns, 1978). In the Netherlands, the rate of death from malignant neoplasms of the upper digestive and respiratory tracts has much increased among men since the war mainly because of an elevated mortality from neoplasms of bronchus and lung (de Lint, 1980). But rates of death from the other malignant neoplasms of the upper digestive and respiratory tracts, such as the malignant neoplasms of buccal cavity and pharynx (140-149), esophagus (150), larynx (161), have not increased during the period 1950-1975. Apparently the higher rate of alcohol consumption has had little effect, statistically speaking, on the incidence of these diseases. Whether the increased alcohol consumption has contributed in any way to the much higher frequency of malignant neoplasms of bronchus and lung remains uncertain.

It is also difficult to connect the higher rates of death from cardiovascular diseases to the recent changes in Dutch drinking behaviour. Follow-up investigations of alcoholics have shown that many of them die from these diseases but — as in the case of malignant neoplasms of bronchus and lung — this may be attributed to their smoking habits. In any event, in the Netherlands the mortality from cardiovascular diseases has much increased among men but has much decreased among women in the age groups 35 to 74 (de Lint, 1980).

In contrast to the rather uncertain role of alcohol use in the etiology of certain neoplasms and cardiovascular diseases, there is generally little doubt about the significance of this behaviour in the development of cirrhosis of the liver. And indeed the rate of death from this disease has increased between the years 1950 and 1975 although not as much as might have been expected on the basis of the 300% rise in average alcohol consumption (de Lint, 1980). Within a five-year period (1970-1975), the number of patients admitted to hospitals for the treatment of liver cirrhosis more than doubled (Hoogendoorn, 1978), although the increase in liver cirrhosis mortality during this same period has not been as rapid. It is of course possible that, in the future, the relationship between liver cirrhosis and alcohol use will manifest itself more clearly as the proportion of non-alcoholic liver cirrhosis to total liver cirrhosis decreases and as excessive alcohol use is no longer a recently acquired habit for many Dutch people.

In the case of death from alcoholism and alcoholic psychosis, very little has happened since 1950 (de Lint, 1980). The ascription of death to these causes is of course done quite arbitrarily (Sundby, 1967; Schmidt and de Lint, 1972) and one, therefore, should not attach too much significance to these findings. It is nevertheless of some interest to note that the admission rate for the treatment of these conditions has much increased (Hoogendoorn, 1978).

Mortality from pneumonia even decreased during the post-war period although this disease occurs frequently among alcoholics (Jellinek, 1942; Sundby, 1967; Schmidt and de Lint, 1972; Nicholls et al., 1974). Again, the increased use of alcoholic beverages in the Netherlands has not affected mortality from pneumonia.

In sum, for the Netherlands we must conclude that the higher rate of alcohol use seems to have affected public health relatively little. This does not necessarily mean that, in the Netherlands, increased alcohol use has not had the influence on public health that it has had elsewhere. It simply may suggest that in the Netherlands, for the time being, the public health effects of much increased alcohol use cannot be made statistically visible.

In this connection, we have already noted how, among Dutch males between the ages 35 and 74, mortality from cardiovascular diseases has much increased. Such a development can easily obscure if not deflate mortality from alcohol-related causes. Similarly death from neoplasm of lung and bronchus has become much more prevalent (an increase of 800% among men 35 to 74 since 1950). Where risks of death from these major causes increase rapidly, it is conceivable that the population at risk of death from alcohol-related causes tends to decrease.

At the same time, the rate of first admissions to alcoholism clinics has risen significantly (van Ginneken and van der Wal, 1980), while both the frequency and acceptance of large quantity drinking per occasion has much increased (Sijlbing, 1978).

THE ALCOHOL-POLITICAL DILEMMA

Whether or not the incidence of alcohol-associated public order and public health problems has really been increasing much in recent decades is not relevant from the alcohol-political perspective. What is important is the growing impression that it has. Thus, at the occasion of the 100th anniversary of the People's League in 1975, the Minister of Health spoke of the need for a "discouragement policy" to stem the tide (Vorrink, 1975).

However, no such policy has thusfar been introduced. As long as there are no clear signals from the public at large that it wants the government to act and as long as the major political parties, the labour unions, the churches, or other influential organizations are not asking for restrictive alcohol control measures, a new alcohol Act discouraging consumption is unlikely to happen in the foreseeable future (Dekker, 1978). To illustrate, in 1978 the abolitionist Society and other anti-drink groups organized a countrywide petition to demand some government action on the "discouragement policy" promised in 1975. About 50,000 signatures were collected representing less than 1% of the drinking age population. In contrast, in 1912, a petition asking for the right of local option was signed by almost 25% of the drinking age population.

Various options for government control have been raised. Some economists have recently pressed for a reduction in the frequency and variety of outlets, a prohibition of alcohol advertising, and much higher duties on alcoholic beverages (van de Tempel, 1977; Cnossen, 1979). However, throughout the alcohol-political history of the Dutch it has never proven possible to implement restrictive alcohol control measures without first generating considerable dry sentiment.

The Netherlands is a welfare state where many aspects of life are controlled. Thus, there are numerous rules pertaining to the expertise of the distributor of a commodity, to the price of products, to the conditions of sale. And so far as the management of alcohol problems is concerned, numerous social welfare provisions exist. If alcoholics do not or cannot work, they receive unemployment benefits, a temporary disability pension, or welfare assistance. Their medical costs are all paid. If they wish, they might obtain light work in State-run industrial or forestry projects together with other mentally or physically handicapped persons. In addition, they may receive treatment in one of the government subsidized alcoholism clinics or they may occasionally visit one of the alcohol consultation offices around the country. In comparison with some other countries, there is little cause for anxiety in the Netherlands as far as income, housing, or medical care are concerned.

In 1976, more than 380,000 Dutch people had been declared disabled for such reasons as chronic depression, back injury, drug or alcohol addiction. Many receive for life up to 75% of their earnings prior to the disabling event with the usual increments. Taken together, the unemployed, sick, disabled, and welfare recipients accounted for 14% of all adults between the ages of 16 and 65 in 1976. It may be recalled that in the late 19th century, alcohol excess used to be associated with poverty, hunger, malnutrition, and other sequelae of capitalist exploitation. In the Welfare State these problems no longer exist. It is, therefore, very unlikely that much dry sentiment can be generated under present conditions. On the other hand, the extensive social benefits now provided by the Dutch government may need to be revised in the near future. Compared to 1960, the proportion of the population 16 to 65 years of age working in farm or factory has gone down from 28.0% to 18.4%. A further cause for concern is the rapid depletion of the once extensive natural gas deposits in northern Holland. Under these conditions it may be difficult to sustain the present level of social welfare. It remains to be seen whether dry sentiment will be reawakened under more strenuous economic circumstances.

REFERENCES

Bruun, K. et al., 1975, *Alcohol control policies in public health perspective*. Helsinki: The Finnish Foundation for Alcohol Studies.

Central Bureau voor de Statistiek (C.B.S.), 1966-1968, *National budget-onderzoek 1963-1965*. 's-Gravenhage: Staatsuitgeverij.

Central Bureau voor de Statistiek (C.B.S.), 1951 and 1976, *Statistisch zakboek*. *'s-Gravenhage: Staatsuitgeverij.*

Central Bureau voor de Statistiek (C.B.S.), 1979-1980, *Werknemers budgetonderzoek 1974-1975.* 's-Gravenhage: Staatsuitgeverij.

Cnossen, S., 1979, Fiscale bouwstenen voor een alcoholpolitiek, *Economisch Statistiche Berichten,* 64: 632-636.

Dekker, E., 1978, Elementen voor een beleid m.b.t. de preventie van alcoholmis-bruik. *Tijdschrift voor Sociale Geneeskunde,* 56: 226-234.

Don, A. and van der Woude, T., 1904, *Het boek van den alcohol.* Amsterdam: Van Looy.

Gadourek, I., 1965, Drinking habits in a developed, non-indulgent society. In: *Selected Papers Presented at the 11th European Institute at Oslo, Norway.* Lausanne: International Council on Alcohol and Addictions.

Gadourek, I., 1963, *Riskante gewoonten en zorg voor eigen welzijn.* Gronigen: Wolters.

van Ginneken, S. and van der Wal, H., 1980, Profile of policies and programmes for the prevention of alcohol-related problems: in the Netherlands. In: *Prevention of Alcohol-Related Problems* (Moser, J. Ed.). Geneva: World Health Organization.

Harmsen, G., 1961, *Blauwe en rode jeugd.* Assen: Van Gorkum.

Hoogendoorn, D., 1978, Het toenemende gebruik van alcohol en de stijgende frequentie van enkele (mede) door alcohol veroorzaakte ziekten. *Netherlands Tijdschrift voor Geneeskunde,* 122: 1275-1280.

Jellinek, E., 1942, Death from alcoholism in the United States in 1940: a statistical analysis. *Quarterly Journal of Studies on Alcohol,* 3: 465-494.

Kautsky, E., 1890, Editorial. *Die Neue Zeit.*

Ledermann, S., 1964, *Alcool, alcoolisme, alcoolisation: mortalité, morbidité, accidents du travail.* Paris: Presses Universitaires de France.

de Lint, J., 1979, Het gebruik van alcoholhoudende dranken in Nederland vanuit het perspectief van de alcoholpolitiek. *Tijdschfíft voor Alcohol, Drugs en Andere Psychotrope Stoffen,* 5: 28-33.

de Lint, J., 1980, De invloed van het toenemende alcoholgebruik op het sterf-tepatroon. *Tijdschrift voor Sociale Geneeskunde,* 58: 547-551.

de Lint, J. & Schmidt, W., 1976, Alcoholism and mortality. In: *Biology of Alcoholism, Vol. 4* (Kissen, B. and Begleiter, H. Eds.). New York: Plenum Press.

Maas, M., 1977, In de spiegel der historie: drankbestrijding in Nederland. *Tijdschrift voor Alcohol, Drugs en Andere Psychotrope Stoffen,* 3: 97-101.

Nicholls, P. et al., 1974, Alcoholics admitted to four hospitals in England: general and cause-specific mortality. *Quarterly Journal of Studies on Alcohol,* 35: 841-855.

Produktschap voor Gedistilleerde Dranken. Verslag over het jaar 1967, 1975, 1977, 1978. Schiedam, 1968, 1976, 1978, 1979.

Proost, E., 1941, *Weg en werk van de N.V.* Utrecht: Centraal Bureau N.V. 1941.

Schmidt, W. & de Lint, J., 1972, Causes of death of alcoholics. *Quarterly Journal of Studies on Alcohol,* 33: 171-185.

Sijlbing, G., 1978, Drinkgewoonten van de Nerderlanders, *Tijdschrift voor Alcohol, Drugs en Andere Psychotrope Stoffen,* 4: 109-114.

Smits, P. & van Loon, J., 1979, *Drank- en horecawet, commentaar, uitvoeringsvoorschriften en jurisprudentie.* Alphen aan den Rijn: Samson.

Sundby, P., 1967, *Alcoholism and Mortality.* Oslo: Universitetsforlaget.

van de Tempel, A., 1977, Alcohol-accijns, alcoholverbruik en consumptiebeleid. *Weekbald voor Fiscaal Recht,* 106: 169-177.

Tuyns, A., 1978, Alcohol and Cancer. *Alcoholism Health Research World,* 2: 20-31.

Vorrink, I., 1975, Alcoholgebruik in Nederland in laatste tien jaar meer dan verdubbeld. *Nederlandse Staatscourant,* September 10.

van der Woude, T., 1903, Emile Vander Velde over de economische factoren van het alcoholisme. *Wegwijzer,* 6(1): 33-43.

6. Drowning the Shamrock: Alcohol and Drink in Ireland in the Post-War Period

Dermot Walsh* and Brendan Walsh**

INTRODUCTION

The Republic of Ireland is a sovereign independent state created by secession from the United Kingdom of Great Britian and Ireland in 1922. It forms 26 of the 32 counties of the island of Ireland; the remaining six counties remained within the United Kingdom. The Irish climate is a temperate one with cool summers, relatively warm winters, and long springs and autumns. The climate is suitable for cereal production but the cereal is not highly suitable for brewing and milling. Nevertheless, considerable quantities of home-grown barley are used for brewing. The summers are too cold to support viticulture and no wines are produced in Ireland. A small number of distillers produce spirits, mostly whisky, although gin and vodka, which are growing in popularity, are also produced.

After a long period of decline, the Irish population is increasing and now numbers over three million. However, this contrasts with an estimated population of six million in 1841. The Irish population is ethnically mixed. The original inhabitants were of Celtic origin, but since the 9th century Ireland has been the subject of successive invasions by Norse, Normans, and English. Originally Gaelic was spoken but the Irish population has become increasingly English-speaking and today only a handful of people use Gaelic as their mother tongue.

More than 94% of the population profess the Roman Catholic faith. Ireland probably has the highest rate of church attendance in Europe today. Religious issues play a very important part in social life. Much of the primary and secondary educational system is managed by the church authorities. Among younger people, however, there is an increasing

---

*The Medico-Social Research Board, 73, Lower Baggot Street, Dublin 2, Ireland.
**Department of Economics, University College, Belfield, Dublin 4, Ireland.

minority who do not formally worship and in middle-class areas of Dublin, for instance, there has been some movement towards non-denominational education.

The family is enshrined in the Irish Constitution as the basis of society. Until recently, marriage rates were low in Ireland and age at marriage was much higher than in other European countries. Ireland still has an unusually high proportion of single people. However, social change since the middle 1960s has altered the picture very considerably and marriage rates have increased substantially. Age at marriage for husband and wife has fallen. Within families, the number of children is also declining, but it is still above the European average. Ireland does not permit divorce with remarriage. Legal separation is possible, but costly. The more "modern" characteristics of Irish demography, such as higher marriage rates and lower age at marriage, are more characteristic of urban than rural areas, although these changes have also affected rural areas in recent years.

Slightly more than 50% of the Irish population live in towns and cities of 1,500 persons or more, the standard that is used as the dividing line between urban and rural. The capital city, Dublin, and its surrounding area now constitute almost one-third of the population. The next largest city, Cork, is little more than one-tenth of Dublin's size and Limerick is smaller again. There are no other towns or cities exceeding 50,000 population.

The Irish workforce consists of 1,100,000 people. Unemployment is currently at 9%, and rising under the impact of the recent recession. Twenty percent of the Irish workforce is engaged in agriculture, 30% in the service industries. As elsewhere in Europe, the agricultural sector has declined as the industrial and service sectors have increased. Per capita income is currently about $5,000 (U.S.) per annum.

Agriculture however, remains the largest single industry. Ireland does not have a long-established industrial and technological tradition, although high levels of foreign investment in the chemical and electronic industries have transformed the country's industrial base during the recent past. It is of interest that one of the largest and one of the oldest (since approximately 1750) of Dublin's industries has been Guinness Brewery, where until recently a job had high status and was exceptionally well-paid. Indeed, many of the brewery jobs descended in families through several generations.

General Political Structure and Processes

Ireland is a democratic republic managed by elected government on the basis of a proportional representational system. The elected deputies form the lower house of Parliament, called the Dáil. Fianna Fail, a moderate right wing party, has governed for the greater part of the existence of the state. The main opposition party, Fine Gael, is also a moderate party. When last in office, Fine Gael formed a coalition with the Labour Party. The Labour Party, itself, is a moderate and relatively conservative socialist party. Local authorities have considerable powers relating to health, transportation, and other administrative areas of function, but depend almost entirely on central sources for financial support.

Decisions concerning alcohol control policies (i.e. price and availability, hours of opening, etc.) are controlled centrally and local authorities have no function in this area. However, local exemption during special functions such as festivals may be granted by local courts.

Government policy in relation to alcohol is dominated by two considerations: first, the revenue interest, and second, the moral interest. In general, a balance between assuring a continuing revenue yield from alcohol consumption and the moral "problem" of public drunkenness as a threat to civic order are the main considerations in Irish alcohol policy.

THE STRUCTURE AND SIGNIFICANCE OF ALCOHOL PRODUCTION AND TRADE

Historically the alcohol industry has always been important in Ireland, in part because of the generally backward state of other Irish industries until recently. In the 18th century there were more than 200 breweries and distillers in Ireland. Alcohol production in Ireland has always been an entirely private enterprise, and there are no special restrictions on entering the manufacturing field. However, over the years, both brewing and distilling in Ireland have become more highly centralized. There are now only two major breweries in the country and one major distillery, with a number of small specialist firms making various liqueurs.

By 1900, certain firms (e.g. Guinness Brewery) had established themselves as important industries both in terms of employment and in terms of exports on the Irish industrial scene. During the first half of the 20th century, Guinness beer, ale and stout were by far the most important non-agricultural exports. However, Guinness has more recently tended to supply the British market from English breweries, and with the rapid increase of many other manufactured exports the relative importance of beer in the Irish trade figures has decreased.

The Structure of Domestic Distribution

The distribution of the manufactured product is a matter for the manufacturers themselves, and there are no specific legal constraints on this activity. Traditionally, the main retail outlet was the public house or bar. In recent years, there has been some erosion of the supremacy of the pub. Restaurants licensed to serve wine only and hotels with restaurants licensed to serve any type of beverage have increased their share of the market. Small private clubs, discotheques, and dance halls have also become important retail outlets for alcohol.

The post-war era has seen the growth of numerous off-premise outlets, usually attached to a licensed facility. These outlets have increased substantially in number and size during the last 10 years. Supermarkets have gained a very high proportion of the market for home-consumed alcohol. In addition, there are some groceries which specialize in higher priced wines.

The Economic Importance of Alcohol in Ireland

The most obvious fiscal role of alcohol in the Irish economy today is the very high burden of taxation it bears. Within the EEC, Ireland, the U.K., and Denmark are exceptional in the extent to which they rely on excise taxation of alcohol (and tobacco) as a source of tax revenue. But even within this group of three, Ireland is exceptional, obtaining about 12% of all tax receipts from the excise taxes on alcohol, compared with from 1% to 5% in other EEC countries (Walsh and Walsh, 1980). Inclusion of the value added tax receipts from the sale of alcohol would make the Irish situation even more unusual.

This heavy dependence of the exchequer on revenue from alcohol taxation is of long standing in Ireland; indeed the growth of other sources of tax revenue has led to some decline in the importance of alcohol taxes, which contributed almost 16% of total revenue in the early 1960s and 18% in the early 1950s. The declining share of excise taxes on alcohol in total revenue is clear from Table 1.

Heavy dependence on revenue from drink taxes was also a feature of the economy prior to Independence in 1922. In the 1880s more than 40% of British Exchequer receipts came from excise taxes on drink (Harrison, 1971: 346). A rapid decline in the relative importance of this source of tax revenue is a natural development as other taxes, notably income and value added taxes, assumed greater importance. Nonetheless, it must be borne in mind in the consideration of alcohol control policies in Ireland that a major decline in alcohol consumption could still have serious fiscal repercussions.

A final measure of the importance of alcohol in the Irish economy is provided by considering the proportion of total exports accounted for by alcoholic beverages. In the early years of Independence, alcoholic beverages accounted for a very large proportion of non-agricultural exports. In 1928, out of non-agricultural export trade of £4.5 million, just over £4 million was due to exports of "ale, beer, porter, and spirits" (Commission of Emigration, 1948-54, Table 36). However, this situation had changed radically by the 1960s, a trend which continued during the 1970s. The value of exports of alcoholic beverages grew fourfold between 1961 and 1978, but total exports grew more than tenfold, so that the share of alcoholic beverages in total exports declined from 4% in 1961 to 1% in 1978. A more detailed examination of the trade statistics reveals that exports of spirits have grown from a very small base in 1961 to the

TABLE 1   *Excise Tax Receipts from Beer, Spirits, and Wine as a Percentage of Total Net Receipts of Exchequer*

Year Ending March 31	Beer	Spirits	Wine	All Alcoholic Beverages
1950	7.72	9.79	.73	17.81
1951	7.71	10.32	.71	18.74
1952	7.68	9.37	.70	17.75
1953	10.00	7.45	.49	17.99
1954	10.15	8.57	.53	19.24
1955	9.41	8.80	.55	18.76
1956	9.22	8.42	.52	18.15
1957	8.66	7.46	.50	16.62
1958	8.83	6.74	.44	16.02
1959	8.56	7.06	.45	16.07
1960	8.65	7.03	.44	16.12
1961	8.26	7.15	.44	15.85
1962	8.02	7.81	.45	16.27
1963	8.37	6.94	.40	15.71
1964	7.84	7.07	.39	15.30
1965	7.50	6.51	.36	14.36
1966	7.55	6.53	.44	14.51
1967	8.25	6.34	.37	14.96
1968	8.17	5.91	.36	14.44
1969	8.50	6.20	.42	15.12
1970	9.45	6.55	.45	16.46
1971	8.42	6.07	.44	14.93
1972	8.23	5.96	.38	14.57
1973	7.68	5.93	.39	14.00
1974	7.20	6.11	.36	13.69
1974 (9 mo.)	7.69	5.81	.37	13.87
Year Ending Dec. 31				
1975	7.34	5.41	.38	13.13
1976	7.46	5.06	.36	12.88
1977	6.79	4.72	.34	11.80
1978*	5.73	4.36	.29	10.38

* Estimate

Source: Total net receipts of Exchequer as shown in *Annual Reports of Revenue Commissioners*

point where they accounted for more than half of total exports of alcoholic beverages in 1978. Until 1977, there was a net deficit in the trade in spirits, but Irish whisky sales abroad now account for almost half of total sales of Irish whisky, and the distillers look to overseas markets for much of their future growth. Beer exports, on the other hand, have consistently made a sizeable net contribution to foreign exchange earnings.

In general, Irish import tariffs are governed by the Treaty of Rome. As a member of the Commission of European Communities, Ireland has to observe prescribed trade agreements. There has been considerable North American investment in Irish distilling, and since the 1930s Guinness has been registered as a United Kingdom Company. With a growing development of supermarkets there is a tendency for some of these chains to import wine directly from the country of origin.

Tourism has always been a significant feature of the Irish national economy even though the number of tourists who visit Ireland tends to be small relative to other European countries. In general, the tourist industry probably does not account for more than a small proportion of the total Irish alcohol consumption. Duty-free concessions operate at Irish points of departure such as airports and seaports and during sailing or in flight.

Direct employment in the production of alcoholic beverages is not of major importance to the Irish economy, and has declined both absolutely and relative to total employment in the last two decades. The retail distribution of alcoholic beverages, especially through public houses, provides more employment than the production of alcoholic drink. Additional employment is, of course, provided in the sectors supplying raw materials and other inputs to the drink industry.

In assessing the economic importance of the alcoholic beverage industry to the economy, what matters is not so much how many people or other resources are currently dependent on the industry for employment, but rather how specific to the industry these resources are. While it is obvious that much of the labour force, plant and equipment, and other resources currently dependent on the industry in Ireland are fairly specific to the industry and would only be redeployed in other sectors at a considerable cost, it is also true that, unlike the wine-producing regions of Europe, Ireland does not have a high regional dependence on producing alcohol from crops grown on land which would have very low productivity in alternative uses. But the endemic high unemployment rate in Ireland lends force to the argument that it would be difficult to replace the jobs lost in any major contraction of the alcohol trade.

In summary, then, the relative importance of the alcoholic beverage industry in the Irish economy has been declining by all the measures considered here — contribution to tax revenues, employment, and foreign exchange earnings. Nevertheless, the exchequer remains very heavily dependent on the excise taxation of alcohol as a source of revenue. Exports of spirits have grown rapidly in recent years, and beer remains an important source of net foreign exchange earnings.

THE REAL PRICE OF ALCOHOL

The price of alcoholic beverages is obviously of great importance in any discussion of alcohol policy. The Irish situation is exceptional because of the very heavy burden of excise taxation borne by beer and spirits. It is not easy to make international comparisons of the price of commodities such as alcoholic beverages relative to the general price levels. However, the most authoritative study of international price levels (Kravis et al., 1978) shows that beer, wine, and spirits are very expensive in the United Kingdom compared with other EEC countries or the United States. Insofar as the relative price of alcohol in Ireland appears to be slightly higher than that in the United Kingdom, it may safely be concluded that alcohol is relatively a very expensive item in this country.

About half the price of alcoholic beverages in Ireland represents taxation. The main rate of taxation is an excise tax which has to be adjusted in the annual budget to keep par with inflation. Other determinants of price are the brewers' and distillers' costs and those of the publican. The relative price of alcohol in this country was higher in the 1950s and 1960s than during the inflationary years of the 1970s. Spirits became a relatively better buy than beer, which proportionately bears a higher burden of taxation, but this situation was altered in the 1980 and 1981 budgets. A bottle of spirits (75cc) costs on average about £8 (U.S. $14) and beer per pint costs 80 pence (U.S. $1.40). A 75 cc bottle of wine can be bought in supermarkets for approximately £2.20 (U.S. $3.80).

The National Prices Commission, in their *Monthly Report* of December 1977, provides a breakdown of retail expenditures on alcoholic beverages in a licensed bar. For Irish whisky, 14% of the selling price went to the distiller, 40% to the retailer, and 46% to the exchequer. For stout, 25% went to the brewery, 29% to the retailer, and 46% to the exchequer. Following various changes in the trade price and in taxation, by 1981 the component of the selling price earmarked for the exchequer was 65% for Irish whisky and 49% for a pint of stout.

These figures illustrate the relatively small proportion of total expenditure on drink that represents the cost of producing the beverages, and the very large share represented by excise and value added taxes. The high proportion of the consumer's budget devoted to purchasing drink in Ireland is, however, important evidence of the attachment of the Irish to alcoholic beverages and their willingness to forego other items in order to secure a desired level of alcohol intake.

The real price of alcoholic drink as seen in Table 2 rose quite significantly between 1961 and 1969, but declined between 1970 and 1974. The fluctuations in this price since 1970 illustrate the effect of inflation on the tax component in the price, and the specific adjustments of the tax in the budgets of 1975, 1979, and 1980. The tax increases introduced in the 1980 and 1981 budgets restored the relative prices of the two beverages to their 1970 levels.

TABLE 2   *Real Price of Alcoholic Beverages, 1961-1980*
                        (Annual Average 1970 = 100)

Year	Alcoholic Drink (1)	Beer (2)	Spirits (3)
1961	82.4	73.6	94.1
1962	89.5	81.5	99.0
1963	90.2	82.6	99.1
1964	92.1	85.4	98.2
1965	92.4	86.3	98.3
1966	95.2	89.2	102.5
1967	96.9	92.0	103.2
1968	96.2	93.9	100.8
1969	100.4	101.8	102.7
1970	100.0	100.0	100.0
1971	99.1	99.5	99.1
1972	94.3	93.1	93.2
1973	91.0	86.9	90.6
1974	85.5	78.3	80.9
1975	89.6	89.3	88.0
1976	97.6	103.4	89.7
1977	91.3	97.8	85.2
1978	90.2	97.7	83.7
1979	90.5	95.0	86.0
1980 (first 2 quarters)	93.5	98.0	90.0

Notes:

Series (1) is the index of alcoholic drink in the Consumer Price Index divided by the All Items index. Prior to 1968 the implicit deflators of expenditure on GNP were used.

Series (2) and (3) are based on indices of the retail price of a pint of stout and a glass of whisky in the Dublin area, divided by the Consumer Price Index. These are not official price indices, but they give a reliable indication of the trend in beer and spirits prices over the years.

Table 2 also presents beer and spirits prices, which illustrate the tendency for beer to become expensive relative to spirits during the period since 1961. This change in relative prices has been mentioned as a reason for the more rapid growth of spirits consumption, but it has proved difficult to support this through econometric studies, which suggests that the two beverages are, if anything, complementary rather than substitutes.

The level of excise taxes during the period 1950-1980 can be measured in current and in constant (1968) prices. In terms of current prices, excise duties increased from £5.60 to £90.12 for beer (per barrel) between 1950 and 1980. For spirits during the same time period, the duty increased from £6.85 to £44.33 per gallon. However, when measured in constant prices the increase is shown to be much less dramatic: from £11.26 per standard barrel of beer in 1950 to £21.9 in 1980. The corresponding numbers for spirits per gallon was £13.77 and £10.8. These series are accurate measures of the excise tax borne by beer and spirits, although changes in the alcoholic strength of the final product should also be taken into account.

The most striking feature of the trend in the tax element in both beer and spirits is that the real (or constant price) tax on beer in 1979 was no higher than it was in 1967, while that on spirits was 22% below its 1961 level. It seems that the government's ability or willingness to maintain the real tax rate on drink declined during the period of accelerated inflation starting in the early 1970s. This is perhaps inevitable in view of the political unpopularity of excise tax increments large enough to offset a rapid rate of inflation. A further reason for the failure to keep alcohol taxes level with inflation may have been the way excise tax increases are themselves reflected in subsequent consumer price increases. The tax increases on beer and spirits announced in 1976, 1980, and 1981 were widely seen as austerity measures, but they merely restored the level of real taxation that prevailed in the early 1970s.

ALCOHOL CONSUMPTION

It can be seen from Table 3 that the per capita consumption of spirits almost trebled in Ireland between 1950 and 1979 and that consumption of beer almost doubled. Wine consumption, though proportionally minor, increased even more since 1950. The level of consumption persons aged 15 and over reached in 1974 has not been surpassed, due to the effects of the recession on living standards and the high real price of drink in recent years.

An important feature of the trend of alcohol consumption in Ireland has been the more rapid growth of consumption of spirits and wine than of beer. In 1950, only 28% of alcohol was consumed in the form of spirits and wine, compared with almost 40% in 1978. Most of the growth in the share of spirits and wine in the alcohol market occurred during the 1960s and 1970s. It is also notable that the rate of growth of alcohol consumption in Ireland has, in recent years, outpaced that recorded in neighbouring countries. Ireland has now drawn level with the United Kingdom in terms of consumption per person aged 15 and over, whereas in the mid-1960s, consumption was about one-quarter below the British level (Keller and Gurioli, 1976). However, despite this tendency for consumption to grow at a faster rate than that observed in other European countries, the Irish still retain a position near the bottom of the international "league table" of alcohol consumption. It is doubtful if there is any unrecorded consumption of alcohol apart from the small amounts illegally distilled and manufactured as poitin. It is not possible to estimate alcohol consumption by visitors but it would account for only a small proportion of overall consumption.

Paradoxically, despite the comparatively low consumption, expenditure on alcohol is very high in Ireland in relation to incomes (Walsh and Walsh, 1973). In Table 4, the proportion of 1. personal disposable income and 2. personal expenditure on goods and services devoted to purchasing alcohol during the period since 1960 is set out. Both these measures of the importance of drinking in Ireland show a marked increase over the two decades, especially during the years up to 1971. The proportion of income spent on alcoholic beverages in Ireland is much higher than that recorded in other western countries today. The nearest rivals are Finland and the U.K. where the proportion of total expenditure devoted to alcohol is about 7%, compared with more than 12% in Ireland. In Poland, the proportion of income devoted to alcohol appears to be very high, but comparisons with a socialist system of national accounting are difficult to make because of the undervaluation of expenditure on services. To find a higher figure than the contemporary Irish one we would have to go back to Victorian Britain, when alcohol expenditures as a proportion of total consumption reached a peak of 15% in the U.K. in 1876 (Dingle, 1972).

CONTROL SYSTEMS

During the 19th century, it was possible to drink throughout the 24 hours in certain places and at certain times in Ireland. However, increasing concern about public drunkenness and its consequences sufficiently exercised policymakers so that, by the 1870s, stricter controls of outlets and opening times were imposed. Before World War I, a system of rigid control was established limiting opening hours. In the 1950s a gradual relaxation set in. At present, Irish licensing laws are more liberal than they were at any time since World War I.

Levels of Decision-Making

All the decisions affecting licensing hours are made by the central government and apply nationally, with certain exemptions. In 1971, there

TABLE 3   *Alcohol Consumption Per Person of Population Aged 15 and Over in Litres of 100% Alcohol 1950-1980*

Year	Beer	Spirits	Wine	Total
1950	3.34	1.20	0.13	4.67
1951	3.56	1.21	0.14	4.91
1952	3.34	0.95	0.12	4.41
1953	3.29	0.98	0.13	4.40
1954	3.29	1.06	0.14	4.49
1955	3.39	1.08	0.15	4.62
1956	3.48	1.05	0.15	4.68
1957	3.40	0.99	0.15	4.54
1958	3.31	1.03	0.15	4.49
1959	3.43	1.08	0.16	4.67
1960	3.48	1.15	0.17	4.80
1961	3.73	1.38	0.19	5.30
1962	3.75	1.30	0.19	5.24
1963	3.84	1.39	0.21	5.44
1964	3.97	1.50	0.24	5.71
1965	4.02	1.56	0.25	5.82
1966	4.03	1.53	0.24	5.80
1967	4.10	1.56	0.25	5.91
1968	4.27	1.73	0.27	6.27
1969	4.59	1.93	0.28	6.80
1970	4.76	2.06	0.31	7.13
1971	5.04	2.21	0.32	7.57
1972	5.31	2.43	0.35	8.09
1973	5.65	2.75	0.40	8.80
1974	6.19	2.82	0.43	9.44
1975	5.81	2.91	0.43	9.15
1976	5.59	2.83	0.43	8.85
1977	5.63	3.00	0.46	9.09
1978	5.79	3.31	0.47	9.57
1979	6.02	3.28	0.70	10.00
1980	5.57	2.99	0.80	9.36

Sources: Annual Reports of Revenue Commissioners; Irish Statistical Bulletin.

Notes:

1. The Revenue Commissioners' data refer to "net duty paid" beer (imported and homemade); spirits and wine "retained for home use."

2. A standard barrel of beer, proof gallon of spirits, and gallon of wine were taken as equal to 8.46, 2.6, and 0.568 litres of absolute alcohol respectively.

3. Up to 1974, the data were for years ending on 31 March. Weighted averages of adjacent years have been taken to obtain calendar year figures.

4. These quantities include consumption by visitors to Ireland but exclude consumption by Irish people while abroad.

TABLE 4 *Expenditure on Alcoholic Beverages as Percentage of 1. Total Personal Disposable Income and 2. Personal Expenditure on Goods and Services, 1960-1978*

Year	Expenditure on Alcohol as % of Disposable Personal Income	Expenditure on Alcohol as % of Personal Expenditure on Goods and Service
1960	7.6	8.2
1961	7.6	8.5
1962	8.2	9.1
1963	8.4	9.2
1964	8.4	9.4
1965	8.7	9.7
1966	8.8	9.8
1967	9.0	10.1
1968	9.1	10.1
1969	9.4	10.9
1970	10.0	11.5
1971	10.2	11.6
1972	9.6	11.4
1973	9.3	11.5
1974	9.4	11.5
1975	9.6	12.7
1976	10.4	13.2
1977	9.7	12.3
1978	9.5	12.4

Source: National Income and Expenditure, (NIE) 1977, Table A.11 and earlier editions.

Notes:

Personal disposable income = personal income *less* taxes on personal income and wealth. NIE items 90 minus 92

Personal expenditure on goods and services = personal disposable income *less* savings. NIE item 121.

All magnitudes measured at current market prices.

These figures include drink purchased by tourists while visiting Ireland, but exclude drink purchased by Irish people while outside Ireland. In 1968, Ireland had a net favourable balance from tourism of 4.3% of personal expenditure but by 1977 this had fallen to 1.4%, so correction for this factor would have very little influence on the more recent figures in this Table.

were approximately 11,000 licensed public houses and off-sale outlets in the Republic of Ireland. The number of public house licences has been strictly limited by past legislation, which determined that no new ones could be granted unless an existing one was "extinguished" or taken over. Due to changes in population distribution, many small rural Irish towns, particularly in the west, were very well served in numbers of public houses and, in some cases, has as many as one public house per 100 inhabitants. A government commission was set up to evaluate the existing situation and to recommend changes if necessary. It criticized the system of allocating licences and recommended a more competitive system of licensing (Restrictive Practices Commission, 1977).

Controls on Availability

Ireland inherited from British rule an elaborate system of controls on the places and time of availability of alcoholic beverages. The Intoxicating Liquor Acts (1924 and 1962) still retain this basic framework, but in 1962 there were major liberalizations. These extended the hours during which public houses could legally sell alcohol and increased the availability of extensions permitting drinking outside normal opening hours. The extension of opening from 10:30 p.m. (or 10:00 in winter) to 11:30 p.m. (or 11:00 in winter) was partly a recognition of the difficulty of enforcing the more restrictive hours, which were not in keeping with social patterns, particularly in rural areas. Following the 1962 legislation, there was a sharp fall in the number of prosecutions of persons for being on licensed premises illegally during closing hours. Few would advocate a return to the shorter opening hours of the 1950s, and many would oppose any such move, but certain aspects of the availability of alcohol have attracted increasing attention from those concerned with evidence of a recent increase in alcohol abuse. Extensions for hours of operation are readily available, the sale of alcoholic drink in off-premise outlets and supermarkets has increased, and the enforcement of regulations regarding sales to people under the minimum age of 18 years has been lax.

The number of exemptions allowing after-hours drinking increased very rapidly during the 1970s, rising from 6,000 in 1967 to 14,000 in 1972, and 42,000 in 1979. Certain public houses situated in areas where night workers are numerous open at 6:30 a.m. and these are much used by alcoholics and heavy drinkers. In addition, individual sports and social clubs are usually free to serve drinks to members and guests until much later (up to 2 or 3 a.m.). Frequent dispensations are given to allow late drinking on the occasion of dances and festivals.

The 1962 legislation did not, of itself, cause these changes. It was several years before the liberalization permitted under this legislation was utilized to any significant degree. It is almost impossible to evaluate to what extent the availability of these exemptions played any role in the growth of consumption. Stricter control might encourage alternative arrangements for social drinking, especially drinking at home rather than in public houses, a trend which is likely to develop in any event. The trend towards greater liberalization in granting exemptions has become deeply entrenched and would be hard to reverse, even where the evidence strongly suggests that exemptions resulted in very heavy drinking. An attempt is now underway to circumvent the prohibition on exemptions for any part of Sunday. Applications for exemptions commencing at 00:01 a.m. Monday morning have been refused on the grounds that such exemptions would violate the spirit of the 1962 legislation. The applicants have succeeded in having the case put to the Supreme Court for a judgement. In general, enforcement relating to licensing hours are fairly strictly observed apart perhaps from certain clubs. Publicans are subject to heavy fines for any infringement of licensing laws and, in general, in metropolitan areas law enforcement and observance are fairly strict.

The legal minimum age of 18 years is not strictly enforced, partly because an offence is committed only if the vendor "knowingly" supplies drink to an underage person. There is also a loophole in the legislation which permits the sale of alcohol to persons as young as 15 years for consumption off the premises in quantities of one pint or less (Irish National Council on Alcoholism, 1978). In general, a problem exists in trying to establish a customer's age because identity cards or other proof of age are not usually carried by customers. However, some supermarkets have introduced their own code of practice and refuse to sell to anyone who, in the opinion of the manager, is a minor.

One of the most noticeable features of the restrictions imposed on the distribution of alcohol in this country is the system for licensing public houses and limiting their number. While this policy may tend to reduce drink sales and promote temperance, its major impact seems to be to create local monopolies in the retail distribution of alcoholic beverages. A liquor licence is a state-backed artificial restraint on competition. If it is believed that this restraint has beneficial effects on the level and pattern of drinking, there are good arguments in favour of reestablishing the administration of this system so that the State gathers most of the economic rent that is thereby created. It is extraordinary to note that in 1976 the State obtained only about £50,000 from retail liquor licences, about £4 per licence. In view of the enormous value that possession of a licence may bestow on a property, there is a case either for making more of them available which would probably have little effect on overall alcohol consumption or for the state to extract most of the economic rent bestowed by the licence. This could be done by periodically selling licences to the highest bidder.

Care has to be exercised to ensure that restrictions on the availability of alcohol intended to curb overall consumption are not maintained in force merely to promote the artificial local monopolies they have created. In Ireland, the Licensed Vintners' Association acts as an advocate for the right of its members to a monopoly of the on-premise sale of alcohol, using arguments that are at times couched in the same language used by those interested in alcohol control policy. This coincidence does not imply, however, that all arguments for restriction of availability are motivated by the self-interest of the drink trade — far from it. If a policy of more restricted availability were espoused, however, care should be taken to avoid creating artificial monopolies that serve no worthwhile social function.

A further aspect of availability that deserves attention is the distribution of consumption between drinking on licensed premises and drinking at home. The importance of the public house in Irish drinking patterns could be viewed as an additional factor, over and above the amount of alcohol consumed, that tends to aggravate the problems arising from drinking. At least two reasons could be suggested for this belief: first, drinking away from home may have adverse effects on family life that would be mitigated if consumption were within the family circle, and secondly, drinking in public houses is obviously part of the reason for the high accident rate on Irish roads during the hours immediately after closing time.

If it were felt desirable to try to switch consumption from the public house to the home, it is not easy to suggest policies that would have this effect. Such policies should discourage on-premise consumption by at least as much as they encourage consumption at home: there would be no gain from a public health perspective if new patterns were merely added to existing ones. One aspect of this side of Irish drinking patterns that requires further study, and that might offer scope for relevant policy initiatives is the small price differential that exists between off-licence and on-licence prices of alcoholic beverages. At present it costs as much, if not slightly more, to purchase bottled beer in retail outlets as in a public bar. This may be a factor reinforcing the traditional Irish preference for drinking in public houses, and might be investigated with a view to changing the balance towards home consumption. However, the price factor is hardly the main consideration for the strong attachment to drinking in public houses and it is unlikely that a major change could be brought about by any change of pricing policy. Consumption in public houses might be much more significantly affected by a very strict enforcement of the legislation on drinking and driving, especially if this were extended to allow the police to screen drivers leaving public houses at closing time.

Consequences of Current Alcohol Control Policies

It is undoubtedly in relation to drunken driving that the strongest support for a less permissive alcohol control policy would be forthcoming. The contribution of drunkenness to road accidents was recognized in Ireland by the late 1950s, and was used as one of the arguments in favour of allowing general Sunday opening in order to avoid the old system of driving to a distant venue in order to drink as a bona fide traveller (Whyte,

1971). Recent studies reveal that up to 40% of driver fatalities, and 50% of pedestrian fatalities, involve people with blood alcohol levels above the legal limit (Crowley et al., 1980).

TABLE 5   *Prosecutions Relating to Drunkenness, Ireland,*
1961-1978, Per 1,000 Population Aged 15 and Over

| Year | Offence | |
	Drunkenness Rate	Drunk Driving Rate
1961	1.6	0.3
1962	1.6	0.5
1963	1.6	0.5
1964	1.7	0.6
1965	1.8	0.7
1966	1.8	0.6
1967	1.8	0.6
1968	1.8	0.6
1969	1.6	0.7
1970	1.4	0.6
1971	1.6	1.0
1972	1.6	1.2
1973	2.1	1.6
1974	2.2	2.2
1975	2.2	1.8
1976	2.1	1.3
1977	2.6	1.8
1978	na	2.8

Source: Statistical abstract, *Offences Relating to Intoxicating Liquor Laws, and Parliamentary Debates,* Dail Eireann, Vol. 320, No. 3, (1 May, 1980).

Notes:

"Drunkenness" refers to prosecutions for drunkenness, simple or with aggravation (there are about equal numbers of each type of offence). "Drunk driving" refers to "driving or attempting to drive while drunk" and, more recently, includes refusals to give a breath/blood/urine sample.

Tougher measures to deal with drunken driving were not enacted until 1968 and their enforcement was delayed by "administrative difficulties" until 1971. Following the use of the Breathalyzer, accidents between the hours most closely associated with drunken driving (9 p.m. and 3 a.m.) declined slightly, but they reached a new peak in 1977. Even more significant is the fact that the proportion of all accidents occurring between these hours showed no sustained fall after the introduction of the Breathalyzer. In 1977, as in 1968, over one-third of fatal road accidents occurred between these hours. The original Breathalyzer legislation was gradually rendered inoperable through persistent court challenges on the way it was administered, and new legislation had to be introduced towards the end of 1978. There was a significant rise in the number of prosecutions in the period following the passage of the new law (see Table 5). These measures were widely credited with significant results over the 1978 Christmas-New Year period, but it appears that the effect was not lasting (An Foras Forbartha, 1979). In Britain as well, the Breathalyzer is reported to have had a marked initial impact which gradually wore off (Howard, 1977).

It is very difficult to say why in Ireland, as in Britain, the courts appear willing to uphold technical defences against charges of drunk driving — defences that would not be entertained in other areas. The complexity of the interactions between social attitudes and rule enforcement in this area can hardly be exaggerated. Paradoxically, it may be that the heavy penalties following conviction — loss of licence, possible gaol sentences — deter judges from convicting. They certainly give the defendant every reason to obtain the best legal advice available, the cost of which is, of course, similar to a fine in its deterrent effects. However, a policy of lighter sentences for first offences might lead to less resistance to the enforcement of laws and ultimately prove more conducive to sobriety on the roads.

DRINKING POPULATIONS, INSTITUTIONS, AND PATTERNS

Over the last century and a half, the Irish have had an ambivalent attitude towards drinking. On the one hand, there is the traditional heroic male attitude which holds that it is honourable and manly to drink. On the other hand, there is a strong abstinence tradition fostered by certain sectors of the religious community and also, of course, by women who have been generally abstinent. In general, drinking has not been connected with food and tended to be an isolated activity indulged in for its own sake. However, drinking was usually social and allowed men to mix and release inhibitions. Drink was also related to business deals such as trading at fairs when the farmers came to sell their produce. In rural areas, business was done and bargains sealed over drink. Alcohol was also linked to sporting events, such as football matches and horse race meetings.

Drinking tends to be a weekend event because of the Saturday and Sunday holidays and the fact that Friday is frequently payday. Among the more affluent sections of the community, this weekly variation does not occur. Holidays are often associated with above average intake, particularly at Christmas.

Drinking Locales and Arrangements

In the past, there were heavy social sanctions against middle class women entering public houses or drinking in public. Drinking locales tended to be uncomfortable, with little by way of chairs or furniture. However, since World War II there has been a gradual erosion of the male dominance in public house settings which have become more civilized and more comfortable in their furnishings and decoration. Drinking groups now often comprise married couples, and young women come in and drink without male escorts. There is a growing acceptance of public female drinking. Many late night restaurants and discotheques provide alcohol, which is regarded as an integral part of these social occasions. Among the business community, wine drinking at lunch and over a business dinner in the evening is considered now the norm, and wine is often supplied at home dinner parties.

Cultural Acceptance of Drinking and Drunkenness

The level of acceptance of excessive drinking and even drunkenness is very high in Ireland. This permissiveness also extends to road vehicle use. The drunk person is often seen as an object of amusement rather than criticism. Nevertheless, attitudes are changing and incompetence at work due to daytime drinking or the effects of the previous evening's drinking are increasingly the object of frequent public criticism. Extreme drunkenness at formal social occasions now tends to be looked at askance and might, if a common feature of an individual's behaviour, lead to ostracism.

At the same time, there is an increasing tendency, due to the efforts of various bodies such as the Irish National Council on Alcoholism, Alcoholics Anonymous, and the medical profession, to regard alcoholism as a "disease." This conceptualization leads to a different type of permissiveness, in that it implies an inability to control drinking rather than an unwillingness to do so. At the same time, many wives as well as husbands see in this disease concept of alcoholism the legitimization of a man's heavy drinking and the condoning of behaviour that otherwise would be condemned.

In recent years, there have been some interview surveys of Irish drinking habits but almost all of these have been carried out by the brewers. The results of these interviews are confidential and have never been published. More recently, social researchers have carried out surveys of the drinking practices of young people and, in a wider study, comparison has been made of the drinking habits of Irish and English youths (O'Connor, 1978).

Temperance and Alcoholism Interest Groups

Since the early 19th century, there has been a considerable emphasis on abstinence movements in this country. The Pioneer Total Abstinence Society of the Sacred Heart, for instance, is a Roman Catholic abstinence society which has flourished for more than a century. It is customary at the religious ceremony of Confirmation for Irish children to take a pledge to abstain from alcohol until at least the age of 21. It is not known, however, how many subscribe to this pledge or indeed how long they maintain it. Likewise, the Pioneer Abstinence Association can indicate how many people join but cannot say when they cease to be members. The Irish National Council on Alcoholism was set up some 10 years ago as an information and referral agency. It is a voluntary organization, state-supported by contributions from various health authorities and, as part of its information service, organizes public discussions on the subject of alcohol addiction to groups throughout the country, including industrial workers.

The first European branch of Alcoholics Anonymous was founded in Dublin in 1946 and the organization is still very active. More recently, a Health Education Bureau has been set up and given a large budget. It provides information to school children about alcohol and its dangers and the needs for sensible drinking habits. Radio Telefis Eireann, the national television station, has entered into a strict code of conduct with the Irish National Council on Alcoholism concerning wine and beer advertising. Spirits advertisements are not carried on television but the press, sports grounds, public hoardings, and the British commercial television stations are free to advertise alcohol as they like.

SOCIETAL DEFINITIONS OF AND REACTIONS TO DRINKING PROBLEMS

Alcohol-related problems are viewed from the perspective of public order. Major concerns include crime and drunk driving, as well as alcoholism in industry and increasing absenteeism from work and reduced productivity. Although many criminal problems would seem to be alcohol-related and there is considerable concern about drunk driving, alcohol-related petty crime, both against property and persons, is not matched by preventive or control activity. Skid row alcoholics are catered to by a branch of the Simon organization which runs a hostel and provides food and essential human requisites such as clothing and housing.

Control and Treatment Facilities and Programmes

In general, treatment for "alcoholism" was conceived in Ireland as a largely medical function. Medical people have almost universally contributed to the expectation that medicine can both treat and possibly cure alcoholism. In consequence, there has been a lack of general community response.

Medical facilities for alcoholism, although not necessarily specialized, have generally developed in association with psychiatric services. The 1945 Mental Treatment Act, which currently governs the mode of admission to psychiatric institutions, has specific provisions for the certification of alcohol "addicts" who are described as people who, by reason of their addiction to alcohol, are incapable of managing their own affairs or ordinary proper conduct. A 1981 health act has no such special provisions for the certification of alcohol "addicts." For years, the private psychiatric sector has been involved with the inpatient and outpatient care of alcoholics. Private psychiatric hospitals have traditionally drawn a very high proportion of their clientele from the ranks of alcoholics. In more recent years, some public psychiatric hospitals have set up specialized alcohol units. This is the basis for professional debates about whether or not special facilities are needed. Whereas most private psychiatric practitioners would feel that alcoholism is a disease and that specialized facilities and approaches are needed for its treatment and recovery, attitudes among psychiatrists practising in public hospitals are not homogeneous and some would completely reject these conceptualizations.

Development of non-residential medical facilities for alcoholism has been relatively neglected. However, the community services of ordinary psychiatric facilities are at the disposal of and are utilized by alcoholics. Also, some non-medical interests, some of them religious, are interested in developing residential and non-residential facilities for alcoholics. Some of these are inspirational, i.e. apostolic rather than medical, and tend to be used by a variety of groups including some skid row alcoholics.

Current medical opinion appears to be mainly of the view that alcoholism is a disease and that the best approach to the problem is to provide more resources for its treatment. The efficacy of various approaches to treating alcoholism has, however, been questioned (see Kendall, 1979, for a summary of the evidence) and it is clear that despite the increase in the resources available for treatment, the incidence of excessive drinking has risen steadily. It could even be argued that the emphasis on the disease concept of alcoholism supports the heavy drinker and encourages him to persist by reassuring him that he is suffering from an illness which is someone else's job to treat. Resources are diverted from other areas of the health services, such as the care of long-stay psychiatric patients, to expensive approaches to the problem of alcohol abuse whose efficacy has not been evaluated. An alternative would be to take a less tolerant view of excessive drinking, adopt a sterner policy against public drunkenness, reduce the availability of paid leave to undergo treatment for drinking problems, provide less support from public funds for centres treating alcoholics, and adopt a tougher policy towards drunk driving.

EXTENT AND TRENDS OF
ALCOHOL-RELATED PROBLEMS

Various estimates have been made of the extent of alcoholism in the Irish community, and figures such as 100,000 alcoholics have been bandied about, but none of these has any scientific basis. Nonetheless, it is clear that the problem is fairly widespread. For example, in 1978 there were 2,538 first admissions to psychiatric hospitals for "alcoholism."

Public intoxication is not generally dealt with by the police unless there are associated problems, such as fights or the breaking of shop windows. However, an individual who is completely incapable of walking or getting home would probably be detained overnight.

A number of Irish studies based on the casualty departments of general hospitals has shown unequivocally that the majority of persons involved in road accidents after 7 p.m. have consumed alcohol, many of them in amounts vastly above the legal blood alcohol level (Crowley et al., 1980). These persons are not just motorists but also include a very high proportion of drunk pedestrians. Data on drunkenness and drunk driving are presented in Table 5 and have been discussed above.

Admission rates to psychiatric hospitals for alcoholism from 1965 to 1978 show a considerable increase. First admissions for both sexes rose from .35 per 1,000 population in 1965 to 1.09 per 1,000 in 1978. The rate of increase for all admissions was even more pronounced, rising from .83 per 1,000 population in 1965 to 3.14 in 1978. In 1978 alcoholism was the most common reason for psychiatric hospital admission. In addition, a substantial number of persons are admitted to general hospitals because of the direct or indirect consequences of alcoholism. These include victims of traffic accidents and accidents in the home. There are, as well, many people admitted to general hospitals because of pancreatitis, esophagitis, gastritis and many other physical complaints. Included among the latter are persons with cirrhosis of the liver. The mortality figures for this condition rose from 3.4 per 100,000 in 1961 to 5.0 per 100,000 in 1977.

SUMMARY

The trend in control policy towards alcohol in Ireland, as in most western countries, has been to treat it more like a normal commodity with relatively few restraints on where, to whom, and when it can be sold. This, in turn, reflects the declining influence of the temperance movement, with its emphasis on the moral evils of heavy drinking. Concern now tends to focus on public health problems generated by alcohol consumption and its role in accidents and family problems.

In Ireland, we have moved rapidly from the situation in which drinking was closely associated with intoxication and disorderly behaviour to a much more diffuse role for alcohol in our society. At the same time, the average level of consumption has risen sharply, reaching a peak in 1974. Some of the indices of alcohol-related problems, such as admissions to mental hospitals for alcoholism or arrests for drunk driving, have also increased.

The appropriate response on the part of public policy to these developments is not easily prescribed. On the one hand, the growing evidence of an increasing public health problem arising from higher levels of alcohol consumption naturally provokes a demand for preventive measures. Current thinking seems to favour measures that would tend to at least moderate the rate of increase in alcohol consumption in general. These measures would include higher taxation of alcohol, stricter enforcement of the laws against drunk driving, and a reversal of the recent trend to ease restrictions on where and when alcohol may be sold. However, critics of this approach point out that higher taxation and reduced availability place penalties on the normal drinker without any guarantee that behaviour of the problem drinker will be affected. They claim that there is very little evidence to show that this approach would have much of an impact on the public health problems caused by heavy drinking, while the costs in terms of limitation of freedom for the majority of moderate drinkers may be unacceptably high.

Apart from the effectiveness of such measures, their political feasibility must also be considered. The long history of attempts to penalize drunk driving in Ireland and elsewhere in the western world illustrates the way in which a policy measure that commands support in principle from almost all quarters may be ineffective. Other measures, such as eliminating drink advertising or heavier taxation of alcohol are not only less clearly appropriate as responses to the problem, but also confront vested interests at least as powerful as those that have persistently rendered legislation on drunk driving ineffective. The state can, of course, continue to spend money on health education designed to provide information on the hazards of heavy drinking and to create a less tolerant climate of opinion towards drunkenness, but the net impact of such publicity is likely to be slight. Faced with these difficulties, it is tempting to suggest that nonintervention is the only appropriate response.

This would, however, amount to an admission that nothing can be done either to advance the preventive approach to the public health problems of alcohol abuse or to reduce the social costs of heavy drinking. Such a pessimistic verdict is not, in our opinion, fully justified by the evidence reviewed in this paper. Detailed proposals designed to achieve desired modifications of drinking practices should be put forward by those more directly involved in policy formulation on the basis of the type of information that has been brought together in this study.

REFERENCES

An Foras Forbartha, 1979, *Road Accident Facts, Ireland 1978*. Dublin: An Foras Forbartha.

Commission of Emigration, 1948-1954, *Annual Reports*, Dublin: Government Publications.

Crowley, F., Curran, A. & Hearne, R., 1980, Road Safety in Ireland. *Irish Journal of Environmental Science*, Vol. 1, No. 1, 1-13.

Dingle, A.E., 1972, Drink and Working-Class Living Standards in Britain 1870-1914. *Econ. Hist. Rev.*, 2nd Series, Vol. XXV, No. 4, 608-622.

Harrison, Brian, 1971, *Drink and the Victorians: The Temperance Question in England, 1815-1872*. London: Faber.

Howard, J., 1977, Alcohol and Road Accidents. In *Alcoholism: New Knowledge and New Responses*, Edwards, G. & Grant, M., 1977 (Eds). London: Croom Helm Ltd.

Irish National Council on Alcoholism, 1978, Alcoholic Beverages — Consumption in Relation to Availability, Discussion Document (mimeo).

Keller, M. & Gurioli, C., 1976, Statistics on Consumption of Alcohol and on Alcoholism. New Brunswick, N.J.: *Journal of Studies on Alcohol*.

Kendall, R.E., 1979, Alcoholism: A medical or a political problem? *British Medical Journal*, 10 February, 367-371.

Kravis, J.B., Heston, A. & Summers, R., 1978, *International Comparisons of Real Product and Purchasing Power*. Baltimore and London: The John Hopkins University Press.

O'Connor, Joyce, 1978, *The Young Drinkers: A Cross-National Study of Social and Cultural Influences*. London: Tavistock Publications.

Report of the Intoxicating Liquor Commission, 1925, Government Publications Dublin.

Report of the Commission of Inquiry into the Operation of the Laws Reporting to the Sale and Supply of Intoxicating Liquor, 1957, Dublin: Government Publications.

Restrictive Practices Commission (1977), Report of Study of Competition in the Licensed Drink Trade. Dublin: The Stationary Office.

Walsh, B. & Walsh, D., 1973, The Validity of Indices of Alcoholism: A Comment from Irish Experience. *British Journal of Preventive and Social Medicine*, Vol. 27, No. 1, 18-26.

Walsh, B. & Walsh D., 1980, The Feasibility of Price Control in Reducing Alcoholism. Reprint from Epidemiological Research as Basis for the Organization of Extramural Psychiatry. *Acta. Psychiat. Scand.*, Suppl. 285, Vol. 62, 265-269.

Whyte, J.H., 1971, *Church and State in Modern Ireland, 1923-1970*. Dublin: Gill and Macmillan.

7. The Alcohol Policy Debate in Ontario in the Post-War Era

Eric Single, Norman Giesbrecht, Barry Eakins*

In Ontario, both the drinking culture and the governmental response to alcohol have undergone marked changes since 1950. This paper concerns the major changes and influences in the alcohol control system of Ontario from the post-war period up to the present time. After introducing some of the essential features of Ontario society, trends in the rates of alcohol consumption and patterns of drinking are presented. It will be seen that alcohol consumption has increased in volume and changed in character. Public attitudes have grown more accepting of alcohol and there has been a gradual liberalization of the alcohol control system. The discussion considers the roles played by temperance groups, public health agencies, the alcohol industry, and the government agencies responsible for the control of beverage alcohol. Examples are provided of changes in the control system, such as the lowering of the drinking age and the introduction of self-serve stores, in order to assess both the origins of policy changes and their impact. The paper concludes with some general comments on the characteristics of the policy-making process and the relative importance of economic and social trends in relation to the alcohol control system.

THE ONTARIO CONTEXT

Ontario is highly diversified — geographically, economically, and socially. It is the second largest of the 10 Canadian provinces with a land area of over one million square kilometres. The greater part of this area is sparsely inhabited timberland or tundra in the northern part of the province. The population of Ontario has increased steadily from 4.5 million in 1950 to 8.3 million in 1976. The vast majority of people reside in southern Ontario near the American border, along the northern shores of

*Addiction Research Foundation, 33 Russell St., Toronto, Ontario, Canada M5S 2S1. The authors gratefully acknowledge the contributions of H. David Archibald, Jan de Lint, Diane McKenzie, Wolfgang Schmidt, Frances Tolnai, Paulette Walters, and all of our colleagues on the ISACE study.

the Great Lakes. By far the largest city is Metropolitan Toronto, with a population of 2.1 million in 1976. The proportion of the population living in urban areas (having at least 1,000 persons per square mile) has increased steadily from 73% in 1951 to 82% in 1971 (Single and Tolnai, 1978).

A large part of this population increase was due to the influx of immigrants from southern and eastern Europe in the 1950s and 1960s. As a result, the population of Ontario has become culturally more heterogeneous. In 1971, 59% reported their ethnic origin to be British Isles, 10% as French, 6% as German, and 6% as Italian. Some 15% of the population in 1971 spoke a language other than English at home, the largest language minorities being French (5%) and Italian (4%). The majority of Ontarians (55%) belong to the Protestant religion, but there is a sizeable and growing majority of Roman Catholics (33%) (Single and Tolnai, 1978).

Ontario has been known as the industrial heartland of Canada. Major industries include manufacturing, mining, construction, and electricity. Nonetheless, by 1976 the majority of workers were employed by service industries, with only 25% of the labour force employed in manufacturing. There is also a distinct trend away from agriculture. The proportion of workers employed in agriculture has decreased from 11% in 1951 to 3% in 1976. Per capita disposable income for Canada as a whole increased dramatically during the study period from $1,286 in 1951 to $5,182 in 1975. Thus, Canadians are among the best paid workers in the world (Single and Tolnai, 1978).

There are three levels of government: federal, provincial, and municipal. Federal and provincial politics operate on a partisan basis whereas municipal politics tend to be non-partisan. There are three major political parties, the Progressive Conservatives, the Liberals, and the New Democratic Party. On the national level, political power has alternated between Liberals and Conservatives. However, the Ontario government has remained Conservative for approximately 35 years.

The provincial political structure is a unicameral parliament which constitutes the legislative arm of government. The executive arm, represented by the Premier and Cabinet, are also controlled by the legislature in that they are traditionally chosen by the governing party in parliament. There is also a titular executive, the Lieutenant-Governor, who is the representative of the Crown in the province. Like other Commonwealth countries, the British sovereign is traditionally deemed sovereign of Canada. Relative to most other countries, the province has more power and autonomy than similar secondary level governments. For example, the power to regulate municipal affairs, social welfare, health care, and education are all under provincial jurisdiction. The province also regulates the marketing and distribution of alcoholic beverages, while the federal government has jurisdiction over the manufacture, import, export, and inter-provincial trade in alcoholic beverages. The province has a monopoly on the off-premise sale of all spirits, imported wines, and imported beer. Domestic wine and beer are sold through monopoly outlets as well as private stores which are closely regulated by the province.

The regulation of alcohol is part of the more general mandate to maintain the public health and the economic well-being of the province. These two aims of alcohol policy are at times in conflict, and, as we shall see, the politics of alcohol in Ontario are typified by a tension between economic and fiscal considerations on the one hand and moral and health considerations on the other.

ALCOHOL CONSUMPTION AND PATTERNS OF DRINKING IN ONTARIO

Both the level of alcohol consumption and patterns of drinking have undergone marked changes in Ontario since 1950. The aggregate consumption in Ontario increased from 24.2 million litres of absolute alcohol in 1950 to 76.2 million litres in 1978. This increase was far greater than the increase in population. Hence per capita consumption rose 68% from 5.4 litres in 1950 to 9.0 litres in 1978. Consumption per person aged 15 and older increased 63% from 7.3 litres to 11.8 litres during this time.

The increase in alcohol consumption may be viewed as composed of two parts: an increase in the proportion of adults who drink alcoholic beverages and an increase in the rate of consumption among drinkers. The available evidence concerning rates of abstention in Ontario during the post-war period indicates a decline in the percentage of abstainers from 30-35% during the late 1940s and early 1950s, to 15-20% at the present time (Single and Giesbrecht, 1979a).

The increase in alcohol consumption has not always been consistent. For example, in 1954 per capita consumption fell by 2.7% and per adult consumption decreased by 1.9%. Definite reasons for this decline cannot be ascribed to any change in control policy or changes in the price or availability of alcohol. In 1958, there was a similar decline in the per capita and per adult rates of alcohol consumption. However, in this case, the decline can clearly be attributed to a particular event. The employees at the Brewers' Retail stores, the major outlet for domestic beer, went on strike for seven weeks during the peak summer period. As a result, beer consumption dropped by 8.8% for 1958 and was only partially offset by disproportionate rises in the consumption of spirits, wines, and imported beer sold at the Liquor Control Board of Ontario (LCBO) outlets. Consequently, overall alcohol consumption declined by 2.5% per capita and 1.5% per adult (Single, 1979a).

There was a temporary levelling off of consumption during the late 1960s. The lack of a consistent increase in alcohol consumption during this time is surprising in light of the fact that there were many small and gradual changes which increased the availability of alcohol (de Lint and Schmidt, 1974; Schmidt and Popham, 1977).

A similar levelling off in the mid-1970s in the per adult rates of consumption has been attributed to a number of factors, including economic recession, change fluctuation, and government policies (Schankula et al., 1981). A more plausible explanation is the demographic impact of the post-war "baby-boom." The progeny of this phenomenon were coming of age in the 1970s. New drinkers enter the drinking population at levels of consumption below the mean. This demographic pattern would explain why per adult rates of consumption levelled off while per capita rates continued to increase.

Despite such fluctuations, it is safe to generalize that there was a large increase in alcohol consumption in Ontario over the study period. It should be noted, however, that this conclusion is based on data derived from sales. Up to 1974, there were two major sources of bias in estimates of alcohol consumption derived from sales (Single and Giesbrecht, 1979b). These were the use of an incorrect conversion factor for wine, which results in an over-estimation of total consumption by about 2%, and unrecorded home production of wine, which resulted in an underestimation of consumption by about 6 to 7%.

Beverage Types

Beer has been the alcoholic beverage of choice in Ontario throughout the study period, but preferences are changing in the direction of greater wine and liquor consumption. The levels of consumption of six major beverage types from 1950 to 1978, presented in Figure 1, show that the increase in the consumption of domestic beer was not nearly as large as the corresponding increases in spirits and wine consumption. Whereas per adult consumption of all types of alcohol increased by 63%, beer consumption increased by only 19%. Levels of beer consumption remained fairly stable throughout the 1950s and 1960s. In the early 1970s, beer sales increased more steadily as part of the general trend towards increased alcohol consumption during this period. However, from 1973 to 1978, per adult beer consumption decreased from 6.1 litres (absolute alcohol) to 5.7 litres.

The second most popular type of alcoholic beverage in Ontario, domestic spirits, showed a steady rise from 1.6 litres (absolute alcohol) per adult in 1950 to 3.7 litres in 1978. Imported spirits appeared to be subject to a great deal more fluctuation. After a relatively stable period in the 1950s and early 1960s, the consumption of imported spirits rose dramatically from 0.4 litres per adult in 1962 to 0.8 litres in 1977.

FIGURE 1 *Consumption of Alcohol Per Person Aged 15 or Older by Six Beverage Types, 1950-1978 (Litres of Absolute Alcohol)*

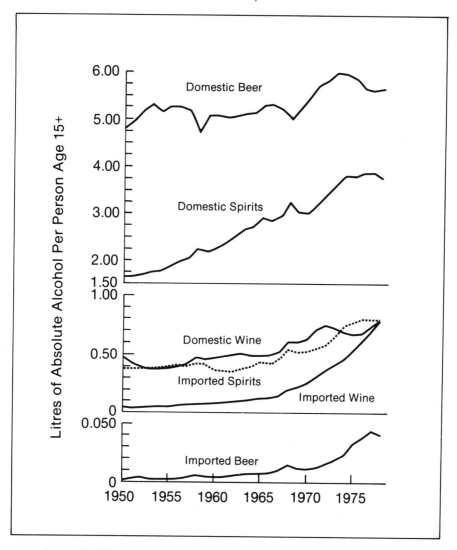

Sources: LCBO Annual Reports.

As with spirits, wine consumption increased at a much greater rate than beer, and there were somewhat different patterns with respect to domestic and imported wines. Taken together, total per adult wine consumption increased more than threefold from 0.5 litres of absolute alcohol in 1950 to 1.6 litres in 1978. Whereas domestic wines rose by 70% during this period, imported wine consumption increased 27-fold from less than 0.1 litres per adult to 0.8 litres.

There has also been a distinct trend toward table wine rather than fortified wines (Single and Giesbrecht, 1979a). In 1969, the Liquor Control Board increased the price of domestic fortified wine to correspond more closely to the mean price per unit of alcohol. Up to this time, domestic sherry and port were priced very low relative to other alcoholic beverages, and partly for this reason were the preferred beverages among skid row alcoholics. The differential price policy apparently succeeded in reducing the consumption of domestic fortified wine.

The overall trend toward increased consumption of wine and spirits relative to the consumption of beer may be summarized by examining the proportion of total alcohol consumption which is accounted for by each of these major beverage types. In 1950, beer accounted for 65.6% of the total alcohol consumption, while spirits accounted for 27.6% and wine for 6.8%. By 1978, however, beer only accounted for 48.0% of total consumption while the portion attributed to spirits and wine increased to 38.5% and 13.5%, respectively. In addition to this general trend, more detailed data reveal a distinct trend towards more diversified drinking within each of the major beverage types. The relative share of total consumption accounted for by the most popular beverages (beer, rye, and domestic fortified wine) is declining as Ontarians are consuming more rum, imported wine, and vodka (Single and Giesbrecht, 1979a).

It should also be noted that these new drinking patterns did not lead to a decrease in the consumption of beer, rye, or domestic fortified wines. As generally has been the case, the development of new drinking patterns did not substitute for old ones, and thus merely served to add to increasing levels of alcohol consumption.

Drinking Patterns

Just as preferences for different types of beverages have become more diversified, so, too, there has been a trend toward greater variation in the types of on-premise outlets for alcohol. In 1950, there were 1,888 licensed outlets (or 5.7 per 10,000 adults) where alcohol was served on-premise. By 1979, there were 7,131 licensed on-premise establishments (10.9 per 10,000 adults), with alcohol available in such places as theatres and recreational facilities. On-premise consumption increased, but off-premise consumption of alcoholic beverages increased at an even greater rate. Available evidence suggests that today only about one-sixth of all alcohol is consumed in on-premise outlets, marking a decrease from the beginning of the study period (Single and Giesbrecht, 1979a).

The typical Ontarian drinks moderately but frequently. Many people have a drink at the end of the work day, usually at home. In a social situation such as a private party, drinking is expected behaviour. Beer is frequently brought when visiting friends and guests will typically bring wine when invited to dinner. Alcohol is also frequently used to socially enhance business transactions. Whereas alcohol was once unavailable in certain situations such as on trains or in theatres, drinking is now accepted and a common accompaniment to travel and entertainment.

There are regional and demographic differences in rates of drinking, with the highest rates of drinking occurring in northern remote areas of the province. Within the more populous southern areas, consumption rates are somewhat higher along the eastern Quebec border than elsewhere, but the most striking pattern is the general lack of variation in drinking rates. Thus, the rate of consumption in Toronto is roughly the same as in most of the rural areas. Even in the Niagara region where a great deal of wine is produced, per adult consumption is close to the overall mean.

As for the relationship between alcohol consumption and demographic variables, abstainers and persons who consume relatively low levels of alcohol tend to be of low income, the elderly, women, members of fundamentalist religious sects, and poorly educated. Males, young persons, persons of high socioeconomic status, and agnostics tend to consume relatively high amounts of alcoholic beverages (Single and Giesbrecht, 1979a).

It is important to remember that even in those groups with the lowest levels of consumption, the majority of persons drink alcohol at some time, and many consume it at levels of high risk. As disposable income continues to rise and the relative price of alcohol continues to fall (Holmes, 1976), the relationship between alcohol use and socioeconomic variables is not as strong as it once was. Today almost everyone can afford to drink. Drinking is no longer considered primarily an activity of urban, working class males who, according to Popham (1976), would often drink to the point of intoxication. Women are drinking in greater numbers and in greater quantities. Drinking on the part of teenagers is increasing. And finally, the new immigrants have brought with them their own tastes and drinking patterns.

As drinking groups become more heterogeneous and drinking becomes more an integral part of social life, new drinking patterns have emerged, such as the drinking of imported wines or spirits other than rye. These new drinking patterns have not replaced old practices, however, as the use of beer and rye has also continued to increase, but at a more moderate rate. The cultural diversity associated with the influx of immigrants after the Second World War has led to a greater variation in drinking styles and preferences. Alcohol is more available, even in remote areas of the province, thus diminishing past differences between urban and rural drinking patterns.

If any generalization is possible, it would be that there is a modern drinking pattern which has generally developed along with traditional drinking practices. The modern drinking pattern is less exclusive and more diversified in its tastes. It involves drinking on the part of youth, women, the less well-to-do. While the frequency of intoxication per drinking occasion may have diminished, the number of drinking occasions has increased. Thus, alcohol consumption has not only increased in volume, it has also changed in character.

Alcohol Problem Indicators

Investigations into the negative consequences of alcohol consumption tend to concentrate on those areas involving chronic health problems such as the prevalence of alcoholism, mortality, morbidity, and accidents where aggregate statistics are collected and maintained.

There has been a substantial increase in the apparent rate of alcoholism in Ontario (Single, 1979b). Estimates of the number of alcoholics in Ontario have increased from 48,800 persons in 1950 to 235,900 in 1976, with the steepest increases occurring in the late 1960s and early 1970s.

These estimates are based on liver cirrhosis mortality (Jellinek, 1956; Popham, 1970) which increased from 7.9 per 100,000 persons aged 20 and older in 1950 to 19.4 in 1976. The rate of death due to alcoholism has similarly undergone a substantial increase, from 1.0 per 100,000 in 1950 to 4.9 per 100,000 in 1976. However, the definition and usage of "alcoholism" in classifying deaths is much more likely to be influenced by extraneous and arbitrary factors than is the case for liver cirrhosis (Giesbrecht and McKenzie, 1980). In any event, for two causes of death where heavy alcohol consumption is a key factor in the majority of cases — namely, liver cirrhosis and alcoholism — there have been significant increases.

There have also been marked increases in reported first admissions to psychiatric inpatient facilities with "alcoholism" and "alcoholism psychosis" diagnoses, as well as reported discharges from all hospitals with "liver cirrhosis," "alcoholism," "alcoholic psychosis," and "accidental poisoning" diagnoses. It is not clear, however, whether these increments represent increased incidence or the expansion of the reporting network. Nonetheless, all of the usual indices of alcohol-related mortality and morbidity have increased, although for discharge data a levelling off was evident in the mid-1970s. The changes in morbidity are in line with the increase in the alcoholism mortality rates, particularly since 1965. The increase in the rate of liver cirrhosis discharges from 60.6 per 100,000 persons aged 20 and older in 1967 to 107.7 in 1975 is congruent with the rising rate of cirrhosis mortality during those years.

The proportion of fatal accidents where the driver was judged by the police or a coroner to be impaired increased from 2.6% in 1958 to 15.6% by 1977. The sharpest rise occurred between 1965 (2.9%) and 1970

(12.1%). It is noteworthy that while the proportion of fatal accidents involving impairment increased, the overall rate of fatal accidents dropped from 3.9 to 1.8 per 100 million kilometres. The major increase in the proportion of fatal accidents attributed to impairment preceded both the lowering of the legal drinking age in 1971 and the 1969 change in legislation which expanded the definition of impairment to include "driving with more than 80 mg. blood alcohol level" and "failure to provide a breath sample." Breathalizer equipment was introduced in two Ontario communities (Toronto and Oshawa) in the late 1950s, but this equipment was not introduced in other jurisdictions until the late 1960s. Therefore, neither legal changes in control nor the introduction of detection equipment would explain the increase in alcohol-related traffic deaths.

It is evident, however, that the change in legislation in 1969 produced a sharp increase in enforcement. The conviction rate for drinking and driving offences per 100,000 persons aged 15 and older increased dramatically between 1950 and 1973 from 5.7 to 56.0. The lowering of the drinking age in September, 1971 may have been in part responsible for a 20% increase in the conviction rate from 1971 to 1972.

One aspect of the shift in control with regard to drinking and driving involves whether the prosecution was by way of summary proceedings (the less serious charge) or by indictment (the more serious). In 1950, only 37.0% of the total drinking and driving convictions were by way of summary proceedings. In 1955, the corresponding figure was 70%, and since 1960, over 99% have been dealt with in this manner. Thus, stronger controls with regard to drinking and driving (i.e. new laws, sophisticated equipment to measure impairment, higher conviction rates) have been accompanied by less punitive procedures.

THE ALCOHOL POLICY ENVIRONMENT

Corresponding to the increase in alcohol consumption and indices of alcohol problems, both the alcohol beverage industry and public health interests in alcohol have grown at a rapid pace. In this section, we examine the overall features of the alcohol beverage industries, public health agencies, temperance interests, and state agencies responsible for alcohol control. We will also discuss the climate of public opinion and its relationship to these interests. In the sections following, we describe the alcohol control system which has emerged from the conflict between these forces.

The Alcohol Industry

The alcohol industry is highly concentrated but not homogeneous. It consists of three parts which are at times at odds with one another. The brewing industry is dominated by three large companies — Molson's, Labatt's, and Carling-O'Keefe. Together they command more than 95% of the Ontario market. Prices are rigid and are not determined by competitive market mechanisms but rather by governmental control. Barriers to entry into the industry are high, and the number of breweries has diminished from more than 30 in 1950 to only 11 in 1975. It is noteworthy that all three major breweries are part of international conglomerates.

The distilling industry is similarly highly concentrated in a few firms which are mainly subsidiaries or affiliates of multinational corporations. Although there are 34 firms which supply products to the Liquor Control Board of Ontario (LCBO), 85% of these are controlled by six multinational corporations. The three largest multinationals — Hiram Walker, Seagrams, and National Distillers — accounted for 74.3% of the market in Ontario in 1975. A major difference between the brewing and distilling industries is that the distillers have a large export market. Indeed, Seagrams receives 94% of its income from exports and Hiram Walker receives 82% of its income from exports. The major market for these exports is the United States. Canada's 1975 exports to the U.S. exceeded domestic sales by 50%.

The wine industry is much smaller than the brewing or distilling industries. It consisted of eight wineries in Ontario in 1975, supplying about half of the total wine consumption for the province, with only a negligible export market. The industry survives primarily because of governmental protectionism. Local wineries are given a preferential markup compared with imported wines, their products are more prominently displayed, and wineries have been permitted to sell their products through special outlets (recently expanded to include winery outlets in department stores). Two companies (Chateau-Gai and Jordan) are owned by major breweries (Labatts and Carling-O'Keefe, respectively). Although it is generally expected that sales of table wine will continue to increase, high costs of land and labour give the wine industry a low profit margin. As a result, the major barrier to growth is not political but economic (Gay, 1979). Unlike the other sectors of the alcohol industry, government is actively promoting domestic wine, but the relatively poor economic performance of the wineries has scared off capital investment.

In a comprehensive analysis of the economic significance of the alcohol industry, Gay (1979) estimates that over 1.87 billion dollars were generated through the manufacture and sale of alcoholic beverages in Ontario in 1975. Spirits contributed 52% of this sum, beer accounted for 37%, and wine production and sales contributed 11% of the total. The major recipient was government. The Ontario government received a total of $532 million from sales taxes, corporate taxes, personal income taxes, and profits attributed to alcoholic beverage sales. The federal government received $409 million from excise taxes, import taxes, corporation taxes, licence fees, and personal income taxes of alcohol industry employees in Ontario. The second largest recipients were the related industries and services, such as the Ontario corn and grape growing industries, packaging industry, and transport. Gay estimates that of the $601 million received by the Ontario alcohol industry in receipts, over $500 million were spent on these related industries. A total of 35,711 persons were employed in the production, sale, and service of alcoholic beverages, with net incomes of over $343 million. In addition, licensed establishments earned $116 million after expenses and wages. Finally, Gay notes that the alcohol industry itself earned $114 million.

Although these data are frequently cited as "benefits" of the industry, factors such as employment and raw materials may be viewed from another perspective as costs to the economy because they involve resources which, in the long run, could be otherwise employed. A redevelopment of resources could not be accompanied immediately or without cost, but the potential to redirect these resources should be kept in mind in evaluating the economic significance of the alcohol industry.

Temperance and Public Health Interests

Although the alcohol beverage industry in Ontario points to a wide variety of economic "benefits" in its arguments against stringent controls, there are several interests opposed to the political power of the industry and the liberalization of the control system. These include temperance groups and public health interests. The temperance organizations are very weak politically and limit their activities to letter-writing campaigns on very specific issues, such as whether to permit beer sales at athletic events, and appearances at licensing hearings.

The public health interests include the so-called "alcoholism" industry and specifically the Addiction Research Foundation of Ontario (ARF). The origins of ARF may be seen in the existence of a position called "director of research" within the Liquor Control Board of Ontario in 1948. The Alcoholism Research Foundation was created by a special Act of the Ontario parliament in the following year. Despite this title, the intent of the Act and the early direction of the work at ARF was in treatment rather than in basic research. Until mid-1970, there was still a stress on treatment, with a substantial share of the Foundation's facilities and budget devoted to a clinical hospital. More recently, the clinic has eschewed the treatment role in favour of research, and now patients are only accepted into the clinical programmes as research subjects.

Although the focus of much of the work at ARF has been treatment, there was a growing interest in the potential use of alcohol control measures to prevent alcohol-related problems. Beginning with various research reports dating back to 1960 and culminating with a formal set of policy recommendations to the Ontario government in 1978, ARF has argued for stricter controls over the alcohol industry.

The State: The Environment of Governmental Alcohol Policy

Government control of beverage alcohol in Ontario involves participation at three levels. The control of production, distribution, and sale of alcohol is subject to the constitutional division of powers between federal and provincial governments in Canada. The present division of power provides the provinces with a general jurisdiction over the retail trade and sales, while the federal government has control of alcohol manufacture and importation. Municipalities have only a slight involvement regarding alcohol control. This is confined largely to a voice in determining the location of retail outlets through zoning by-laws, and indirectly through local option provisions of provincial legislation.

At a national level, the development of policy strategies and programmes with a federal state such as Canada is fraught with difficulty. Despite the fact that provincial structures are generally similar, differences in the degree of liberalization as well as different experiences with alcohol problems render uniform priorities and approaches difficult to achieve. For example, Quebec is more permissive than British Columbia in its alcohol policy. As the central government has no direct constitutional authority in alcohol control, there has been a lack of consensus as to exactly what legitimate role it might play. Moreover, recent developments in federal-provincial regulation have made the federal government somewhat less than willing to assert or involve itself in areas of dual responsibility or where jurisdiction is undefined. There has been a tendency to rely on inter-provincial committees, such as the Federal-Provincial Working Group on Alcohol Problems, consisting of representatives of federal and all provincial and territorial governments. Consequently, a strong or coherent federal policy regarding the problem of alcohol control has not been forth-coming.

The locus of control is thus at the provincial level. For much of the period, decision-making concerning the changing structure of control appears to have been conducted on an ad hoc and incremental basis in response to specific problems. Although a 1972 Ontario government reorganization grouped several departments into three broad policy fields in order to eliminate this type of decision-making, provincial alcohol policy did not escape the tendency toward fragmented and uncoordinated policy-making. Alcohol policy remains divided between economic ministries on the one hand, and health and welfare ministries on the other. Agencies with relevant expertise such as the Addiction Research Foundation and the Liquor Control Board of Ontario (LCBO) are somewhat removed from the process. There is a lack of coordination between these agencies, as ARF reports to the Minister of Health while the LCBO reports to the Minister of Consumer and Corporate Affairs. Further, industry submissions are generally confidential so that outside critical analysis and evaluation of many such proposals does not occur.

Thus, the structural environment in which policy is formulated has not encouraged a comprehensive approach to alcohol control. The response to alcohol-related problems has been a piecemeal development of treatment facilities rather than the adoption of a preventive strategy. In the absence of a general policy, the Ontario government has been simultaneously engaged in promoting the consumption of alcohol while underwriting the alcoholism treatment and research effort.

The Climate of Opinion

The "liberal" direction which alcohol control policy has assumed in recent years is indicative not only of trends in control but also of changes in the underlying social and intellectual climate. This has involved at least three influential elements: a decline in the association of alcohol with immorality; the shift from a concern with alcohol and its control on a community level to an emphasis on individual consumer rights as the appropriate decision-maker; and the predominance of the disease concept of alcoholism and the influence of the "integrationist" approach to the prevention of alcohol-related problems.

The association of alcohol with immorality would seem particularly dated and outmoded today. Although it stems from prohibitionist sentiment which equated alcohol (in particular, Prohibition) with moral reform, this notion persisted into the post-World War II period. For example, in 1946 an Ontario legislator remarked that, " . . . if you let down the bars now and provide greater freedom for people to consume wine and beer and liquor, this province is going to have a reduction in its moral standards" (McLeod, 1946: 1,871). During the past three decades, however, the association of alcohol with immorality has declined considerably. Temperance influences have diminished and to a certain extent, been replaced by a concern for individual rights. As an Ontario legislator observed in 1970:

If one peruses the liquor legislation of the province under the Liquor Control Act, which has to do with the private drinking, or the Liquor Licence Act presently under surveillance having to do with public drinking, one can see the plethora, the maze, and the stupidities through which we have drawn through the centuries in the name of an outworn, purged, and wholly immoral morality, which has led to more ignominious terms and human relationships than it has ever sought to solve, has broken families, has disrupted the relationships between individuals.

That tortured, repressive, unhappy imposition through a particular ethos, namely the puritannical, is long obviated and overdue (Lawlor, 1970: 1340).

The growth of strong sentiments against the "puritanical" denial of individual rights is further evidenced by the erosion of certain elements of the local option provisions and the removal of ration books and permit requirements for alcoholic purchases. Revisions to the province's liquor laws in 1975 carefully defined the administrative powers and procedures of both the Liquor Licence and Liquor Control Boards in accordance with principals of natural justice in administrative law which recognize individual rights. Indeed, Simpson examined the conflict over prevailing views of alcoholism and concluded that the liberalization of control " . . . represented a fundamental shift and transferred additional responsibility for the control of drinking from the government to the individual concerned" (Simpson, 1977: 8).

A factor which has further contributed to the climate of liberalization has been the predominance of the disease concept of alcoholism. The conceptualization of problem drinkers or alcoholics as being very distinct from normal, social drinkers is particularly appealing to the alcohol industry since it shifts the focus of alcohol problems to the individual. Accordingly, increased consumption by normal drinkers would presumably not affect alcohol problems.

A related development was the emergence of the "integrationist" or "socio-cultural" approach to the prevention of alcohol-related problems in the 1960s (e.g. Wilkinson, 1970). This approach held that many problems were a product of the mysticism which surrounded many drinking activities. This could be resolved, it was reasoned, by the early introduction and inculcation of responsible drinking habits and through the removal of certain legal constraints and regulations. Thus, it encouraged the liberalization of many elements of control as consistent with a healthy drinking culture and population. This approach was particularly supported by the alcohol industry, most notably the Brewers and on-premise licencees. On a number of occasions, the Brewers Association has argued for the promotion of beer drinking on the grounds that beer is less harmful and represents a more responsible drinking pattern than spirits (see, e.g. Alcoholic Beverage Study Committee, 1973). Many of the changes in control, such as the introduction of self-serve stores, longer hours of operation, and the expansion of licence types and eligible premises, might be attributed to the influence of this approach.

THE ALCOHOL CONTROL SYSTEM

Current alcohol control legislation in Ontario originated with the repeal of Prohibition. The Ontario Temperance Act of 1916 had prohibited the sale of alcoholic beverages containing more than 2.5% proof spirits except for medicinal, sacramental, industrial, or scientific purposes. Manufacture of alcohol for export continued, and individuals were permitted to import small quantities for home consumption. The Ontario Temperance Act was repealed in 1927. It was superseded by the Liquor Control Act which created the Liquor Control Board of Ontario (LCBO) to regulate all sales of alcoholic beverages. On-premise consumption was only permitted for light beers (under 2.5% alcohol), and all sales of alcoholic beverages were prohibited in local areas which chose to remain dry under the Liquor Licence Act of 1877. The two principal amendments were in 1934, providing for the licensing of establishments for on-premise sales of beer and wine, and in 1944, when on-premise consumption was placed under the control of a new board, the Liquor Authority Control Board.

The Liquor Licencing Act of 1946 further extended the powers of the board which controls on-premise consumption, renamed the Liquor Licence Board of Ontario (LLBO). The LLBO was empowered to provide for the licensing of private clubs and four types of public establishments: dining lounges (where all types of alcoholic beverages could be served with meals); dining rooms (where beer and wine could be served without meals); lounges (where any type of alcoholic beverage could be sold without meals); and public houses (where beer could be sold without meals). This Act, as amended in 1947, is the basis for the alcohol control system in Ontario. Its essential feature is the division of authority into two boards, one dealing with off-premise consumption and the other dealing with on-premise consumption. Although the explicit rationale for granting this authority to relatively autonomous boards is that this arrangement is more efficient, the underlying reason may well be the political sensitivity of the alcohol issue (Silcox, 1975: 147).

Licensing Policy

The licensing policy of the LLBO has been built around four principles: 1. that the applicant's premises and facilities be suitable and meet the standards set by the board; 2. that the operation of the establishment be financially viable and responsible; 3. that there be no involvement by, or close connection with, any criminal element; and 4. that the issuance of on-premise licences meet community needs and interests. Prior to 1975, licensing policy was largely unwritten and was subject to the discretionary authority of the board. The requirements were frequently unknown or misunderstood by applicants and many applications were rejected because they did not meet standards or were not congruent with the board's "policy." Since then, licensing policy has been explicated and made available to applicants in advance. The result is that more applicants are now successful than previously.

The LLBO has changed regulations expanding the days of sale and hours of operation several times. In 1950, the sale of liquor was prohibited on Sundays, Good Friday, Christmas, and election days. On-premise hours were generally from noon to 10:30 p.m. Pubs, however, had to close from 6:30 p.m. to 8:00 p.m., and certain dining rooms and lounge licencees were permitted to serve liquor after 10:30 p.m. (until 2:00 a.m.) provided food was served with the beverage. In 1965, the hours for dining rooms, dining lounges, and lounges were extended to 1:00 a.m. on weekdays and 11:30 p.m. on Saturdays. In 1969, Sunday sales were permitted under a Special Occasion Permit from noon to 10:00 p.m. provided a meal was served. Pub hours were extended to 1:00 a.m. Monday through Saturday. In 1970, uniform hours for all licencees were established from noon to 1:00 a.m. The prior restrictions regarding on-premise sales on special days are no longer in effect.

Advertising

The advertising of alcoholic beverages requires the approval of the LCBO and since 1975, the LLBO. At present, a "preclearance" system of prior approval is in place, and approvals remain in effect for 12 months. As of March 1978, approval must also be secured from the federal Department of Consumer and Corporate Affairs, which enforces some sections of the Food and Drugs Act.

In the 1950s, beer commercials on television were permitted only a brief flash of their trademark at the end of the commercial. Bottles could not be shown. Current policy permits bottles to be shown in the hand, but advertisements are not allowed to portray drinking scenes, show pictures of minors, or unduly exploit the face or figure of any person as the central theme of the advertisement. A continuing controversy surrounds the use of so-called "lifestyle" advertising techniques. A 1975 LCBO directive prohibits the association of alcohol consumption with a "lifestyle or way of life, such as prestige, success in business, relationships with the opposite sex, improving performance in sports, or helping to solve personal problems." In general, advertising is allowed in most media. The major exception is that advertising of spirits is not permitted on radio or television. There are also limitations on the frequency and size of advertisements.

Price Policy

One of the most significant ways in which the LCBO has influenced the availability of alcohol has been through its pricing policies. In the past, pricing policy has reflected a variety of concerns including revenue requirements, public health problems, and the protection of domestic industry. A central element of the LCBO policy is uniform pricing. Prior to 1971, beer had cost one cent extra per bottle in northern Ontario due to higher transportation costs, but this is the only exception to the pattern of uniform prices.

Another central feature of the price policy is the use of uniform mark-ups for specified categories of wines and spirits. The mark-up on imported beverages is higher than domestic products. In 1975, the mark-up for major beverage classes were as follows: Canadian whisky 82%, other Canadian spirits 85%, Scotch 103%, other imported spirits 104%, Ontario wines 60%, imported wines 108% (Gay, 1979: 52).

Two aspects of the mark-up policy bear notice. First, the differential mark-up of imported goods amounts to a protectionist policy. A committee investigating the tax structure of Ontario (Smith, 1968) concluded that protectionism had no place within a provincial revenue system and this policy was supposed to be phased out. While differences have narrowed, they have not disappeared. A second feature of the mark-up system is the lack of uniformity on levels applied to spirits and wines. Spirits are taxed more than wines, and the differential between imported and domestic products is much greater for wines than spirits. The Smith Committee on Taxation could find no rationale for these differentials and concluded that "the size of the mark-up varies from item to item, and to the best of our knowledge is based more on custom than reason" (1968: 390).

In addition to the LCBO mark-ups, there are provincial and federal taxes added to the cost of alcoholic beverages. There is a provincial sales tax of 10% on all alcohol sales. In the case of domestic beer, however, a gallonage tax is levied in place of the LCBO mark-up. Federal taxes consist of excise duties on domestic products and import duties on imported beverages, plus an additional 12% sales tax on all alcoholic beverages. Essentially, three justifications for alcohol taxation have been put forward: 1. alcohol as a luxury, 2. expediency as a means for obtaining necessary funds, and 3. as a control mechanism for reducing consumption (see e.g. Johnson, 1973; Smith, 1968). There is little evidence that control is anywhere near a primary consideration in price policy. Levels of taxation are decided by the Ministry of the Treasury in consultation with LCBO officials. The principal consideration in pricing is the size of a price increase needed to generate a desired level of revenue.

The net impact of the LCBO mark-up and the various taxes is shown in Table 1. A bottle of Canadian spirits selling for an average of $6.48 in 1975 actually cost the LCBO only $1.10. The producer price of a domestic wine selling for $1.97 was $.89 and the production cost of a bottle of domestic beer retailing for $.24 was $.14. The proportion of the selling price accounted for by provincial and federal taxes or profit was 83% for domestic spirits, 55% for domestic wines, and 42% for domestic beer. The taxes and mark-up on imported alcoholic beverages was even greater. For each of the three major beverage types, the imported product had a lower production cost but sold at a higher price than the comparable domestic beverage. It is noteworthy that most of the differential between imported and domestic prices was due to the provincial mark-up rather than the federal import duties.

TABLE 1   *The Per Bottle Cost of Alcoholic Beverages in Ontario in 1975, Broken Down into Its Component Parts*

Cost Item	Spirits		Wine		Beer	
	Domestic	Imported	Domestic	Imported	Domestic	Imported
Producer Price	1.10	1.05	.89	.82	.14	.09
Excise/Import Duty	1.77	1.83	.12	.26	.08	.04
Federal Sales Tax	.35	.35	.11	.10	.02	.02
Freight	—	.14	—	.13	—	.05
Mark-up	2.67	3.51	.67	1.42	.03*	.30
Provincial Sales Tax	.59	.69	.18	.28	.02	.05
Final Price	6.48	7.57	1.97	3.01	.29	.55

Source: Recomputed from Table 2:16 and Table 2:3 in Gay (1979).

* Gallonage tax

The importance of revenue considerations in price policy is evident not only from the price of alcohol but also from the manner in which price decisions are carried out. When the LCBO increases the price of various brands, it typically does so with advance notice and a good deal of publicity. Rather than increasing the price of all beverages across the board, once a year or at a given time, the LCBO increases prices only on a small portion of the total brands available at a number of times throughout the year. As a result, the public is given the impression that alcohol prices are increasing substantially and regularly when, in fact, the real dollar price of alcohol has been declining. The nominal prices of all the major beverage types have increased: a case of two dozen 12-ounce bottles of beer which cost $3.40 in 1953 cost $5.00 in 1973; a 25-ounce bottle of Canadian whisky (least expensive brand) which cost $3.20 in 1953 sold for $5.50 in 1973; a 26-ounce bottle of Canadian sherry (least expensive brand) which was $.75 in 1953 cost $1.20 by 1973. However, these increases were not as great as the general increase in the consumer price index, which rose by 68% during this time. Further, real disposable income increased from $1,553 in 1953 to $2,565 in 1973. Holmes (1976) has computed the income adjusted real price per litre of absolute alcohol and found that the cost of alcoholic beverages actually declined from $10.08 per litre in 1953 to $5.91 in 1973. Thus, the price of alcoholic beverages has in effect declined relative to real disposable income.

Revenue considerations alone do not fully account for the decline in the real price of alcohol. Indeed, it is possible that greater profits could be generated by price increases but the LCBO operates under certain constraints. The proximity of the vast majority of Ontario residents to the U.S. or Quebec borders places a limit on the extent to which prices can be manipulated. The existence of a relatively large number of home wine-makers limits the price which can be charged for wines. Further, pressure from the alcohol industry and small business interests to demonopolize alcohol sales may have rendered the LCBO reluctant to institute major price increases.

Although the dollar receipts from alcohol taxation have grown enormously, their proportional contribution to the total budgetary revenue of the government has, in fact, declined. At the federal level, alcohol excise and import taxes for all of Canada increased from $132 million in 1953 to $548 million in 1975. During the same period, the proportion of the total budgetary revenue accounted for by these alcohol revenues declined from $2.8% to 1.6%. The declining fiscal significance of alcohol is more pronounced at the provincial level. While revenues of the Liquor Control Board of Ontario increased from $41 million in 1950 to $335 million in 1975, they have declined in importance. LCBO profits accounted for 15.6% of Ontario's budgetary revenues in 1950 but only 3.4% in 1975.

Enforcement

Enforcement of liquor laws is the responsibility of the various police forces in Ontario. Federal offences such as the illegal importation of alcohol are enforced by the Royal Canadian Mounted Police. Municipal police forces enforce Liquor Control Act provisions such as underage drinking, drinking-driving offences, and public order concerns in their respective locales. The Ontario Provincial Police are responsible for enforcement in rural areas and small towns and villages where there is no municipal police force. It has also established a separate Liquor Laws Enforcement Section which is responsible for the investigation and enforcement for various Liquor Control Act and Liquor Licencing Act violations.

The licensing laws and regulations for on-premise consumption are enforced through a system of inspection attached to the licensing function. On-premise licencees are inspected a minimum of twice a year and usually monthly in unannounced visits by the district inspector. There is also an annual inspection by a supervisory inspector. Enforcement policy has a selective emphasis so that those considered to be problem cases receive the most frequent attention (Cooper, 1978). Those suspected of continued violation of regulations may be checked by "special" undercover investigators.

The conviction rate for public drunkenness or other Liquor Act offences (combined) increased from 1950 to 1965 and then declined after

1970 at the time of the most dramatic increases in drinking and driving convictions. This process culminated in the partial decriminalization of public drunkenness in 1971, when there began a programme of referring public inebriates to detoxification centres as an alternative to laying a charge (Annis et al., 1976). Even before the arrest rates for public drunkenness diminished, the conviction statistics indicate a declining utilization of coercive measures to deal with public drunkenness in the province (Oki et al., 1976).

The decline in "public order" convictions in the late sixties was accompanied by an increase in drinking and driving convictions about the same time. It appears that whether by explicit design or in response to broader social pressures, the drunk on the street was increasingly perceived as less of a serious problem, while the drinking driver became the target of more intensive enforcement measures (Giesbrecht and McKenzie, 1980).

THE IMPACT OF ALCOHOL AND RELATED INDUSTRIES

The principal mechanism by which the alcohol industry has attempted to influence policy is through lobbying organizations, specifically the Brewers Association of Canada, the Association of Canadian Distillers, and the Canadian Wine Institute. The overall effectiveness of the industry's lobby has probably been enhanced by the manner in which gradual changes in the structure of control have been sought. The alcohol industry has tended to concentrate its efforts on one or two issues at a time rather than by encouraging major policy changes, thereby increasing the effectiveness of its efforts.

The alcohol industry, and especially the distilling industry, has maximized the legitimacy of its case further by addressing the government almost exclusively in economic terms. Briefs and proposals are generally directed to the economic ministries of government. The economic significance of the industry is hard to ignore. As noted earlier, Gay (1979) has estimated this to be more than $1.87 billion in 1975 for Ontario. Emphasis is placed on alcohol revenues. By stressing the additional revenue possibilities available to the government from specific tax changes and increased sales, the industry has often taken advantage of the somewhat natural alliance and mutual interest of both government and industry in alcohol sales and revenue.

The solidarity of the industry has been fractured periodically. The brewing industry has attempted to portray beer as a beverage of "moderation" by arguing that, based on alcohol content, alcoholics typically drink spirits and wine, and thus those beverages are proportionately larger contributors to levels of alcoholism. In opposing a system of absolute alcohol taxation proposed to the Ontario Committee on Taxation in 1967, the Brewers Association of Canada contended that it was the proper role and duty of government to promote "healthy" as opposed to "unhealthy" consumption. In 1971, the Brewers Association of Canada commissioned the Alcoholic Beverage Study Committee headed by Lancelot Smith, the former chairman of the Ontario Committee on Taxation, to research their position. Published in 1973 under the title *Beverage Differences and Public Policy in Canada,* the report covered a wide range of topics, from epidemiological evidence to revenue analyses supportive of preferential tax policies favouring beer. The Brewers Association efforts have been thus far successful in avoiding absolute alcohol taxation.

The relationship between wine producers and the Ontario government and the position which domestic wines are accorded within the control system is qualitatively different from either of those of the brewing industry or distilling industries. Domestic wines have traditionally been given preferential treatment (Gay, 1979). In fact, the Ontario Temperance Act of 1916 provided for the exemption of native wines from its provision.

However, the Ontario Wine industry has often been at a disadvantage in that many production costs were higher than their competitors and Ontario wines, which must be made entirely from Ontario grapes, have had a poor image in the marketplace. Further, certain federal policies have hurt the industry. On trade missions abroad, entry of foreign wines has been used as a bargaining tradeoff and Canada became a dumping ground for foreign wines. Federal excise taxes were significantly lower for imports so that when custom duties were added, the retail price was equalized. Thus, there was no actual tariff protection for domestic wine producers.

The Ontario government has, in recent years, taken an active part in redressing the balance of conditions for the wine producers and its related industry, the grape growers. The Ontario Grape Growers Marketing Board has been established and financial aid from the Ministry of Agriculture has assisted research into the development of new strains of grapes to improve wine quality. The Horticultural Research Centre at Vineland in the Niagara region was established in this way. In 1977, the Liquor Control Board improved listing, distribution, and display opportunities in government stores. Ontario wines, unlike other listings, are automatically given preferential treatment and guaranteed listings in a certain number of stores. They are also given preferential mark-ups over imported wines.

One reason for the success of the Canadian Wine Institute in securing preferential treatment over the objections of the Ontario Imported Wine and Spirits Association is a concern with maintaining the Niagara Peninsula as agricultural land. This, in turn, is contingent on the economic success of the wine industry. Although the government is moving toward reduction of the differential mark-up between domestic and imported wine (as it is in reality a tariff barrier which is outside of provincial jurisdiction), it is openly pursuing a policy preferential to the wine industry.

The distillers do not receive preferential treatment in relation to the other alcohol manufacturers but they have had some influence in the gradual liberalization of alcohol policy and they have managed to avoid stringent controls. Emphasis has been placed on the economic benefits of the industry, with particular attention directed to the large export production. The distillers have argued against the notion that spirits are the beverage of excess. It is probable that the disagreement between the distillers and the brewers has limited their collective influence.

The hospitality and tourism industries have had an active and constant interest in liberalizing Ontario's drinking laws since 1950. These industries have been represented by the Canadian Restaurant Association, the Ontario Hotel Association, and Tourism Ontario, along with other smaller organizations. In 1974, tourism and restaurants were Ontario's third largest industry, accounting for 10% of Ontario's Gross Provincial Product and 10% of the province's workforce (Davis, 1974). The industry has been united in its representations to the Ontario government on various issues concerning alcohol control. The emphasis of their presentations has been on changing what they felt were archaic restrictions in order to make drinking a more "normal" and attractive activity for customers. The principal issues to which they have addressed themselves have been lengthening hours of sale, establishment of sidewalk cafes (patio licences), the serving of alcoholic beverages without food in taverns provided an overall 50/50 sales ratio is met, the removal of sexual restrictions on public house licence classifications, and the serving of liquor without food on Sundays. With a few exceptions, the industry has been successful in securing the changes it has sought. The major exception to this is in pricing and taxation considerations. Although the industry has unsuccessfully lobbied for volume discounts and the removal of the double layer of provincial sales taxation on on-premise sales, they have otherwise been successful in liberalizing on-premise restraints.

PUBLIC HEALTH INTERESTS: THE ADDICTION RESEARCH FOUNDATION

The influence of the public health interests in alcohol control policy has been guided in Ontario largely through the presence of the Addiction Research Foundation. Since its creation in 1949, the organization has acquired and developed the major research expertise in the province in the fields of alcohol addiction and treatment. The inclusion of prevention in its legislative mandate provides it with an obvious interest in the direction of alcohol control policy. The Minister of Health expects policy advice from the Foundation and even though that advice may be made public, the government may choose not to act on it (Macdonald, 1979: 11).

Since the early 1960s, the Foundation has attempted, through its research programmes, educational materials, and policy statements, to increase public awareness of the relationship between control policy, levels of consumption, and alcohol-related problems. It has underlined the desirability of price controls and other mechanisms aimed at restraining aggregate consumption in order to prevent further increases in the incidence of alcohol-related problems (see, e.g. ARF, 1978).

In 1975, the Minister of Consumer and Commercial Relations did acknowledge that "there is a direct relationship between freer drinking and the social problems of alcohol abuse . . ." (Handleman, 1975). However, the continued relaxation of restrictions and the government's interest in maximizing revenues from alcohol would indicate that the ARF has not had a great deal of influence on alcohol control policy.

The Foundation's failure to persuade the Ontario government to adopt a public health oriented policy does not indicate that it has been without influence. The mere presence of a provincial alcohol research agency, monitoring consumption levels and alcohol-related problems, has enabled the government to resist pressures for greater liberalization when it so desired.

THE ROLE OF TEMPERANCE INTERESTS

Temperance interests are very weak in Ontario. The principal temperance organizations were at the peak of their activity and power during the period of prohibition from 1916-1927. Since then, the movement has entered a long period of decline in which only a few organizations have survived. In the period under review, temperance interests have been primarily represented by the Ontario Temperance Federation (and its successor, Alcohol and Drug Concerns, Inc.), the Women's Christian Temperance Union, and the Inter-Faith Liquor Legislation Committee.

The decline can be at least partially attributed to the great psychological sense of defeat of the movement with the repeal of prohibition (Reeve, 1976: 7). As the climate of opinion has become more liberal, the movement has had difficulty in keeping its treatment of the issues both socially and politically relevant. The popular base of support has declined. For example, in 1951 the Ontario Temperance Federation claimed a membership of 75,000 (OTF, 1951) whereas its successor, Alcohol and Drug Concerns, now optimistically estimates a following of 25,000 to 35,000 (Reeve, 1978). The Women's Christian Temperance Union, which dates from 1875 and once had 11,000 members in Ontario, now has fewer than 800 (*Toronto Star*, 1977).

There remains a strong church presence in the movement. In the past, Protestant denominations have tended to be over-represented and the United Church, in particular, has been very active. More recently, there has been a greater Roman Catholic presence and denominations as diverse as the Salvation Army and the Church of Scientology have voiced temperance sentiments on alcohol issues. The church presence has introduced a moralistic element counter to the prevailing trends in public sentiment.

Although several temperance personalities were associated with the Cooperative Commonwealth Federation, predecessor of the leftist New Democratic Party, the major political parties have avoided any association with temperance interests. Most of the temperance organizations are no longer politically oriented. The principal activities centre around local option votes and actively opposing individual on-premise licence applications. (Ironically, temperance interests are sometimes allied with tavern and pub operators who are opposed to increased competition from a licence applicant.)

There is a split between those groups which advocate abstinence and those which are moderationists. While the WCTU and Salvation Army are abstinence-oriented, most of the other organizations today take a moderationist stance. Although based on different rationales, the positions adopted by the temperance organizations have been generally congruent with the position of the Addiction Research Foundation. In 1973, in response to anticipated revisions in the Ontario laws, the Inter-Faith Liquor Legislation Committee was formed to oppose any liberalization in the control system and advocated control changes which would 1. increase pricing, 2. restrict availability, 3. reduce the alcohol content of wine and beer, and, 4. shorten hours of sale. Almost all temperance groups have concerned themselves with alcohol advertising and have advocated everything from a total ban to simply the elimination of lifestyle advertising.

The influence of the temperance movement on government policy has declined markedly. In previous years, the movement could count on an attentive ear in their presentations to the Premier and various ministers. In more recent times, the government has tended to listen politely and simply not act on temperance proposals. During the 1970s, the access of such groups to the Premier and those in authority has been more difficult. Educational grants given to certain temperance organizations have ceased. The Minister of Consumer and Commercial Relations stated in 1974, "Prohibitionist sentiment has no place in this government's attitude toward the regulation of alcohol sales and distribution" (Clement, 1974: 15).

EXAMPLES OF CHANGE IN THE CONTROL SYSTEM

The following discussion focusses on some examples of the gradual liberalization of control policy in Ontario. The examples serve to illustrate the multiplicity of influences on the control system and the manner in which changes in control may have unanticipated consequences.

The Decriminalization of Public Drunkenness

Decriminalization of the offence of public drunkenness and the attendant emphasis on treatment for the offender was an outgrowth of several developments during the 1960s and early 1970s (Bottomley et al., 1976; Giesbrecht et al., 1981). In some cities, urban renewal of downtown core areas threatened the established habitat of many skid row inhabitants, helping to draw attention to their plight. Police forces expressed concern about the amount of time and resources expended in enforcing public drunkenness laws and questioned their values, particularly for chronic offenders whose recidivism suggested that criminal penalties were having little deterrent effect. In 1966 alone, 52,290 convictions for this offence were registered and more than 8,000 persons were considered to be chronic offenders (Bottomley et al., 1976: 36). This coincided with the general opinion in Canada which favoured decriminalization of all "victimless" crimes. Further, the disease concept was increasingly accepted at this time. Thus, instead of being seen as a matter of public morality assigned to the police courts, public drunkenness and the skid row inebriate were gradually accepted as social problems lying more properly within the domain of the social welfare and public health system.

The change in the treatment of public inebriates was accomplished by a gradual process of granting the police and the courts greater discretion in handling cases, culminating in a 1971 amendment to the Liquor Control Act which empowered police to take offenders to detoxification centres in lieu of a charge. Ironically, there is considerable evidence that this more benign approach actually had a negative impact on the health and well-being of the skid row population (Giesbrecht et al., 1981). With less police intervention and less time spent in gaol, the public inebriates suffered from poorer diets, greater exposure to the cold, and a higher rate of beatings and muggings.

Changes in the Drinking Age

The legal drinking age in Ontario was lowered from 21 to 18 years in July of 1971. Several factors were clearly involved in this decision. There was a rather widespread movement to lower drinking ages throughout Canada and the United States around this time. Five other Canadian provinces and both territories had lowered the legal age of consumption prior to Ontario. Political considerations were undoubtedly involved. The reduction in the age increased the privileges and legalized a social activity for approximately 412,000 young people, who simultaneously acquired voting privileges as well. The reduction was passed into law shortly before a provincial general election. The occasion allowed Premier Davis to claim that the age reduction was proof that the Progressive Conservative party was more "progressive" than the opposition parties were (Davis, 1971: 5048).

Another important factor was the linkage of the drinking age with the overall age of majority. The government held, and it was generally supported by public opinion, that to separate the age for alcohol consumption from the age at which people were otherwise considered adult would be inconsistent and would create a double-standard. The lowering of the age of majority was considered a "legislative package" and involved amending some 37 individual statutes to which age applied. Debate was thus framed within the context of an overall age reduction and as a result, the decision to lower the drinking age was not examined solely on its own merits but rather became tied to a reduction in the overall age of majority.

The subsequent decision to raise the age to 19 indicates that the magnitude of the social problems emanating from the lowering of the age were largely unanticipated by government. Teenage drinking was increasingly implicated as an important factor in alcohol-related traffic accidents. From 1970 to 1973 there were significant increases in the proportion of drinking drivers involved in all collisions for the 16-19 age group, and this finding was attributed to the reduction in the drinking age. Other indicators showed a marked increase in alcohol-related problems among teenagers. Admissions to alcoholism facilities and detoxification centres for those under 21 increased from almost none to 4.4% and 3.5% respectively (Smart and Finlay, 1975). Reports of high school students drinking during lunch hours and being intoxicated in class and at school functions became more frequent.

In reaction to such reports, public sentiment towards the lowered drinking age began to shift. A public opinion survey done for the *Toronto Star* in 1978 indicated that 71% of the Metropolitan Toronto residents favoured raising the drinking age to 19. In 1978, the government raised the legal drinking age to 19 years, effective January 1, 1979. The rationale for choosing the age of 19 was that it would remove legal drinking from the high school population.

Introduction of Self-Serve Stores

The advent of self-serve liquor stores has altered the character of retail beverage alcohol sales in Ontario. Their introduction marks a basic change in LCBO sales activities and philosophy toward a more distinctly market orientation. From its inception in 1927, the LCBO has operated outlets under a non-direct access or clerk service system. Bottles were kept behind the counter away from the view and direct access of the customer. Until 1962, ration books or a permit were required for presentation before a sale was made.

With the opening of the LCBO's first self-serve outlet in 1969, customers acquired direct access to all products. Bottles were displayed on open shelves and those making purchases simply made their choice and took it to the cashier for check-out. After initial testing, the new format was deemed successful. Less staff were required to handle sales and it was easier to maintain inventory under the new system. A policy of making all new outlets the self-serve type was adopted in 1970 and by March of 1979, 397 or 67% of all LCBO outlets were of this type (LCBO, 1979).

The change to self-serve stores is significant in two respects. First, self-serve stores appear to have increased consumption. Smart (1974) found that self-serve outlets tend to encourage impulse buying. Second, and perhaps more importantly, the introduction of self-serve stores may be viewed as a symbol of the greater acceptance of alcohol in Ontario. As the purchase of alcoholic beverages resembled that of other commodities, the advent of self-serve stores signified a new and more liberal attitude towards alcohol.

More recently, the alcohol industry in alliance with food stores, has lobbied for the sale of beer and wine in grocery stores. This would permit small groceries to maintain their existence in the face of competition from supermarkets and large chain stores. Thus far, pressure for this change has been resisted, not because of public health concerns but rather due to the opposition of monopoly store employees who perceive the proposal as a threat to their jobs.

SUMMARY

Alcohol consumption and the alcohol control system have undergone a period of marked change since 1950. At the beginning of the study period, drinking was associated with the urban, male proletariat and alcoholism was associated with moral weakness. Stringent controls existed over the purchase of alcoholic beverages for home consumption or for on-premise consumption. These controls reinforced prevailing attitudes toward alcohol use and drunkenness.

By the end of the 1970s, the drinking culture was radically changed. Popular attitudes have grown more accepting of alcohol use. New groups of drinkers have become more prominent: women, youth, immigrants. The composition of drinking groups has become more heterogeneous and drinking culture has become more diversified. Alcohol is available in a greater variety of products and locations. Alcoholics are given treatment rather than moral condemnation. Just as the previously strict controls were congruent with prevailing social attitudes, so, too, it may be claimed that the liberalization of control policy is consistent with the liberalization of attitudes towards alcohol abuse and alcohol problems.

As the influence of temperance interests has declined, the power and influence of alcohol interests has increased. The alcohol industry can legitimately claim to be a significant force in the Ontario economy and a benefactor to the government itself. By effectively targeting lobbying efforts toward the economic ministeries in the provincial and federal governments, the alcohol interests have generally succeeded in attaining a gradual relaxation of restrictions on alcohol. The drinking age was lowered, alcohol has been available in a greater number and variety of settings, and perhaps more importantly, the price of alcohol has not kept pace with the consumer price index or with increased personal disposable income.

There has also been a marked change in the organizations and interests opposed to the continued increase in alcohol consumption. At the beginning of the study period, the predominant political force opposed to alcohol interests was the temperance movement. Strongly affiliated with religious groups, these organizations adopted basically a moral position against alcohol. Over the following three decades, however, the influence of temperance groups has diminished enormously and the major opponents of alcohol interests have become public health interests. In particular, the Addiction Research Foundation has advocated a programme of policies aimed at restraining further increases in aggregate consumption. This position is based on empirical evidence concerning the relationship between consumption and alcohol-related problems. Although the government has not adopted a public health oriented alcohol policy, the Foundation has played a role in preventing greater liberalization.

As to the consequences of the alcohol control system, it is at best a difficult task to determine the impact of regulatory measures on alcohol use and alcohol problems. In many ways, the increase in alcohol consumption and the relaxation of control measures are not in a cause-effect relationship but rather concomitants of the same social and economic processes which have produced liberalized public attitudes toward alcohol and alcohol abuse. Nonetheless, one can point to a number of specific effects of the control system. For example, changes in the drinking age had a demonstrable impact on traffic accidents and fatalities among teenagers. Differential price policies have been used to manipulate drinking preferences with regard to fortified domestic wines (Single and Giesbrecht, 1979a). Protectionist policies have undoubtedly benefited the domestic wine industry. But an examination of the long-term trend in alcohol consumption would lead to the conclusion that economic factors have played a greater role in determining consumption levels than have control policies.

If any overall conclusion is possible regarding the alcohol control experience in Ontario over the past three decades, it would be that the alcohol control system has been more a servant than a master of the social and economic forces which have led to the increase in alcohol consumption and alcohol abuse.

REFERENCES

Addiction Research Foundation (ARF), 1978, *A Strategy for the Prevention of Alcohol Problems*. Recommendations to the Ontario Parliament from the Executive Committee of the Addiction Research Foundation.

Alcoholic Beverage Study Committee, 1973, *Beer, Wine and Spirits: Beverage Differences and Public Policy in Canada*. Ottawa: Brewers Association of Canada.

Annis, H.M., Giesbrecht, N., Ogborne, A. & Smart, R.G., 1976, *Task Force II Report on the Effectiveness of the Ontario Detoxification System*. Toronto: Addiction Research Foundation.

Bottomley, K., Giesbrecht, N., Giffen, P.J., Lambert, S. & Oki, G., 1976, *A History of Recent Changes in the Social Control of Public Inebriates, with Special References to Ontario and Toronto*. Toronto: Addiction Research Foundation, Substudy No. 813.

Clement, J.T., 1974, *Alcohol: A Provincial Problem*. Address to the Brewers Association of Canada, September 23.

Cooper, R., 1978, Personal Interview with R. Cooper, Director of the Ontario Liquor Licence Board.

Davis, Hon. W., 1971, *Debates*. Legislature of Ontario, p. 5048. Toronto: Queen's Printer.

Davis, Hon. W., 1974, Speech to the Annual Meeting of the Ontario Hotel Association, Toronto.

Gay, K., 1979, *Benefit Analysis of Beverage Alcohol — Ontario 1975*. Toronto: Addiction Research Foundation, mimeo.

Giesbrecht, N., Giffen, P.J., Lambert, S. & Oki, G., 1981, Changes in the Social Control of Skid Row Inebriates in Toronto: Assessments by Skid Row Informants. *Canadian Journal of Public Health,* 72: 101-104.

Giesbrecht, N. & McKenzie, D., 1980, *A Brief Overview of Trends in Selected Public Health Order Consequences of Alcohol Consumption in Ontario*. Toronto: Addiction Research Foundation, Substudy No. 1134.

Giffen, P.J. et al., 1969, Task Force on Detoxification Planning, *Report*. Toronto: Addiction Research Foundation.

Handleman, Hon., S., 1975, *Debates,* Legislature of Ontario, p. 2503. Toronto: Queen's Printer.

Holmes, K.E., 1976, *The Demand for Beverage Alcohol in Ontario 1953-1973.* Toronto: Addiction Research Foundation, Substudy No. 815.

Johnson, J.A., 1973, Canadian Policies in Regard to the Taxation of Alcoholic Beverages. *Canadian Tax Journal,* 21: 6, 553.

Lawlor, Hon. P., 1970, *Debates,* Legislature of Ontario, p. 1340. Toronto: Queen's Printer.

de Lint, J. & Schmidt, W., 1974, Control Laws and Price Manipulation as Preventive Strategies, in Room, R. & Sheffield, S. (Eds.), *The Prevention of Alcohol Problems.* Berkeley: U. of California Press.

Liquor Control Board of Ontario (LCBO), *1949-1979 Annual Reports.* Toronto: Ministry of Consumer and Commercial Relations, Government of Ontario.

Macdonald, J., 1979, *The Mission of the Addiction Research Foundation.* Paper presented at the Senior Executive Seminar, School for Addiction Studies, Toronto.

McLeod, Hon. R.T., 1946, *Debates,* Legislature of Ontario, p. 1871. Toronto: Queen's Printer.

Oki, G., Giesbrecht, N., Giffen, P.J. & Lambert, S., 1976, *Decriminalization of Public Drunkenness: A Statistical Profile of Patterns and Trends.* Toronto: Addiction Research Foundation, Substudy No. 740.

Ontario Temperance Federation (OTF), 1951, Submission to the Ontario Government Regarding an Act to Amend the Liquor Licence Act.

Popham, R.E., 1976, *Working Papers on the Tavern, 1. Social History of the Tavern* Toronto: Addiction Research Foundation, Substudy No. 808.

Reeve, D., 1976, *Abstinence: Reassessment and Recommendations.* Paper presented at the annual meeting of the Canadian Foundation on Alcohol and Drug Dependence, Toronto.

Reeve, D., 1978, Personal interview with J. Kaczmarski.

Schankula, H. et al., 1981, *Alcohol: Public Education and Social Policy.* Report of the Addiction Research Foundation Task Force on Public Education, Toronto.

Schmidt, W. & Popham, R.E., 1977, *An Approach to the Control of Alcohol Consumption.* Paper presented at the Addiction Research Foundation — World Health Organization Conference, Toronto, November 1977.

Silcox, P. 1975, The ABCs of Ontario: Provincial Agencies, Boards and Commissions, in Macdonald, D. (Ed.), *The Government and Politics of Ontario.* Toronto: MacMillan.

Simpson, R., 1977, *Alcohol Control Policies in Ontario 1966-1976*. M.A. Thesis, McMaster University.

Single, E., 1979a, The "Substitution" Hypothesis Reconsidered: A Research Note Concerning the Ontario Beer Strikes of 1958 and 1968. *Journal of Studies on Alcohol,* 40: 5 (May 1979), 485-491.

Single, E., 1979b, Estimating the Number of Alcoholics in Ontario: A Replication and Extension of a Previous Study. *Journal of Studies on Alcohol,* 40: 11 (November 1979), 1046-1052.

Single, E. & Giesbrecht, N., 1979a, *Rates of Alcohol Consumption and Patterns of Drinking in Ontario 1950-1975*. Toronto: Addiction Research Foundation Working Paper Series.

Single, E.W. & Giesbrecht, N., 1979b, The 16% Solution and Other Mysteries Concerning Estimates of Alcohol Consumption Based on Sales Data. *Br. J. Addict.,* June 1979.

Single, E. & Tolnai, F., 1978, *Profile of Programmes and Policies for the Prevention of Alcohol-related Problems*. Paper prepared for the WHO Project on the Prevention of Alcohol-related Problems. Toronto: Addiction Research Foundation.

Smart, R., 1974, *The Effect of Self-Service Stores on the Purchase of Alcoholic Beverages*. Toronto: Addiction Research Foundation, Substudy No. 595.

Smart, R.G. & Finley, J., 1975, Increases in Youthful Admissions to Alcoholism Treatment in Ontario. *Drug Alc. Depend.,* 1: 83-87.

Smith, L.J., 1968, *Report of the Ontario Committee on Taxation*. Toronto: Queen's Printer.

Toronto Star, 1977, Demon Rum: Aging Warriors in Losing Battle, May 14.

Wilkinson, R.L., 1970, *The Prevention of Drinking Problems: Alcohol Control and Cultural Influences*. New York: Oxford University Press.

8. California's Alcohol Experience: Stable Patterns and Shifting Responses

Richard Bunce, Tracy Cameron, Gary Collins, Patricia Morgan, James Mosher and Robin Room*

One of the most striking aspects of California policies between 1950 and 1979 is the relationship between the general stability of drinking patterns and the shifting societal responses to the consequences of alcohol consumption. This can be seen in part by the strict separation between the alcohol beverage control and alcohol problems domains. Policies concerned with both alcohol-related problems and alcohol beverage controls were shaped by common political and economic forces and shifts in public values, but they have followed separate agendas, addressing themselves to different audiences and generally not influencing each other's paths of development. Changes in control policies favoured increasing availability and the spread of consumption, a stable marketing climate for the growth of the alcohol beverage industry, and increased revenues to the state. The shift of policies on alcohol-related problems during this time from a moral/policing to a medical/administrative model was accompanied by a marked increase in expenditures on alcohol-related problems (Reynolds, 1973). This paper outlines the historical development of alcohol consumption, control, and problems from 1950-1979, and examines their relationship to each other, to state policies, and to the social, political, and economic milieu.

Overview of California

California is a land of contrast and paradox, a patchwork of ethnic, social, economic, and geographical diversity. Among the 48 contiguous states it contains the highest mountains, the lowest desert, the most

*Alcohol Research Group, Institute of Epidemiology and Behavioral Medicine, Berkeley (formerly the Social Research Group, School of Public Health, University of California, Berkeley). Preparation of this report was supported by a National Alcohol Research Grant (AA-03524) from the National Institute on Alcohol Abuse and Alcoholism.

productive farmland, a 1,000-mile seacoast, and a vast reserve of forest and timberland. This diversity has contributed to California's standing as the wealthiest state in the nation, and the most populous — 22 million people in 1979.

California's growth was based on its land. First, gold, then concentrated corporate farming, led to the development of trade, transportation, and industry. The wealth from these three sources overlapped significantly. The Southern Pacific Railroad remains one of the largest landowners in the state, and Foremost-McKesson, the state's largest agricultural firm, is also involved in property development and the manufacture of drugs and chemicals and the distribution of alcoholic beverages (Budde and Bar-Din, 1979). Today, aerospace, electronics, oil, and agriculture are the industries vital to California's economy. The major California ports, in San Diego, Los Angeles, Oakland, and San Francisco, have helped to develop and maintain the state's leading position in international trade. The state's agricultural, industrial, and trade enterprises have provided a base for the tremendous growth of financial institutions, currently representing a combined net income of over $15 billion yearly.

Through much of California's history, greater numbers of immigrants arrived from other nations than from other parts of the U.S. In the 19th century, Chinese, Japanese, and Filipinos came from Asia, and from Europe came Armenians, Italians, Irish, and Portuguese. In the 20th century, they were followed by South Americans and Mexicans (McWilliams, 1949). The immigrants came to work the fields, the mines, the railroads, and the burgeoning related industries in the state. Referred to as the "quilt of many colours," California's population includes 29% who have a mother tongue other than English, an estimated 3 million of whom are Spanish-speaking residents of Southern California (California Statistical Abstracts, 1976).

The period after World War II witnessed a tremendous growth in aerospace, defence, and electronics industries, associated with a doubling of population from 10 to 22 million between 1950 and 1979. The overwhelming proportion of the state's population has been urban, and urbanization has continued throughout the study period. In 1950, 60% of the people lived in areas of over 2,500 population; by 1970, this had increased to 86%. The post-war "baby boom" was particularly strong in California. The rise in the under-20 population was most dramatic up to the mid-1960s when it began to decline. The over-50 population, however, has remained relatively stable throughout the study period.

California has also displayed a cultural and political diversity, often expressed by sectional differences and rivalries. The southern part of the state has always been more politically and ideologically conservative, more religiously fundamentalist, and more anti-union than the northern area, reflecting, in part, differences in historical and economic development and migration patterns. The north has enjoyed most of the wealth in natural resources. Prior to World War II, the northern part of the state held the major portion of the population, the industry, and the political power in the state legislature. The balance in all of these areas had shifted heavily to the south by the first part of the study period.

California's governmental process is divided into legislative, executive, and judicial branches. Changes initiated during the Progressive Era (1900 to 1920) diminished political party strength for many years and curtailed executive power. This resulted in a powerful legislature and equally powerful special interest lobbying groups. Candidates for office could file under either Democratic or Republican party tickets, and even today most local and county elective offices remain "nonpartisan." To an unusual degree, direct lawmaking powers are retained by the state's citizens: referendum, initiative, and recall provisions enable citizens to vote in new laws directly, rescind old ones, and recall both state and local officials from office. While these powers have often been manipulated by special interests, their existence increases legislative accountability (Morgan, 1978a; Mowry, 1951; Rusco, 1960). Legislative power, strong lobbying groups, and direct citizen input all figure significantly in California's alcohol control experience.

STRUCTURING THE MARKET FOR ALCOHOL

The manufacture and distribution of alcoholic beverages in California is formally regulated by three tiers of government — federal, state, and local. The state government has primary authority by virtue of the Twenty-first Amendment to the U.S. Constitution which ended Prohibition in 1933. However, the federal government exercises considerable authority at the production level. Local governments in California have played only a minimal role in determining the nature of the distribution system because the state has maintained preemptive control over the alcohol trade. However, local communities have been given a major responsibility for enforcing state regulations and may, through zoning regulations, initiate some controls (Mosher, 1979a; Wittman, 1980).

Reorganization Without Change

California was one of several states which, at the time of repeal, assigned responsibility for administering alcohol beverage control policies to a taxing agency responsible for maximizing revenues for the state (Morgan, 1979; Baird, 1945). From 1933 to 1954, the sale and distribution of alcoholic beverages in California were administered under a licensing system run by the State Board of Equalization (SBOE). The SBOE, the state's general tax collection agency, is headed by elected officials and operates independently of the governor's office. The legislature gave the SBOE power over alcoholic beverages for three reasons: 1. to maximize legislative power by keeping control of alcoholic beverages away from the governor's office; 2. to vest power in an agency which was not specific to alcohol and would not interfere with the growth and development of the alcoholic beverage industry and of tax revenues from that industry; and 3. to maintain centralized state control and counter temperance efforts to enact local control over the sales and distribution of alcoholic beverages (Morgan, 1979).

In 1954, corrupt practices of California's SBOE in alcohol control were exposed in a scandal which forced a reorganization. Reform efforts to move alcohol control away from "politics" to a neutral administrative agency led to the creation of a separate, "independent" Department of Alcoholic Beverage Control in 1954, directly under the responsibility of the governor's office (Morgan, 1979). Pressure from industry lobbying groups also led to the creation of an Alcohol Beverage Appeals Board — a three-member body, appointed by the governor, with the authority to review and restrict the ABC Department's licensing power. Over the years, the Board has generally acted to limit the scope of the department's decisions, and the legislature has acted to further restrict the department's regulatory power (Mosher, 1979a, b; Morgan, 1980). Thus, the alcohol control reform of the 1950s resulted in a control agency with substantially reduced powers. The department has, as a result, pursued relatively minor retail violations. Throughout most of the study period, the agency retained an ideal vision of itself as an "honest cop," with no aspirations or jurisdictions over alcohol-related public health or welfare issues. Thus, the ABC Director strongly repudiated a suggestion in 1974, from the state Finance Department, that it adopt responsibility for "promoting temperance" (Clark and Owsley, 1974).

In 1975, a proposal by the new gubernatorial administration to combine the ABC and alcoholism treatment bureaucracies into a single state agency was overwhelmingly defeated in the legislature, where it was opposed by both beverage industry interests and the alcoholism treatment constituency. Thus, although there was a reform in the management of alcohol controls, the separation between issues of alcohol marketing policy and issues of alcohol problems continues to characterize California's system.

Control of Alcohol Retailing

After the repeal of Prohibition, California opted for a licensing system, whereby the state licenses private businesses to sell alcohol and places limits on the number, type, and location of licences. Despite delegating much authority to the county level on other issues, California has chosen to centralize alcohol control at the state level, strictly limiting local control of sales and licensing (Morgan, 1979; Mosher, 1979a, b). This contrasts with many states that permit local option and control. Centralized state control has insured the availability of alcohol throughout the entire state.

The stated purpose of California's alcohol beverage control system, in addition to the collection of revenues, is the "promotion of temperance" (California Business and Professions Code 23001). In actual practice, promoting temperance has been viewed primarily as a matter of regulating retail outlets (Mosher, 1979b). Through the 1960s, two important mechanisms for this purpose were the tied house and fair trade laws (Mosher, 1979b). Tied house laws prohibit vertical integration within the alcohol industry and establish a strict three-tier structure (producer, wholesaler, and retailer). Fair trade laws (which were ruled unconstitutional by the California Supreme Court in 1978) granted unique powers to the alcohol manufacturers. They required all wine and spirits producers (and brewers, if they so chose) to set minimum retail prices which the government would then enforce.

Both the tied house and fair trade laws were seen as promoting temperance because, in theory, they protected small retailers and deterred aggressive retail sales techniques. Tied house laws were justified as a means to keep producers from operating saloons, a practice that was viewed as having been a serious problem prior to Prohibition. (Mosher, 1979a, b; California Business and Professions Code 24749; California Beer Wholesalers Assn. vs. Alcoholic Beverage Control Appeals Board, 1971; Room, 1973). However, tied house laws also insulated the producers, and fair trade laws secured the economic growth of the wholesalers and producers by inflating prices and minimizing competition. Tied house laws, when originally enacted, tended to isolate retailers as the source of alcohol problems while ignoring producers' marketing and producing activities. They also helped, particularly in conjunction with related laws which strictly limited the number of wholesale and general retail licences, to maintain a stable, financially secure marketing structure. Beginning in the late 1950s, tied house laws have been altered by a series of special exceptions, resulting in a crazy quilt of regulations which maintains some but not all of the three-tier structure (Mosher, 1979a). Fair trade laws were developed in the 1930s, when the wine industry was plagued with chronic oversupply. Permitting the industries to administer their own prices proved to be an ideal instrument for stabilizing the growth of the industry overall (Bunce, 1979).

California also maintains other regulations designed at least in theory to promote temperance (Mosher, 1979b). These include the prohibition of sales to those under 21 and to those who are obviously intoxicated and the prohibition of nude dancing and restrictions on barmaid practices in on-sale premises. In fact, most enforcement efforts are geared to these regulations.

There were major changes in the composition of outlets during the study period. Bars became legal in 1955. Up to that time, on-premise sale of alcohol was permitted only in establishments which served food. Seasonal licences became increasingly prevalent in tourist areas, and special licences for a variety of groups and events were greatly expanded. Beer and wine outlets, strictly limited according to density of population until 1943, became readily available to a variety of businesses such as supermarkets, sports areas, fast food markets, and restaurants.

Although general licences (which permit sale of all types of alcoholic beverages) are restricted according to county population (one per 2,000 inhabitants on-sale, and one per 2,500 off-sale), the availability of all types of alcoholic beverages has increased throughout the study period. One important factor has been the growth in off-sale general licences for supermarkets and convenience stores which themselves have expanded considerably since 1950. These stores are also able to carry a larger shelf stock and a greater variety of alcohol beverages. Permissible locations for alcohol licences have also increased (Mosher, 1979b). During the late 1950s, the Board of Equalization was given broad discretion to determine the appropriateness of licence locations, and outlets were prohibited near universities, churches, and schools. Today, the ABC Department has far less discretion, and the location restrictions have been amended virtually out of existence.

The number of retail licences both in absolute terms and per 10,000 adult population (15 years and over) increased markedly between 1934 and 1942 (Mosher, 1979b). From 1942 to 1970, there was a steady decline in the number of licences per capita, as new and existing licences did not keep pace with the rapid increase in population (see Figure 1). Sharp declines in the number of on-sale beer-only and off-sale beer and wine licences accounted for most of this trend. Since 1975, there has been a slight increase, primarily due to a dramatic rise in the number of on-sale beer and wine licences (particularly restaurant licences). Beer and wine off-sale licences have also increased slightly. The number of both on-sale and off-sale general licences (spirits, beer, and wine) per capita have remained almost stable throughout the period, as the total number is carefully regulated on a per capita basis by the state. This has resulted in a steady increase in the absolute number of these establishments (Mosher, 1979b).

The changes in licence concentration reflect several trends. As alcohol purchases have shifted from on-premise to off-premise establishments (discussed below), the number of neighbourhood bars has declined sharply. Meanwhile, the makeup of off-sale premises has changed dramatically. Beer and wine, and often spirits, are regularly given very large shelf space in supermarkets and discount houses (Wittman, 1980). As retail availability has become more concentrated in California so too has the availability of alcoholic beverages.

FIGURE 1   *Number of Retail Outlets for Alcoholic Beverages Per 10,000 Members of the 15 Years and Older Population in California, 1950-1978*

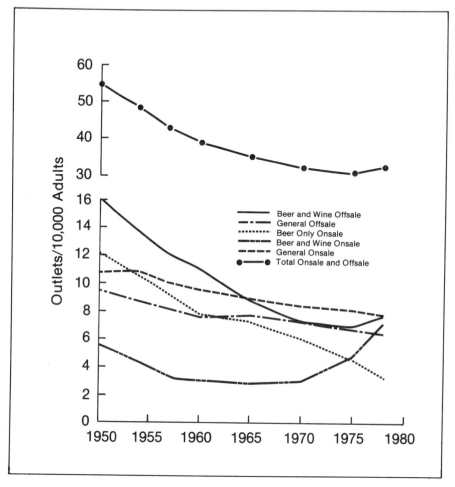

Source: James F. Mosher, "Retail Distribution of Alcoholic Beverages in California. Prepared for the Second Conference of the International Study of Alcohol Control Experiences, Asilomar, California. April, 1979.

While there are still restrictions on availability in California, which serve in part to preserve partial monopolies for business interests, the general effect of California control laws, particularly at the end of the study period, is to establish ready availability of alcohol. Liquor stores and bars, which must close only between 2 and 6 a.m., generally keep the longest hours of any businesses in their community. Wine and beer, particularly, are treated increasingly as ordinary foodstuffs, readily available in supermarkets and in "convenience" late-hours stores. Whatever the official structure of the control laws, there are few places in the world with greater *de facto* availability of alcohol, day or night, than California.

Taxing Policies

Trends in alcohol excise taxation reflect the economic interests that California and federal governments have in the alcohol industries. Repeal was enacted during the Depression, partly in order to raise desperately needed government revenues. This fiscal interest declined significantly in the period after 1950; in fact the proportion of alcohol tax to total tax revenue has declined steadily since Repeal at both the federal and state levels (Morgan, 1978b). Further, although the total tax collected (in dollar amounts) has more than doubled at both levels of government, the increases are caused as much by increased sales as by increased tax rates, particularly at the federal level. The federal government raised alcohol tax rates 15% in 1951 (in part to fund the Korean War) but has kept the rate constant since that time. California increased spirits taxes 250% and beer taxes 100% between 1950-1975, but has kept taxes for table wine at a penny a gallon, making California wine tax 10 to 80 times less than for other states. For both the state and national governments, revenue collected on a given volume of alcohol has, in most cases, actually declined in real dollars during the study period due to inflation. In California, the industry has been particularly successful in its efforts to prevent, or at least limit, tax increases (Bunce, 1976; Morgan, 1978b).

Concentration of Production

Between 1950 and 1979, alcohol production on the national level was characterized by increased concentration and integration. At the opening of this period, only spirits were being marketed nationally. By its close, beer and wine had also become affixed to national marketing networks, a change achieved typically through corporate mergers and the increasing concentration of production in a smaller number of large firms.

The eight largest brewers, which accounted for 30% of the U.S. beer market in 1947, controlled 70% by 1972. In 1950, there were 407 breweries nationwide, but by 1975 there were only 117. Concentration of wine production followed a similar course. Eight wineries controlled 68% of the U.S. market in 1972, compared to only 42% in 1947. The spirits industry, which was already highly concentrated in 1947 (the eight largest firms controlling 86% of the U.S. market), actually showed a slight diversifying trend, but remained concentrated with the largest eight firms still controlling 73% of the market (Mottl, 1979).

At the same time, the boundaries between the wine and spirits sectors had broken down. The general trend toward corporate mergers during this period included the alcohol industries, where it was spurred by the deteriorating condition of the former centrepiece of the spirits business — its whisky trade — and by the general economic climate which required larger economies of scale to maintain both profit margins and market share. Seagram's, Heublein, and National Chemical and Distillers led a move to buy out wine firms, followed closely by multinational food marketers such as Pillsbury and Nestle (Bunce, 1979).

The smaller firms that were forced out — and the trade press — claimed that bribery payoffs were an important strategy in this process. Chains of grocery stores, eating places, hotels, airlines, and sport concessionaires are mentioned as the main focus of bribery efforts aimed at alcohol retailers. Spirits distributors fought for market shares and shelf space through a variety of illegal beverage practices that Foremost-McKesson — California's largest spirits wholesaler and probably the largest in the U.S. — defended as being "consistent with competitive practices in the industry" (Burck, 1977).

The federal government took little action despite the evidence of illegal activities on the part of the large firms. Only one federal anti-trust suit against any beer or wine producer was filed between 1950-1975, when most of the alleged illegal practices took place. Yet Foremost-McKesson, Seagram's (the largest spirits multinational), Anheuser-Busch (the world's largest brewer), and Gallo (the largest vintner), have all recently admitted to substantial political payoffs, bribes, or similar illegal marketing practices during that time (*San Francisco Chronicle,* 1979; *New York Times,* 1975, 1978; *Wall Street Journal,* 1976). The federal government, in exchange for these admissions, has permitted the companies to keep secret the nature and extent of the illegal practices and has, except in the Seagram's case, imposed only light fines. (The fact that Seagram's is a Canadian-based firm may have been a factor in its sentence.)

The state of California has done even less to confront illegal producer practices. Virtually no enforcement action has ever been taken against any California producer by the California ABC Department. Legislative action and state court decisions have at least encouraged, if not mandated, an ABC enforcement focus aimed primarily at the retail level. For example, the state legislature has imposed a ceiling of $5,000 as a maximum fine against licencees, an inconsequential penalty against producers. Although the ABC could, in theory, revoke or suspend a producer's licence, neither the ABC nor its predecessor, the Board of Equalization, has ever done so. Instead, California's ABC enforcement activity has remained primarily focused on retail practice issues: drinking by minors, preventing immoral practices in licensed retail establishments, and the trading in retail licences (Mosher, 1979a, b).

Alcohol Takes Its Place in a Consumption-Priming Economy

The development of national marketing networks was speeded by social changes occurring outside of the alcohol supply-demand interface. New mechanisms for national mass marketing invited such exploitation, and producers of most consumer goods, from soap to cars and oil, responded similarly.

Alcohol marketing over this period was principally a competition between beer and spirits, which account for roughly 80% of absolute alcohol consumption in California. The period opens in 1950 with Californians drinking most of their alcohol in the form of spirits, and closes with beer drawing ahead, spirits having lost market share chiefly to wine (see Figure 2). National television advertising — now seen by the industry as a key activator of consumer demand — played an important role in this competition. Beer advertising grew enormously (66%) with the introduction of television in 1950-1955, although per capita beer consumption in California declined slightly during these years. Over the next decade (1955-1965), beer advertising increased, but only slowly, matched by consumption increases which took off after 1967. Beer advertising declined somewhat during the early 1970s but experienced rapid growth after 1975 (from $100 million in 1974 to $301 million in 1978) (*Bottom Line*, 1978, 1979; Mosher and Wallack, 1979a).

Spirits producers, on the other hand, excluded themselves entirely from radio and television advertising by intra-industry trade agreements formed in the 1950s under threat of federal legislation (Mosher and Wallack, 1979a). Nevertheless, spirits producers and wholesalers initially made a relatively greater investment in advertising than did beer interests, channeling their funds into billboards and financing a proliferating magazine market. Spirits advertising increased most dramatically from 1950-1955, a period of declining per capita spirits consumption, with advertising growing more slowly from 1955-1965, and declining thereafter in real dollars. Thus, by the mid-1970s, spirits interests were spending, on the average, 80% of what the beer industry spent on advertising, giving up parity largely because of losses in market share and profit margins (Liquor Handbook, 1955-1976).

The wine industry is centred in California and was isolated from most of alcohol's corporate and financial infrastructure during the first half of this period. Thus, it was the last to experience the impact of economic concentration, national distribution, mass marketing, and advertising. All of these factors have begun to reshape the industry since 1967, fueling and fueled by a substantial growth in wine consumption which occurred over the same time (Bunce, 1979). National distribution and national advertising have contributed to greater product differentiation and greater availability. This impact is more significant for the national wine market than for the market in California, because wine distribution and advertising has always been more extensive in California than in the rest of the United States.

Wine's advertising has been overwhelmingly concentrated in broadcast media (Wine Marketing Handbook, 1978). It has been substantially less than its share of the alcohol market, but has shown considerable growth since 1967 (Mottl, 1979). Yet throughout the 1970s, even at its peak in 1975, wine's advertising share was barely more than half its market share. Wine advertising is still checked by two factors: limits on wine availability (outside California), and autonomous shifts in consumer preference signalled by the industry's inability to maintain demand for its higher proof (18%+) products despite disproportionate advertising expenditures over the first half of this period.

Neither the California nor the federal government chose to interfere with this overall increase in alcohol advertising. Even though the explosion of alcohol advertising in the 1950s was focused on television, itself a regulated medium, no significant new federal advertising standards or regulations for alcohol advertising were adopted. The U.S. Congress threatened on several occasions to regulate aspects of alcohol advertising, and various states (other than California) passed advertising restrictions. Although these actions limited the scope of the alcohol industries' advertising tactics the industries were, for the most part, allowed to determine and control their overall advertising strategies (Mosher, 1979c). The reason for this lies, at least partly, with the producers' sophistication in matters of marketing strategy, self-regulation, and public image (Morgan, 1980).

Changing Products Reinforce Changing Consumer Tastes

Beer, wine, and spirits suppliers each successfully experimented with product differentiation during this period. The spirits market became more diversified between 1950 and 1979, with "white goods" (vodka, tequila, and rum) cutting into whisky sales. Furthering this trend was a simultaneous "recipe" promotion in spirits advertising, suggesting an infinite variety of mixed drinks (which themselves became available in bottles and cans) tailored to the individual and the occasion (Liquor Handbook, 1955-1976).

Beer and wine producers followed suit, the spirits industry's experience being interpreted as evidence that product differentiation tends to expand consumption, and thus has an additive, rather than substitutive effect. The promotion of fruit-flavoured sweet wines, "light" low-calorie beers (at lower alcohol contents than traditional wines and beers), and stronger beers (malt liquors) began in the late 1960s and early 1970s, following the distilled spirits producers' moderately successful marketing of canned mixed drinks (margaritas, pina coladas, etc.). These new beer and wine drinks were very successful initially, although the market for fruit-flavoured wines declined sharply by 1975.

Product differentiation is best illustrated by examining labelling practices, particularly in the spirits industry. Although the top 25 spirits labels account for an estimated 40% of the spirits market, the total number of alcohol beverage labels registered in California by 1975 topped 26,000, a large percentage of these being spirits labels. In many cases, one product is marketed under numerous labels. Fair trade laws also contributed to the proliferation, by encouraging discounted "house labels."

Based on its market research, the industry believed that drinking occasions were increasing, that new and occasional drinkers were the source of market growth, and that drinking patterns were changing from "purposeful" to "temperate" (Liquor Handbook, 1976). Sales of high-proof sweet or fortified wine — a beverage type associated since Prohibition with the "biggest-bang-for-the-buck" market — declined steadily. In addition, there was an increased preference for mixed drinks (lower-proof) and colourless, almost tasteless and odorless vodka over whiskys. Marketing analysts explained this trend as expressing new consumer preferences for diluted alcohol — i.e. relaxing but non-inebriating beverages. The growing frequency of consumption was claimed to derive from increases in leisure time and from specific increases in home entertainment in the late 1950s and dining out in the late 1960s (Liquor Handbook, 1976).

All of these trends — in "lightness," in mixing (diluting) alcohol with other beverages, in expanding the propriety of drinking alcohol to more frequent and new occasions (plane travel, sports audiences), in differentiating labels, brands, and products — were heavily promoted as themes of industry advertising as quickly as they were introduced and/or detected. Not all of these marketing strategies were effective. For instance, light whiskys were introduced in 1972 to defend against the inroads of Scotch and Canadian whiskys as well as "white goods" — only after whisky distillers had succeeded in pushing through federal legal changes in their own standards (Liquor Handbook, 1976). Considered a financial failure, they were largely withdrawn from the market by 1975. As discussed earlier, "pop" wines, which led a leap in wine consumption in the late 1960s, had by 1975 declined substantially, and many were withdrawn. Nevertheless, on balance, these trends had an important impact on industry practices during the study period.

Conclusion

In structuring the market for alcohol, control of the industries has come through the state rather than by the state. California's and the federal government's principal regulatory role in the period can be seen as that of mediator of both horizontal (inter-industry) and vertical (intra-industry) rivalries and conflicts. Although California has the power to restrict and control all segments of the industry, the power is largely not exercised to control aggregate consumption of alcohol.

The accommodation or facilitation of the industries' interests by state and federal control policies is illustrated in a number of other ways. For instance, federal regulations on whisky were amended in 1968 when the industry saw them as limiting their marketing strategies (Liquor Handbook, 1976). Under the banner of agriculture research and promotion, California appropriated public funds to develop new wine grape hybrids tailored to each of the state's micro-climates; until 1975, collected a producer's tax which the wine industry could use for lobbying, advertising, and promotion; collected and reported crop and related wine grape industry statistics at taxpayers' expense; and funded development of the mechanical grape harvester, thus reducing labour costs and weakening the bargaining position of agriculture labour (Bunce, 1979; Amerine, 1971; Olmo, 1976; Winkeler, 1973).

ALCOHOL CONSUMPTION IN CALIFORNIA, 1950-1980

The United States currently ranks near the median when compared with 30 or so countries for which overall alcohol consumption statistics are readily available (Hyman et al., 1980). California in 1976 showed a 25% higher consumption per capita aged 15 and over than the U.S. generally (U.S. National Institute on Alcohol Abuse and Alcoholism, 1978a). Among states without substantial distortion by tourism or crossborder buying, only Alaska showed a considerably higher consumption. In international comparisons, California is well above the median level of consumption.

The changes which occurred in California's aggregate consumption from 1950 to 1979 followed the same general pattern as the U.S. as a whole (Hyman et al., 1980; Collins and Milkes, 1980; Collins, 1980a). In terms of overall consumption, California figures show the same flatness as national figures until the late 1950s. California's consumption level started to rise in 1959, a little before a similar national change, and, after a slight dip in the mid-1970s, continued to rise through 1979. National consumption leveled off in the 1970s, although there was a slight rise again by the end of the decade.

The United States has a much higher proportion of total abstainers in the population than other countries with equivalent consumption levels (Armyr, 1978). In addition, unlike most other countries, the proportion of abstainers has stayed relatively stable in a period when per capita consumption rose substantially (60% drinkers among adults in 1950, 62% in 1960, 68% in 1974 [Gallup, 1977]). Unlike the U.S. as a whole, however, California is not extraordinary in its rate of abstainers, (80% drinkers among adults in 1960, and 82% in 1980 [Field Institute, 1960; Cameron, 1981]). Consumption per drinker in California is thus nearly the same as consumption per drinker in the U.S. as a whole.

As for beverage choice, both beer and spirits consumption in California started rising in the late 1950s, with spirits consumption levelling off after 1969 at approximately 4.3 litres of ethanol per capita while beer consumption continued to rise. By the mid 1970s, beer consumption passed spirits (Figure 2). California is often thought of as a wine-drinking state, and indeed Californians drink more than twice as much wine per capita as the national average. Nonetheless, wine accounted for only about one-fifth of total alcohol consumption in California during the study period. Wine consumption stayed quite stable until 1968 and then rose throughout the 1970s (Collins and Milkes, 1980; Collins, 1980a).

FIGURE 2   *Apparent Per Capita Consumption of Various Alcoholic Beverages in Litres of Absolute Alcohol Per Year by Members of the 15 Years and Older Population in California, 1950-1979*

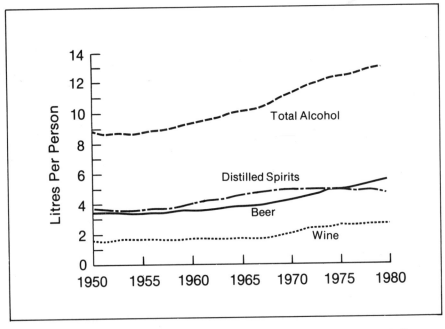

Sources: Gary Collins and John Milkes. "Aggregate Consumption of Alcoholic Beverages in California — Some Quantitative and Qualitative Changes, 1950-1975." Berkeley: Social Research Group, University of California. March, 1980.

Gary Collins. "Aggregate Consumption of Alcoholic Beverages in California — Some Quantitative and Qualitative Changes: An Update of Selected Tables, 1976-1979. Berkeley: Social Research Group, University of California. August, 1980.

Trend data in terms of ethanol content for general beverage types disguise some substantial changes emerging within each type, particularly the trend toward beverages of lower alcohol content. In California, the most dramatic change was in wine consumption: in 1950 more than twice as much fortified wine as table wine was sold, while over five times as much table wine as fortified wine was sold in 1975. This huge shift towards lighter alcohol content wines reflected substantial changes in the social definition and position of wine drinking.

Spirits consumption was also shifting to more dilute forms of alcohol, a phenomenon which began in the 1950s and accelerated rapidly after 1970 (Collins and Milkes, 1980). By 1979, the majority of major spirits brands, except Scotch and Canadian whiskys, had been reduced from 43%, or higher, to 40% alcohol (Collins, 1980a). Although stronger beers (malt liquors) and imported beers were promoted in this period, light beers, with a lower alcoholic content than regular beer, have become a more important market phenomenon, particularly since 1975.

Although no data specific to California are available, drinking patterns in the state undoubtedly mirrored a major change in national drinking habits during the study period. In the late 1940s, 90% of all alcohol was sold "on-premises" (in bars and restaurants); by 1970, the proportion was one-third (Kluge, 1971). This shift meant a substantial drop in the effective price of alcohol to the consumer. As a rough estimate, alcohol in 1979 would have been from two to six times as expensive when bought by the drink in a bar as when bought by the bottle. The change also reflected a substantial broadening of the situations in which drinking was considered an appropriate activity — drinking became less enclaved and more a part of everyday activities.

Drinking Patterns and Norms among the General Population

There are relatively little data available for California on the distribution of drinking among the population, let alone on trends in drinking patterns. Available information for California must thus be rounded out with data for larger areas (the U.S. and its regions) and for smaller (e.g. San Francisco).

A study of U.S. drinking patterns for the period 1964 to 1971 (Room and Beck, 1974) found that the only major change in drinking patterns was an increase for both sexes in the proportion of drinkers who drank fairly heavily, at least occasionally. Other patterns — frequent heavy drinking, infrequent drinking, and abstaining, etc. — did not show large changes. An analysis of a series of commercial surveys of the U.S. general population conducted in 1971-1976 showed relatively stable drinking patterns, with some tendency for heavier drinking to increase among men but not among women during the period (U.S. National Institute on Alcohol Abuse and Alcoholism, 1978b).

A trend analysis of the adult population in California for the period 1974 to 1980 (Cameron, 1981) found that there were slight increases (on the order of 2%-3%) at both ends of the drinking continuum — among frequent heavy drinkers as well as among infrequent drinkers and abstainers — and a decrease in the middle — among less frequent heavy drinkers and light drinkers (Table 1). These shifts in drinking patterns among the population as a whole were more characteristic of men's drinking than of women's. Women exhibited little change in the frequent heavy drinking end of the continuum, but did reveal a decrease in the middle categories and an increase in infrequent drinking. Thus, a slight increase in heavy drinking between 1974 and 1980 was tentatively suggested for men in California, but the opposite was true for women — among women in California there was a movement toward infrequent drinking during the period 1974 to 1980. These trends in drinking patterns among men and women in California were similar to those reported for the U.S. as a whole during the first half of the 1970s (U.S. National Institute on Alcohol Abuse and Alcoholism, 1978b).

It has generally been found both in the U.S. and in California that drinking is more common among men than women and among the young than the old, and less common in the lowest income and education groups than in higher status groups (Cahalan and Room, 1974; Clark and Midanik, 1980; Cameron, 1981). Frequent heavy drinking is also more common among men and among younger persons. Both the 1974 and 1980 surveys of the California adult population found this to be the case. However, frequent heavy drinking among youth (aged 18 to 24) in California appears to have declined between 1974 and 1980 (Cameron, 1981).

In 1974, the proportion of frequent heavy drinkers among blue collar and white collar workers was quite similar. As a result of a large increase in frequent heavy drinking during the six-year period, blue collar workers had almost twice as many frequent heavy drinkers (19%) as white collar workers (10%) in 1980. Frequent heavy drinking did not vary substantially by educational status. Despite the history of Southern California as "dry" during the Temperance era and Northern California as "wet" (Ostrander, 1957), few sectional differences in drinking patterns appear to be evident during this period.

American drinking norms vary not only according to the status of the drinker but also according to the situation involved (Room and Roizen, 1973). While drinking on the job is allowed and even expected in some specific occupations, drinking is generally proscribed at work. In fact, drinking is used as a signal for ending times of serious responsibility. Drinking in family situations probably increased during the study period, but parental responsibilities are generally seen as inhibiting drinking. Relatively heavy drinking is not officially approved by a majority for any drinking situation, but is most tolerable in a party situation or at a bar with friends. Alcohol is commonly a medium for gestures of friendship: drinks are offered when friends visit; buying someone a drink is a conventional friendly gesture; guests often bring wine or other alcohol when invited to dinner; a gift bottle of liquor between business associates is regarded as a friendly gesture not constituting a bribe.

TABLE 1   *Drinker Typology by Sex, 1974 and 1980 (in percent)*

Drinker Typology	1974			1980		
	Total	Males	Females	Total	Males	Females
(n)	(980)	(412)	(568)	(1,016)	(442)	(574)
Frequent heavy drinkers (Drinks some alcohol at least weekly and drinks five or more drinks at least once weekly)	9	16	4	12	19	5
Weekly moderate drinkers (Drinks some alcohol at least weekly and drinks five or more drinks occasionally but not as often as once a week)	23	30	16	22	29	16
Monthly moderate drinkers (Drinks some alcohol 1 to 3 times a month and drinks five or more drinks occasionally but not as often as once a week)	11	12	10	7	9	6
Weekly light drinkers (Drinks some alcohol at least weekly and never drinks five or more drinks at a sitting)	13	13	14	12	10	13
Monthly light drinkers (Drinks some alcohol 1 to 3 times a month, but never drinks five or more drinks at a sitting)	10	6	13	9	8	10
Infrequent drinkers (Drinks some alcohol less often than monthly)	18	13	23	20	12	27
Abstainers (Did not drink in the past year)	16	11	21	18	13	23

Source: Tracy Cameron, "Alcohol and Alcohol Problems: Public Opinion in California, 1974-1980." Social Research Group Report C31. Paper prepared for the California Department of Alcohol and Drug Programs, February, 1981.

Alcohol has almost certainly become more a part of everyday life in the study period. California abstainers are likely to give inconsequential or health rationales for not drinking (Knupfer and Room, 1970); moral fervour for abstention tends to be rare and only occurs within fairly narrow religious and health-cult circles. But Californians, like Americans generally, see alcohol as having potentially powerful adverse effects (Aarens et al., 1977; Levine, 1977). Alcohol is popularly thought to diminish responsibility for (without excusing) serious crimes like homicide and to explain family violence; it is readily viewed as the cause of chronic failures in family and work roles.

POPULAR SENTIMENT ON DRINKING AND DRINKING PROBLEMS

Public attitudes about drinking and drinking problems during the study period were influenced by two formidable interest groups, the alcohol beverage industry and the National Council on Alcoholism and associated organizations. In earlier times, public attitudes about drinking were strongly affected by temperance ideology, supported by longstanding temperance organizations with grass roots religious and community affiliations. But in the post-war period, the institutions and public presence of the temperance movement withered. The rise of the alcoholism disease model in the 1940s, and the corresponding trend toward professionalizing the handling of alcohol problems, transferred the onus of the problem from "the bottle" to "the man." The disenfranchisement of temperance thought was generally complete by 1960. Public information programmes of the alcoholism treatment movement became the dominant alcohol ideology in the public arena.

It is relatively easy to document and analyze the efforts of the various interest groups to set the tone of public discourse and form public opinion on alcohol issues. It is much harder to measure and analyze the structure and weight of public opinion itself. This difficulty is itself a finding: data on public opinion are sparse because alcohol issues were generally low on the horizon of public discourse and consciousness throughout the study period. In the relative vacuum thus created, interest groups held considerable sway, although events often reflected bureaucrats' and legislators' sense of limits on how far policy could diverge from latent public sentiment.

Public Opinion Polls on Alcohol Issues

Reflecting the fact that alcohol issues were largely removed from public debate during this period in California, state-wide political opinion polls on major public issues included only a very small number of alcohol-related questions (Mitchell, 1980). From 1950 to 1979, only one state-wide initiative concerned with alcohol appeared. Placed on the ballot by the legislature in 1956 at the request of the beverage industry, the measure removed the requirement that bars sell food. Although written in such a way as to appear to be a "dry" sponsored measure (by incorporating a clause transferring the prohibition of drinking under the age of 21 from the statute law to the state constitution), it barely passed.

The *de facto* "wettening" of California, which was actually accomplished by legislation and regulation in the period, often occurred in the face of dryer but politically unfocused popular sentiments. The clearest example of this was the abolition of the ban on alcohol sales on general election days in 1961. A 1960 survey had indicated that 85% of California adults were opposed to this measure (Field Institute, 1960).

A general "dryness" of popular sentiment on drinking was expressed in other survey responses. During this period — 1973-1975 — three-quarters of respondents thought 18-20 year-olds should be allowed "to incur debts and be legally responsible for them," and 57% said they should be "allowed to gamble at state licensed race tracks," but only 50% approved of allowing 18-20 year-olds to purchase liquor (Field Institute, 1973, 1974, 1975). The even split on the liquor purchase item represented the zenith of popular support for lowering the drinking age. Only 32% gave an affirmative answer to this survey item in 1971 (Field Institute, 1971), and only 30% were favourable to a similar item in 1979 (Field Institute, 1979).

The most complete survey information on California popular sentiment in the period 1950-1980 comes from Fieldscope questions asked in 1974 (Cahalan, Roizen, and Room, 1976) and repeated in 1980 (Cameron, 1981). Although results indicate that the public was concerned about the "wettening" of the state, alcohol was not considered a major issue. Respondents were asked whether governments "should do more" than was currently being done for each of several specific prevention and treatment measures. There was a strong agreement with offering treatment for drinking problems to those who want help (90% in 1974 and 88% in 1980) and for being tougher with drunk drivers (88% in both years). Substantial minorities wanted bars to close earlier (41% in 1974 and 36% in 1980) and to make drinking more expensive by raising taxes (38% in 1974 and 36% in 1980); however, only 8% in 1974 and 9% in 1980 wanted total prohibition of alcohol. However, in the 1980 survey, 40% supported putting labels on all alcoholic beverages warning that "Too much drinking can be harmful to your health and happiness," and 35% supported the prohibition of all advertising of wine, beer, and spirits.

In an overall ranking of major societal problems, alcohol problems were rated at the lower end by both California samples. Asked to compare whether "alcoholism and excessive drinking" was more severe than each of a list of nine other problems, respondents ranked only two problems in 1974, and three in 1980 as less severe than alcohol problems (discrimination against women, cigarette smoking, and, in 1980, racial troubles). Inflation, environmental pollution, the energy shortage, unemployment, and drug use and drug traffic all ranked above alcohol problems in both years. Between 1974 and 1980, economic problems — particularly inflation, unemployment, and the energy shortage — were seen as increasingly more important than alcoholism. Similar results were obtained in U.S. surveys between 1972 and 1974 which found that alcoholism and drinking ranked far below such issues as inflation, crime, and drugs as "major problems facing your community today" (Louis Harris and Associates, 1974).

The Field surveys offer some information on the degree to which social problems were defined as alcohol problems in the popular mind. Respondents were asked, for a list of seven problems, how serious they were for American society, and to what extent alcohol or alcoholism was a factor in each. Between 1974 and 1980, for all seven social and health concerns there was at least some increase in the extent to which alcohol was viewed as a major factor. Thus, despite the decline in importance of alcoholism itself as a social problem, alcohol was more often seen as a major factor in other sorts of social problems, particularly traffic accidents. Drunk driving substantially dominated the public consciousness as the most serious alcohol problem. California opinion appeared to reflect national sentiment in the U.S. in this respect. A 1971 nation-wide Harris Poll showed 77% of adult Americans agreeing that "the worst danger of drinking is the traffic accidents it causes" (Louis Harris and Associates, 1971).

For most of the public, alcohol issues conjured up only a vague unease, general tolerance for and perhaps support of treatment efforts, and a conviction, especially after 1960, that something should be done about drunk driving.

Public Discussion of Alcohol Issues

Research on the structure of public discourse on alcohol issues in the study period is limited to content analyses of two sources, the *San Francisco Chronicle* and the U.S.-wide *Reader's Guide to Periodical Literature*. The *Chronicle* index shows considerable attention to alcohol control issues such as licence availability, the question of dry zones around university campuses, and scandals and reforms in the control system. Articles on these issues were quite common between 1955 and 1967 but tapered off considerably after 1967 (averaging about 12 per year between 1967 and 1975). Articles on alcoholism as a general problem were never frequent (less than 10 articles per year for most years) with attention to this area peaking in the early 1960s. Articles related to treatment issues — generally presenting state plans and programs — were most frequent in the early

1950s when the legislature was establishing state alcoholism treatment agencies. Media attention to drunk driving problems increased during the mid-1960s (Morgan, 1980).

An analysis of the *Reader's Guide to Periodical Literature* shows substantial attention to alcohol-related topics; there were almost 3,000 relevant articles in popular magazines and periodicals in the U.S. between 1950 and 1975 (Smith, 1980). The most prevalent subjects were related to alcoholic beverages as consumer goods and to the beverage industries. Discussions of alcoholic beverages, generally more positive than negative in tone, showed a steady increase. Articles on alcohol problems such as drunk driving and teenage drinking and on the alcoholic beverage industry were much more prevalent than treatment/rehabilitation or control issues. This reflects, at least in part, a continuing focus on alcohol problems as individual and private rather than public or state issues.

Articles referenced in the *Reader's Guide* often represented the views of those interested or most involved in supporting a particular image of alcohol, that is, the beverage industries and the alcoholism treatment movement. The National Council on Alcoholism, for instance, had from its beginning a major focus on public relations. The Council saw as an important task the placing of articles reflecting its purpose in as many popular magazines and periodicals as possible. The beverage industries, besides spending several million dollars each year on advertising, devoted much time and energy to promoting their image. Until the end of the 1970s, the two interest groups generally did not work at cross-purposes: the alcoholism movement tended to eschew "political" questions like alcohol availability, and the beverage industries recognized the emphasis on "the man" rather than "the bottle" as harmonizing with the industries' interests.

Overall, public discourse in California tended away from discussions of alcohol control or treatment as political issues for public concern and decision-making, and towards a much more passive and depoliticized image of the citizen's relation to alcohol issues. In the daily diet of news and features, discussions of alcohol availability shifted from political decisions about the control structure to "consumer education" on wine releases and taste comparisons. Similarly, the political dialogue around the establishment of state alcohol problems responsibility and other reform efforts in the early 1950s had given way by the 1970s to public information on "alcoholism" from professional sources.

ALCOHOL-RELATED PROBLEMS

There was a dramatic shift in the social handling of alcohol-related problems in California in the period 1950-1979, reflecting U.S. trends but within California's particular circumstances. The change is

usually summarized as a shift from a criminal/legal rubric to a disease/
medical rubric — a description also applied to the social handling of other
intractable problems in American society (Room, 1978; Conrad and
Schneider, 1980). The changes were actually more multi-dimensional,
reflecting the net effects of numerous interacting currents:

Deinstitutionalization.   The 1960s and 1970s were marked by a swing
away from the policy of segregating problem populations in large institutions and toward treatment in smaller institutions within the home community. A large segment of the state mental hospital system was dis-
mantled and partly replaced by community mental health centres and
board-and-care facilities. To a small extent, the "drunk tank" in the local
gaol was replaced with pick-up services and detoxification facilities. The
"deinstitutionalization" scenario recurred throughout the social services
systems, sometimes accompanied by an increase in individualized case-
work.
     The deinstitutionalization movement was motivated ideologically
by growing concerns over individual liberties, and over the dehumanizing,
deviance-reinforcing atmosphere found in large institutions. A more conservative rationale for deinstitutionalization was the belief that it would
save money.

Fiscal crises and levels of government.   Local governments have traditionally had the primary governmental responsibility for social welfare services. Demands for expanded social programmes increased dramatically
during the study period, however, particularly so in the 1960s. Local jurisdictions were financially incapable of satisfying the perceived needs, and
new and enlarged programmes became dependent on federal and state
financing. Given their chronic fiscal crisis, local governments were only too
willing to give up jurisdiction — if the state or federal government were
willing to pay the bill.
     In the late 1970s, the "taxpayer's revolt" against property taxes
exacerbated the fiscal problems of local government and their dependence
on financing from above. In addition, moves to limit federal and state taxing powers generally threatened financing for governmental services.

Medicalization of deviance.   There is by now considerable sociological
literature on the shifting of a variety of social problems in the U.S. during
the last 30 years into a health/medical rubric (Conrad and Schneider,
1980). For alcohol-related problems, there was not necessarily a conviction
that doctors were the best equipped to handle the problem or that hospitalization was the best remedy. In fact, at the beginning of the period in
California, two major social institutions with custody over alcohol problems — mental hospitals and county general hospitals — already operated
under a medical rubric. Instead, the motivation was to establish a "public

health" rubric for alcohol problems — a move which offered the greatest possibility for humane treatment.

There is, in fact, a conflict between the medical *rubric* for the management of alcohol problems and the generally nonmedical *nature* of the treatment. The basic therapy for alcoholism is verbal persuasion, often delivered by nonprofessionals, about the nature of the client's problem (Roizen, 1977). Halfway houses, "social model" detoxification units, behavioural therapy clinics, drunk driver re-education programs, are all examples of essentially nonmedical services which deal with alcohol problems under a medical rubric — i.e. with government funding from a health agency, perhaps with coverage from group health insurance, and sometimes under the formal leadership of a physician.

Individualization of problem definition. The expansion of social welfare services and the medicalization of deviance promoted the tendency to define social problems as individual rather than societal (structural) failings. Attributing social problems to the individual's failure or inability to control his/her drinking behaviour is a particularly strong avenue for the individualization of problem definition, a rubric under which even political conservatives could support increases in state services.

The Diversification of Alcohol Problems Management

The interplay of the factors outlined above complicates the history of the institutional handling of alcohol problems in California in the study period. At the state level, the public health-oriented alcoholism movement, which started in the eastern U.S. in the mid-1940s, did not have a substantial public presence in California until the mid-1950s when the State Alcoholic Rehabilitation Commission was formed. The Commission was a byproduct of legislative investigations of scandals in the alcoholic beverage control system. It established several pilot alcoholism treatment clinics state-wide and began to examine the handling of alcohol problems in existing state institutions. The functions of the Commission were abruptly transferred by the Legislature in 1957 to the State Department of Public Health, and later to the State Department of Vocational Rehabilitation where they remained without a substantial increase in state-funded programs for a decade (Morgan, 1980). After 1967, there was a massive infusion of federal funds for treatment, and a concomitant (somewhat surprising and unexplained) rise in state funds.

In an effort to organize the expanding number of treatment programs and facilities and to qualify for financial support from the federal government, the California state legislature created the Office of Alcohol Program Management (OAPM) in 1970 (California Office of Alcoholism, 1975, 1976; California Office of Alcohol Program Management, 1974). The OAPM was set up to function as the single state agency in contact with the federal government, while coordinating treatment services provided by various state and local facilities. This was accompanied by the growing political presence of an alcoholism field based increasingly in the constituency of public presence and private service "providers" rather than in community or public interest movements.

Many developments were neither controlled by nor mediated through the state government. Counties and cities, acting relatively autonomously, adopted a wide variety of institutional arrangements for handling alcohol problems in the court system (particularly with respect to public drunkenness), the health and mental health systems, and, to some extent, the welfare system. The fate of alcohol problems in county hospitals is largely uncharted, despite the role of these institutions as major providers of alcohol problem services at the beginning of the study period. The federal government also acted in a number of ways which did not involve the state. A large part of the U.S. alcoholism treatment establishment is in federally-funded Veterans Administration Hospital programmes. Similar direct entitlements exist for such categories as active-duty military and their families, Indians, and merchant seamen. Through the federal grants programmes, direct subventions are made to local private or public treatment, training, prevention, and research programmes, although treatment grants at least are increasingly subject to state influence.

A variety of new institutions for handling alcohol problems has also emerged and burgeoned. Halfway houses for alcoholics appeared in the 1950s as a relatively early and self-conscious element in the California treatment scene. Detoxification facilities, as mentioned, have existed in specific places in a variety of institutional settings. Recent court decisions have raised speculation that there may eventually be a state-wide system of such facilities. Scattered experiments have been made with drop-in centres, dry hotels, and even a few wet hotels on skid row, and there are some civilian pickup services for drunks, such as San Francisco's Mobile Assistance Patrol. Hotlines, which emerged to handle youth and drug culture problems and threatened suicides, have also served as referral sources for alcohol problems. The National Council on Alcoholism has operated referral services in most cities, primarily supported by "donations" from those referred. A large cadre of labour-management alcoholism consultants has arisen to advise on "industrial alcoholism programmes." A very large number of counsellors are employed in one or another form of drunk driver reeducation, financed by mandatory fees from those convicted and diverted to such reeducation or treatment.

In this patchwork "system," however, the most visible institution has become the publicly-funded alcoholism treatment centre, which usually offers a broad spectrum of therapies both on an inpatient and outpatient basis. Every county has a state-approved alcohol plan which provides for such categorical alcoholism treatment. A resurgent element on the scene is the private alcoholism clinic. While there have always been small clinics for discreetly drying out the wealthy, the extension, under governmental pressure, of group health insurance to cover alcoholism has created a new, profitable niche for treatment of working patients. A California-based corporation, CompCare, has been a pace-setter in this movement, leasing unused hospital wings for a relatively expensive ($8,000) inpatient program with an aggressive "public service" recruitment campaign.

By 1975, then, the surge of alcoholism treatment facilities had been greatly expanded over that available 25 years earlier. Services were offered at 559 outpatient clinics, recovery homes, and halfway houses, 150 general and psychiatric hospitals, 146 referral agencies, 166 employee alcoholism programmes, 2,824 Alcoholics Anonymous groups, 661 Al-Anon family groups, and 161 Alateen groups (California Office of Alcohol Program Management, 1974).

Finally, despite the proliferation of treatment facilities, California continues to rely on the criminal justice system to handle public inebriates, although to a significantly lesser degree than at the beginning of the study period. Beginning in the 1960s, alcoholism lobbies, court decisions, and federal policies all created pressures in California for a legal reform that would decriminalize public drunkenness. Partial legislation was passed in 1972, but it has proven ineffective (California Office of Alcoholism, 1975, 1976; California Office of Alcohol Program Management, 1974). Under its provisions, local jurisdictions may choose to commit public inebriates to a civil facility for 72 hours in lieu of bringing criminal charges. The state has been willing to fund pilot and demonstration projects in detoxification facilities, but has refused to assume from local governments any ongoing fiscal responsibility. As a result, only a few counties have opted for this programme while the majority have continued to rely on the criminal justice system.

Indicators of Alcohol Problems: Alcohol-Related Mental Hospital Commitments

Any interpretation of alcohol problem indicators must take account of major shifts in the management of alcohol-related problems, since the indicators reflect both the shifts in problem *policies,* and the shifts in the problematic behaviours or occurrences themselves. California legislation during the study period stiffened regulations so as to limit the number of all involuntary commitments to mental hospitals (including involuntary alcoholic commitments), and greatly discouraged treatment for alcoholism at state hospitals through fiscal disincentives for local referring agencies. By the early 1970s, the shift was so complete that the State

Department of Drug and Alcohol Abuse no longer systematically collected information on involuntary alcoholic commitments to state mental hospitals. For both California and the U.S., the number of alcoholics admitted to state and county mental hospitals declined during this period. Further, in California the proportion of all first admissions to these hospitals which were diagnosed as alcoholic, decreased from 20% to 6% between 1950 and 1972 (Figure 3).

FIGURE 3   *Mental Hospital Admissions for Alcoholism and Cirrhosis Mortality Per 100,000 Members of the 15 Years and Older Population in California, 1950-1978*

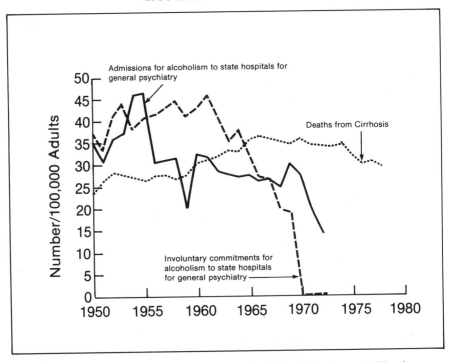

Sources: Tracy Cameron. "Tables on Alcohol-Related Problems, California 1950-1975." Prepared for Third Working Session of the International Study of Alcohol Control Experiences, Warsaw, Poland, April 1980.

Gary Collins. "Tables on Alcohol-Related Problems in California: An Update of Selected Tables 1976-1979." Berkeley: Social Research Group, School of Public Health, University of California, August 1980.

Alcohol-Related Mortality

Mortality statistics for California include three alcohol-related causes of death: cirrhosis of the liver, alcoholism/alcohol dependence, and alcoholic psychosis (U.S. Department of Health, Education, and Welfare, 1950-1978). Of these three, cirrhosis is by far the largest contributor to alcohol-related deaths in California. Between 1950 and 1978, total cirrhosis deaths increased from 1,714 to 4,346 (see Figure 3). This represents an increase from 1.74% of all mortality in California in 1950 to 2.47% in 1978. The cirrhosis mortality rates per 100,000 individuals for men and women rose from 30.7 and 17.0, respectively, to 42.8 and 21.7 in 1975. Trends in cirrhosis mortality relative to trends in alcohol consumption for the same time period show only minor fluctuations. Cirrhosis mortality per 100,000 litres of absolute alcohol increased from a low 2.4 in 1950 to 3.0 in 1966, after which it declined steadily to 2.0 in 1978 (Figure 6). Not all cirrhosis deaths, of course, are attributable to alcohol. However, careful study in San Francisco put the proportion due to alcohol at 93.7% (Puffer and Griffith, 1967), and it seems certain that the preponderance of cirrhosis deaths in California are alcohol-related.

Until quite recently, cirrhosis mortality, in the form of the Jellinek Estimation Formula, was used in official California reports to estimate rates of alcoholism in the state. However, there was relatively little attention to cirrhosis mortality as a problem in its own right.

Deaths officially listed as due to alcoholism/alcohol dependence fluctuated between 150 and 250 annually until 1965, when an increase began, resulting in 650 such deaths in 1979. Deaths due to alcoholic psychosis have shown no consistent trends, with the number of deaths fluctuating between 12 and 72 annually. These last two causes of death are most probably skewed toward skid row populations.

Alcohol-Related Arrests

California has experienced dramatic changes in both public drunkenness and drunk driving arrests since 1950. Caution should be exercised when interpreting these statistics, however, as arrest data are subject to reporting biases and discrepancies in alcohol-measurement, both across local jurisdictions and over time. As shown in Figure 4, per capita public drunkenness arrests have declined steadily since 1960, when the statistics were first collected on a state-wide basis, with the sharpest decline occurring in the later 1960s and early 1970s (California Department of Justice, 1950-1964, 1965-1978). Relative to trends in alcohol consumption, adult misdemeanour public drunkenness arrests declined during this period, from 249.1 arrests per 100,000 litres of absolute alcohol in 1960 to 97.3 in 1979 (Figure 6).

In the period 1950-1960, public drunkenness arrests appear to have been at a historic high in many large California cities (California Department of Public Health, 1964), where they served as a weapon in programmes of "urban renewal." The steady decline in arrests since then reflects the shift in both official and public attitudes and sentiments toward the decriminalization of public drunkenness. Decreases in the number of arrests have occurred despite the lack of effective decriminalization legislation in California.

In sharp contrast to public drunkenness, arrests for drunk driving have increased dramatically between 1960 and 1979 (Figure 4) (California Department of Justice, 1950-1964, 1965-1978). After increasing gradually until 1967, per capita adult misdemeanour drunk driving arrests rose markedly in 1968 and continued to climb rapidly until the peak year 1973, after which the energy crisis and reduced driving and speed limits contributed to a slow decline in per capita arrest rates. Relative to trends in alcohol consumption, adult misdemeanour drunk driving arrests increased from 37.6 per 100,000 litres of absolute alcohol in 1960 to 119.2 in 1979 (Figure 6).

FIGURE 4   *Adult Misdemeanour Arrests for Drunk Driving and Public Drunkenness Per 100,000 Members of the 15 Years and Older Population in California, 1950-1979*

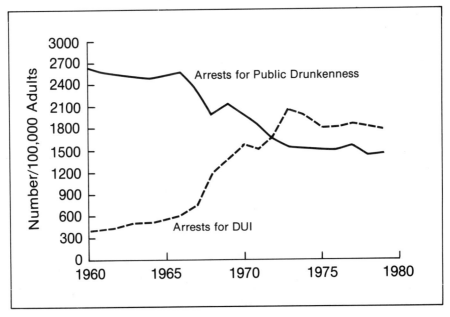

Sources: Tracy Cameron. "Tables on Alcohol-Related Problems, California 1950-1975." Prepared for Third Working Session of the International Study of Alcohol Control Experiences, Warsaw, Poland, April 1980.

Gary Collins. "Tables on Alcohol-Related Problems in California: An Update of Selected Tables 1976-1979." Berkeley: Social Research Group, School of Public Health, University of California. August 1980.

Several factors contributed to the sharp increase in the number of arrests for drunk driving in California in the late 1960s and early 1970s. Implied consent legislation, which increased policy authority to require roadside breath or blood alcohol tests, was enacted in California in 1966. The United States as a whole (as well as other North American and European countries) was focusing more intensely on the problem of drunk driving in the late 1960s and 1970s than it had in previous years. The Federal Highway and Safety Act of 1966 resulted in an elaborate nation-wide effort to reduce the problems of drinking and driving, including a range of programmes aimed specifically at increasing the level of police enforcement of drunk driving laws. Thus, the increased focus on drunk driving in

FIGURE 5   *Number of Drinking Drivers Involved in Traffic Accidents Per 100,000 Members of the 15 Years and Older Population in California, 1950-1979*

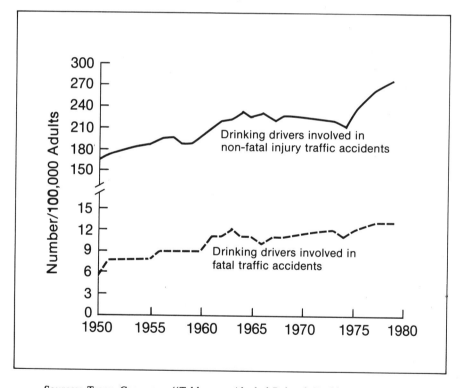

Sources: Tracy Cameron. "Tables on Alcohol-Related Problems, California 1950-1975." Prepared for Third Working Session of the International Study of Alcohol Control Experiences, Warsaw, Poland, 14-23 April 1980.

Gary Collins. "Tables on Alcohol-Related Problems in California: An Update of Selected Tables 1976-1979." Berkeley: Social Research Group, School of Public Health, University of California. August 1980.

the late 1960s and 1970s, and the various enforcement, arrest, and conviction policies it generated, strongly influenced the statistics on drunk driving arrests in California, and in the United States as a whole (Cameron, 1979).

Alcohol-Related Traffic Accidents

Serious traffic accidents — those involving at least some bodily injury — increased from 65,506 to 215,498 between 1950 and 1979 in California, while at the same time the number of registered vehicles climbed from more than 4 million to more than 16 million, and the annual number of vehicle miles driven rose from 41 trillion to more than 160 trillion by 1979. The death rate per 100 million miles driven decreased from 7.3 to 3.4 during this period, due in part to improved post-crash medical care and improved safety conditions in vehicles and roadways (California Department of Highway Patrol, 1950-1961, 1962-1965, 1966-1979).

There were some substantial changes in the proportion of serious traffic accidents which involved drinking drivers. The proportion of drivers in fatal accidents who had been drinking more than doubled, from 14% in 1950 to 33% in 1975. The rise was particularly sharp in 1973-1974, when the total miles driven and the overall rate of fatal accidents fell in the first shock of OPEC price rises and petroleum shortages. The proportion decreased somewhat to 30% in 1979. However, it must be kept in mind that fatal accidents account for only a slight proportion of all serious accidents — 4.1% in 1950 and only 2.2% in 1979. The role alcohol played in non-fatal injury accidents did not change markedly during the study period: the proportion of drinking drivers in such accidents decreased from 12.5% in 1950 to 10.5% in 1967, then increased by 1975 to stabilize at 13.1% in 1979 (California Department of Highway Patrol, 1950-1961, 1962-1965, 1966-1979).

These results might be interpreted as indicating that drinking-driving occasions proved to be less elastic than other driving occasions with respect to the gasoline price rises and shortages of 1973 and 1974. Figure 5 shows indeed that, on a per capita basis, fatal accidents involving drinking drivers have risen slowly and steadily from 6 to 13 per 100,000 in the period 1950-1979 — showing little responsiveness to the 1973-1974 shortages or to drunk driving enforcement efforts. The rate of nonfatal injury accidents involving drunk drivers (Figure 5) has also showed a long-term tendency to rise, at about the same rate both as alcohol consumption (Figure 6) and as the rise in non-drinking injury accidents. The drinking-related injury rise was arrested by the beginning of the period of maximum increase in drunk driving law enforcement activity (1966-1973, Figure 4), but resumed at a steeper rate after 1975.

FIGURE 6   *Rate of Occurrence for Various Alcohol Problems Per 100,000 Litres of Absolute Alcohol (Note that the vertical axis is logarithmic)*

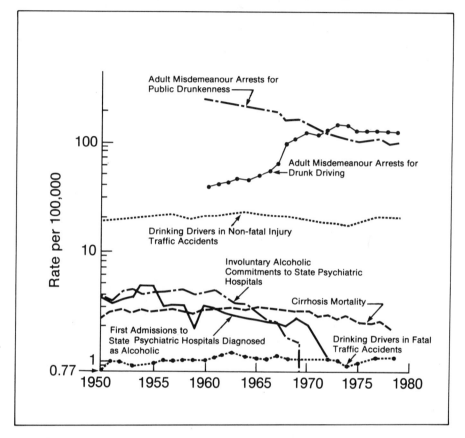

Sources: Tracy Cameron. "Tables on Alcohol-Related Problems in California, 1950-1975." Paper presentedat the Third Conference of the International Study of Alcohol Control Experiences, (ISACE), Warsaw, Poland, April 1980.

Gary Collins. "Tables on Alcohol-Related Problems in California: An Update of Selected Tables, 1976-1979." Berkeley: Social Research Group, University of California. August 1980.

Alcohol-Related Problems Relative to Consumption Levels

Figure 6 shows, on a semi-logarithmic scale, the relative prevalence of and trends in the various available social statistics on alcohol-related problems. The logarithmic vertical scale allows the presentation of indicators of very different orders of magnitude but, by the same token, in terms of visual impression, tends to flatten out substantial absolute changes in an indicator. It can be seen that there are large differences on the basis of the available statistics in the involvement of the state in different alcohol-related problems. By far the most frequent involvement is in alcohol-related arrests. The rates of alcohol-related injuries in traffic accidents and cirrhosis mortality also suggest a substantial involvement of the general health system in alcohol-related problems. As noted above, the state mental hospital system disappeared as a factor in handling alcohol problems during the study period.

The rates in Figure 6 are computed on a base of litres of alcohol rather than population. Since alcohol consumption grew relatively steadily during the study period (Figure 2), a figure computed on a population base looks very similar to Figure 6 — all lines would be slightly skewed upwards to the right. Given the base computation, a flat horizontal line on the graph would indicate a perfect temporal correlation between an alcohol problem indicator and the level of alcohol consumption — a pattern often interpreted as indicating a causal connection. However, our attention is directed instead to the question: In a period of rising consumption, did the problems associated with a given amount of drinking rise or fall? With the exception of indicators which reflect clear policy shifts (mental hospital admissions and drunk driving and public drunkenness arrests), the general answer seems to be that "problems per litre" held steady or fell.

Overall, alcohol-related problems in California have shown no unified trend over the past 30 years. Social policy decisions on the federal, state, and local levels have substantially influenced many of the indicators traditionally used to measure the magnitude of "alcohol problems" in California. Decreases in mental health hospital admissions for alcoholism and in public drunkenness arrests between 1950 and 1979 reflect changes in the national and state mental health care policy and the partial shifting of the public inebriate problem out of the criminal/legal arena to the medical arena. Likewise, the increases in drunk driving arrests and in drinking drivers involved in fatal traffic accidents reflect a nation-wide policy emerging in the late 1960s which placed greater emphasis on the problem of drinking and driving. Statistics on alcohol-related problems serve as indicators of social policy as well as indicators of the actual extent of problems serve as indicators of social policy as well as indicators of the actual extent of problems in California during this period.

CONCLUSION

The California alcohol control experience in the past 30 years is marked by several trends. First, the state's unique political, economic, and demographic environment must be taken into account. The young and mobile population, drawn into the state by the promise of an expanding economy and a new suburban lifestyle, set the stage both for changes in the nature of alcohol consumption and for increases in the availability of alcoholic beverages. Second, the period of the greatest demographic changes, from 1956 to 1970, was also marked by the greatest political changes in the alcohol control structure. The shift here was to narrow the focus of control, allowing the new state control structure to act increasingly as a conduit for and mediator between special interest lobbies. The third trend of increasing alcohol beverage availability, is related partially to the lessening political power of the state control system. Licence restrictions themselves were loosened, making beer and wine in particular much more available by the end of the study period. In addition, the nature of off-sale retail outlets changed as small retailers were replaced by large chain and convenience stores able to carry a much greater shelf stock of alcohol beverages.

Finally, the definition of alcohol problems during the study period changed, moving away from a prevention and alcohol control model and toward a professionalized medical/treatment model. This trend has resulted in a greatly expanded structure for managing alcohol problems, a specialized alcohol treatment profession, and a tremendous growth in federal and state fiscal responsibility for alcohol problem services. Meanwhile, the alcohol control system has become increasingly divorced from alcohol problems issues. The creation of the ABC Department in 1956 formalized a system which stressed economic management of, and mediation between, the various tiers of the alcohol industry with little regard to the department's potential role in managing and minimizing alcohol problems.

There have been some preliminary signs in the last five years that this trend may be reversing. Although proposals to integrate the alcohol control and alcohol problems departments were soundly defeated in the Legislature, current ABC Department policies reflect some concern that control decisions may influence the incidence of alcohol problems (Mosher and Wallack, 1979b; Wittman, 1980). Moreover, scholars have begun to study the relationships of control decisions to problems management. Several resulting studies indicate that alcohol control may be a source for new prevention strategies (Bruun et al., 1975; Wittman, 1980). The present study may be seen as one aspect of this new trend.

REFERENCES

Aarens, M. et al., 1977, *Alcohol, Casualties and Crime.* Report C18. Social Research Group, School of Public Health, University of California, Berkeley.

Amerine, M.A., 1971, *The University of California and the State's Wine Industry.* California Wine Industry Oral History Series. Regional Oral History Office of the Bancroft Library, University of California, Berkeley.

Anderson, D., 1942, Alcohol and Public Opinion. *Quarterly Journal of Studies on Alcohol,* 3(3): 376-392.

Armyr, G., 1978, Number of Total Abstainers from Alcohol and Socio-Economic and Life Style Characteristics of Total Abstainers and Alcohol Consumers in Some Countries. Paper presented at the Epidemiology Section, 24th International Institute on the Prevention and Treatment of Alcoholism, Zurich.

Baird, E.G., 1945, Controlled Consumption of Alcoholic Beverages. In *Alcohol, Science and Society.* New Haven, Conn.: Quarterly Journal of Studies of Alcohol.

The Bottom Line, 1978, 2(3): 2-12.

The Bottom Line, 1979, 3(2): 22-24.

Bruun, K., Edwards, G., Lumio, M., Mäkelä, K., Pan, L., Popham, R., Room, R., Schmidt, W., Skog., O., Sulkunen, P. and Österberg, E., 1975, *Alcohol Control Policies in Public Health Perspective.* Publication No. 25, Helsinki: The Finnish Foundation for Alcohol Studies.

Budde, S. and Bar-Din, I., 1979, California: General Social Structure and Demographic Composition. Paper presented at the Second Conference of the International Study of Alcohol Control Experiences (ISACE), Asilomar, California.

Bunce. R., 1976, Alcoholic Beverage Consumption, Beverage Prices and Income in California, 1955-1975. Report No. 6 to the California Office of Alcoholism. Social Research Group, University of California, Berkeley.

Bunce, R., 1979, The Political Economy of California's Wine Industry. Prepared for the Second Plenary Meeting of the International Study of Alcohol Control Experiences, Asilomar, California. (Revised, December 1979).

Burck, C.G., 1977, The Whiskey Distillers Put Up Their Dukes. *Fortune,* 46(3): 155-168.

Cahalan, D., Roizen, R. and Room, R., 1976, Alcohol Problems and Their Prevention: Public Attitudes in California. In *The Prevention of Alcohol Problems: Report of a Conference.* R. Room and S. Sheffield (Eds.). Office of Alcoholism, Sacramento.

Cahalan, D. and Room, R., 1974, *Problem Drinking among American Men.* Monograph No. 7. New Brunswick, N.J.: Rutgers Center of Alcohol Studies.

California Beer Wholesalers Assn. vs. Alcoholic Beverage Control Appeals Board, 1971, 5 Cal. 3d. 402.

California Department of Highway Patrol, 1950-1961, *Annual Statistical Report.* Sacramento.

California Department of Highway Patrol, 1962-1965, *Traffic Accident Statistics.* Sacramento.

California Department of Highway Patrol, 1966-1979, *Report of Fatal and Injury Motor Vehicle Traffic Accidents.* Sacramento.

California Department of Justice, 1950-1964, *Crime in California*. Bureau of Criminal Statistics, Sacramento.

California Department of Justice, 1965-1978, *Crime and Delinquency in California*. Bureau of Criminal Statistics, Sacramento.

California Department of Public Health, 1964, *California's Alcoholism: Problems, Resources*. Division of Alcoholic Rehabilitation, Berkeley.

California Office of Alcohol Program Management, 1974, *California Alcohol Data 1973*. Sacramento.

California Office of Alcoholism, 1975, *Recent Available Figures on Selected Alcohol-Related Indicators*. Sacramento.

California Office of Alcoholism, 1976, *California Alcoholism Program 1976, Report to the Legislature: Current Status and Future Directions*. Sacramento.

California Statistical Abstracts, 1976, State Printing Office, Sacramento.

Cameron, T., 1979, The Impact of Drinking-Driving Countermeasures: A Review and Evaluation. *Contemporary Drug Problems,* 8(4): 495-565.

Cameron, T., 1980, Tables on Alcohol-Related Problems, California 1950-1975. Paper presented at the Third Conference of the International Study of Alcohol Control Experiences (ISACE), Warsaw.

Cameron, T., 1981, Alcohol and Alcohol Problems: Public Opinion in California, 1974-1980. Social Research Group Report, C31. Prepared for the California Department of Alcohol and Drug Programs.

Clark, M.E. & Owsley, L.L., 1974, *Alcohol and the State: A Reappraisal of California's Alcohol Policies*. Report No. PR-111. California Department of Finance, Sacramento.

Clark, W.B. & Midanik, L., 1980, *Alcohol Use and Alcohol Problems among U.S. Adults: Results of the 1979 National Survey*. Draft report prepared for the National Institute on Alcohol Abuse and Alcoholism under contract ADM-281-77-021.

Collins, G., 1980a, Aggregate Consumption of Alcoholic Beverages in California: An Update of Selected Tables, 1976-1979. Working Paper F124. Social Research Group, School of Public Health, University of California, Berkeley.

Collins, G., 1980b, Tables on Alcohol-Related Problems in California: An Update of Selected Tables 1976-1979. Working Paper F120. Social Research Group, School of Public Health, University of California, Berkeley.

Collins, G. & Milkes, J., 1980, Aggregate Consumption of Alcoholic Beverages in California, 1950-1975 — Some Quantitative and Qualitative Changes. Working Paper F91. Social Research Group, School of Public Health, University of California, Berkeley.

Conrad, P. & Schneider, J.W., 1980, *Deviance and Medicalization: From Badness to Sickness*. St. Louis: C.V. Mosby.

Field Institute, 1960, California Field Poll 6003. San Francisco.

Field Institute, 1971, California Field Poll 7101. San Francisco.

Field Institute, 1973, California Field Poll 7304. San Francisco.

Field Institute, 1974, California Field Poll 7401. San Francisco.

Field Institute, 1975, California Field Poll 7501. San Francisco.

Field Institute, 1979, California Field Poll 7902. San Francisco.

Gallup, G., 1977, Drinkers at 38-Year Record Level Due to Changing Habits of Women February 13 press release. *The Gallup Poll.*

Hyman, M.H., Zimmerman, M.A. Gurio, C., & Helrich, A., 1980, *Drinkers, Drinking and Alcohol-Related Mortality and Hospitalizations: A Statistical Compendium*. New Brunswick, N.J.: Center of Alcohol Studies, Rutgers University.

Keller, M. & Gurioli, C., 1976, Statistics on Consumption of Alcohol and on Alcoholism. New Brunswick, N.J.: *Journal of Studies on Alcohol.*

Kluge, P.F., 1971, Neighbourhood Bars Are Left High and Dry as Tipplers Flee City. *Wall Street Journal,* 84(103):1.

Knupfer, G. & Room, R., 1970, Abstainers in a Metropolitan Community. *Quarterly Journal of Studies on Alcohol,* 31(1): 108-131.

Levine, H., 1977, Colonial and Nineteenth Century American Thought about Liquor as a Cause of Crime and Accidents. Paper presented at the annual meeting of the Society for the Study of Social Problems, Chicago.

Liquor Handbook, Annually, 1955-1976, Title varies. Benjamin Corrado Marketing Consultants, New York, publishers, supplanted by Gavin-Jobson Associates, New York.

Liquor Handbook, 1976, The 1955-1975 Market. P. 48ff. New York: Gavin-Jobson Associates.

Louis Harris and Associates, Inc., 1971, *American Attitudes Toward Alcohol and Alcoholics: A Survey of Public Opinion*. Study 2138. Prepared for National Institute on Alcohol Abuse and Alcoholism, New York.

Louis Harris and Associates, Inc., 1974, *Public Awareness of the NIAAA Advertising Campaign and Public Attitudes Toward Drinking and Alcohol Abuse: Phase Four: Winter 1974 and Overall Summary.* Study No. 2355. Prepared for National Institute on Alcohol Abuse and Alcoholism, New York.

McWilliams, C., 1949, *California: The Great Exception*. New York: Current Books.

Mitchell, A., 1980, Unpublished data collected from a series of the California Field Poll Reports, 1956-1979.

Morgan, P.A., 1978a, *The Political Uses of Moral Reform: California and Federal Drug Policy,* 1910-1960. Ph.D. Dissertation in Sociology. University of California, Santa Barbara.

Morgan, P.A., 1978b, Examining United States Alcohol Policy: Alcohol Control and the Interests of the State. Paper presented at the meetings of the International Sociological Association, Uppsala, Sweden.

Morgan, P.A., 1979, The Evolution of California Alcohol Policy. Paper presented at the Second Conference of the International Study of Alcohol Control Experiences (ISACE), Asilomar, California.

Morgan, P.A., 1980, The State as Mediator: Alcohol Policy Management in California, 1955-1975. Paper presented at the Third Conference of the International Study of Alcohol Control Experiences (ISACE), Warsaw.

Mosher, J.F., 1979a, The Alcohol Beverage Control System in California. Paper presented at the Second Conference of the International Study of Alcohol Control Experiences (ISACE), Asilomar, California.

Mosher, J.F., 1979b, Retail Distribution of Alcoholic Beverages in California. Paper presented at the Second Conference of the International Study of Alcohol Control Experiences (ISACE), Asilomar, California.

Mosher, J.F., 1979c, Marketing of Alcoholic Beverages in California. Paper presented at the Second Conference of the International Study of Alcohol Control Experiences (ISACE), Asilomar, California.

Mosher, J.F. & Wallack, L.M., 1979a, Proposed Reforms in the Regulation of Alcoholic Beverage Advertising. *Contemporary Drug Problems,* 8(1): 87-106.

Mosher, J.F. & Wallack, L.M., 1979b, *The DUI Project: A Description of an Experimental Program to Address Drinking-Driving Problems.* California Department of Alcoholic Beverage Control, Sacramento.

Mottl, J.R., 1979, Economic Structure and Significance of Alcohol Production and Trade. Working Paper F114. Social Research Group, University of California, Berkeley.

Mowry, G., 1951, *The California Progressives.* Chicago: Quadrangle.

New York Times, 1975, Jan. 3, p. 39.

New York Times, 1978, April 1, p. 29.

Olmo, H.P., 1976, *Plant Genetics and New Grape Varieties.* California Wine Industry Oral History Series. Regional Oral History Office of the Bancroft Library, University of California, Berkeley.

Ostrander, G.M., 1957, *The Prohibition Movement in California, 1848-1933.* University of California Publications in History, Vol. 57, Berkeley.

Puffer, R. & Griffith, G.W., 1967, Alcoholism, Alcoholic Psychosis, and Cirrhosis of Liver, pp. 160-168 in: *Patterns of Urban Mortality.* Scientific Publication No. 151. Washington, D.C.: Pan American Health Organization.

Reynolds, L.M., 1973, *The California Office of Alcohol Management: A Development in the Formal Control of a Social Problem.* Ph.D. Dissertation in Education. University of California, Berkeley.

Roizen, R., 1977, Comment on the Rand Report. *Journal of Studies on Alcohol,* 38(1): 170-178.

Room, R., 1973, Regulating Trade Relations and the Minimization of Alcohol Problems. Statement to the California Senate Committee on Governmental Organization. Hearing on Tied House Provisions of the California Alcoholic Beverage Control Act. San Francisco, November 26, 1973.

Room, R., 1978, *Governing Images of Alcohol and Drug Problems: The Structure, Sources, and Sequels of Conceptualizations of Intractable Problems.* Ph.D. Dissertation in Sociology, University of California, Berkeley.

Room, R. & Beck, K., 1974, Survey Data on Trends in U.S. Consumption. *Drinking and Drug Practices Surveyor,* 9:3-7.

Room, R. & Roizen, R., 1973, Some Notes on the Study of Drinking Contexts. *Drinking and Drug Practices Surveyor,* 8:25-33.

Rusco, E., 1960, *Machine Politics, California Model: Arthur H. Samish and the Alcoholic Beverage Industry.* Ph.D. Dissertation in Political Science, University of California, Berkeley.

San Francisco Chronicle, 1979, Sept. 28, p. 25.

Smith, D.C., 1980, Unpublished data. Social Research Group, School of Public Health, University of California, Berkeley.

U.S. Department of Health, Education, and Welfare, 1950-1978, *Vital Statistics of the United States.* Washington, D.C.

U.S. National Institute on Alcohol Abuse and Alcoholism, 1978a, *Third Special Report to the U.S. Congress on Alcohol and Health.* DHEW Publication (ADM) 78-569. Washington, D.C.

U.S. National Institute on Alcohol Abuse and Alcoholism, 1978b, *Technical Support Document: Third Special Report to the U.S. Congress on Alcohol and Health.* DHEW Publication (ADM) 79-832.

Wall Street Journal, 1976, May 20, p. 22.

The Wine Marketing Handbook, 1978. New York: Gavin-Jobson Associates.

Winkeler, A.J., 1973, *Viticultural Research at UC Davis (1921-1971).* California Wine Industry Oral History Series. Regional Oral History Office of the Bancroft Library, University of California, Berkeley.

Wittman, F., 1980, Tale of Two Cities: Policies and Practices in the Local Control of Alcohol Availability. Social Research Group, School of Public Health, University of California, Berkeley.

9. *Postscript*

Seven cases of alcohol use and control, drawn from seven nations — or parts thereof — from two continents, from East as well as in West Europe, from extremely rich nations as well as the relatively poor. What has been presented to us is an exceptional variety of nations. And yet: an amazing similarity when it comes to alcohol.

First, the extent of alcohol use within all these nations. A very large proportion of citizens in these countries are by now regular users of a substance with such highly debated qualities that most of these nations outlawed it, or attempted to do so, some 60 years ago. It is a strong substance, indeed. Several of these countries had large segments of teetotallers. Today they are gone — replaced by drinkers. Industrialized man is also an industrialized drinker. He consumes alcohol as he consumes other commodities.

A second observation is the *similarity* in the spacing and form of drinking behaviour. The gradually decreased variance between industrialized nations is exemplified in alcohol use. It is as if a powerful mastermind were behind it all and carefully making us behave in a similar way in Helsinki, in Toronto, in Los Angeles. Some peculiarities in national habits might remain, but more important seems to be a move towards a common denominator.

Among the many striking similarities is the reduced importance of the large, ritualistic alcohol explosions. In their place has come the more trivialized use of alcohol — from the rare encounter with powerful magic, to consumption as part of the daily food, one even advertised as of low caloric content. Initially occurring in the public arena — restaurants, bars — now this activity is also to a large extent taken home. To the privatization of family life in general is added the privatization of drinking life. It is changing from being the catalyst of a display of emotions on a public stage, to being no more than a private intake of beverage.

On that private stage, alcohol itself is also converted: from a trigger mechanism, a licence for atypical behaviour, into a daily tranquillizer. Are we again confronted with the effects of industrialized life? One where the importance of expressive ritual generally seems to have been reduced? Maybe the demands for smooth productive activity are incompatible with the large outbursts. Funerals take half an hour. Marriages can be entered into during lunch hours. Central heating and cooling take care of the variations between winter and summer; what remains of hallowed religious days has been converted into a time for intensified commerce. Of all the nations described, Poland is the only one which, in modern times, seriously initiated a ban on alcohol — and got it approved. The political struggle in Gdansk demanded social involvement to a degree which made alcohol unnecessary; indeed, possibly dysfunctional. Solidarity and the government competed in getting it banned from the arena and in getting the credit for having succeeded. Here was expressed so much existential drama that public use of alcohol would only distract attention, and reduce the performance of the major actors. The detachment and non-expressiveness of social behaviour in most consumer democracies stand out in relief against the happenings in Gdansk. Besides rare happenings like those in Gdansk, great sports events — seen from a cool sociological standpoint — provide some of the few public outlets for great emotions. But here, for the spectators, there are no obvious reasons to abstain from alcohol. They are not there to perform. They are there to consume. Here we are back to more old-fashioned forms of strong, public drinking — so strong that they are seen as a problem which threatens the very existence of the sport events themselves.

Looking into the future, one wonders: will that *future* — if we have any — also be the same for all these countries. I think it can be argued that it will go in that direction. And my further guess would be that we can expect a repetition of a very old history. Several of the cases in this book make it clear that the countries went through a greatly troubled epoch towards the end of the last century. That was the epoch of industrialization without welfare. In that miserable situation, alcohol got a lot of the blame. Political action against alcohol won broad support. Now we are up against new troubles. Chances are that we will enter an epoch of de-industrialization in the seven countries considered in this book. If this does not result in war, it will at least trigger off unrest. The welfare system will become strained. It is possible that this will lead to a renewed interest in alcohol as the cause of the trouble. Drugs are already being used as a scapegoat for the youth troubles created by a social organization that makes youth superfluous to any rewarding task. Alcohol might become the next target and be seen again as a major danger. Which it also is.

Nils Christie
Oslo, October 1981